Lukács Reappraised

Edited by
AGNES HELLER

New York · Columbia University Press · 1983

© in this collection Agnes Heller 1983

Printed in Great Britain

Library of Congress Cataloging in Publication Data
Main entry under title:
Lukács reappraised.

Bibliography: p.
Includes index.
1. Lukács, György, 1885 – 1971—Addresses, essays,
lectures. I. Heller, Agnes.
B4815.L84L883 1983   199′.439   83-7182
ISBN 0-231-05802-0
ISBN 0-231-05803-9 (pbk.)

Contents

Acknowledgements   vi

1   Life and the Soul: the Young Lukács and the Problem of Culture   1
GYÖRGY MÁRKUS

2   Georg Lukács and Irma Seidler   27
AGNES HELLER

3   Lukács and Bloch   63
SÁNDOR RADNÓTI

4   Lukács in Weimar   75
FERENC FEHÉR

5   Lukács and Husserl   107
MIHÁLY VAJDA

6   Notes on Lukács' *Ontology*   125
FERENC FEHÉR, AGNES HELLER, GYÖRGY MÁRKUS AND MIHÁLY VAJDA

7   Lukács' *Ontology*: a Metacritical Letter   154
GÁSPÁR TAMÁS

8   Lukács' Later Philosophy   177
AGNES HELLER

Index   191

Acknowledgements

Versions of five of the articles included in this book were published first in the journal *Telos*. They appear here under the titles 'Life and the Soul' (György Márkus), 'Lukács and Bloch' (Sándor Radnóti), 'Lukács in Weimar' (Ferenc Fehér), 'Lukács and Husserl' (Mihály Vajda) and 'Notes on Lukács' *Ontology*' (Ferenc Fehér, Agnes Heller, György Márkus and Mihály Vajda).

The publishers are grateful to *Telos* for permission to reprint these articles in this volume.

1

Life and the Soul: the Young Lukács and the Problem of Culture

GYÖRGY MÁRKUS

Every human being of substance has just one thought; indeed, one may ask whether thought can ever have a plural.
George Lukács

'. . . from one Sunday to the next he turned from Saul into Paul,' says Anna Lesznai,[1] one of Lukács' closest friends, writing in her own memoirs of the philosopher's conversion to Bolshevism in 1918. Not only does this picture of sharp rupture recur constantly in the reminiscences of former students and friends, but it is also one of the basic themes of the ever-increasing body of interpretative literature on Lukács' philosophical development – and not without reason. An examination of his early career seems to confirm this picture. In December 1918 the philosopher and critic, at 34 by no means still a young man, joined the Hungarian Communist Party and from then on dedicated his life and work to the realization of the ideas and ideals of his chosen movement. It was a commitment that was to survive both historical and personal crises. With baffling suddenness, without any transition it seemed, Lukács made a radical break with all his earlier work, work that, if only on account of its influence on his contemporaries, cannot simply be labelled dismissively as 'immature' or 'escapist'. The year 1918 did not, however, mark Lukács' first intellectual encounter with Marxism and socialism as representing both a problem and an alternative. They were present in his first important work *History of the Development of the Modern Drama*, and he himself characterized his study *Remarks on the Theory of Literary History*, written in 1909, as an attempt to provide a coherent explication of his position regarding historical materialism, a position that was 'complex and difficult to explain'.[2] And nothing demonstrates better the paradox of the road that led him to Marxism than the fact that up until the turning-point in 1918 his view of it, as it emerged in repeated intellectual confrontations, became increasingly critical and

1

– especially in regard to its practical importance – increasingly resigned. (One only has to compare the relevant passages in his history of the development of the drama, completed in 1909, with the essay 'Aesthetic Culture', written just a year later, or with his verdict on Marxism in the study *Fatal Youth* of 1916.)

The picture becomes even more paradoxical when we consider those aspects of Lukács' thought that were central to his intellectual conversion. If one compares the essay *Bolshevism as an Ethical Problem*, which appeared in 1918, with *Tactics and Ethics*, written only a few months later (before the Räterepublik was proclaimed in 1919), one finds that the same problem is raised in both pieces. Parallel trains of thought can be identified at more than one level, and even identical formulations. But whereas the first piece reaches the conclusion that the 'ethical dilemma' of Bolshevism is fundamentally insoluble, and rejects the Bolshevist position, the second takes upon itself, with passionate commitment, the task of finding an active historical solution to this dilemma.[3] In the first article Lukács could still write that 'the choice between the two positions therefore is, like every ethical question, a question of faith'.[4] And it does indeed seem as if the *hiatus irrationalis* between the two positions can be bridged – in some impenetrable way – only by a climactic, voluntaristic decision, by a conversion of faith.

Yet, paradoxically, the extraordinary sharpness of the break, which emerges quite clearly from a comparison of these two works, points immediately to the fact that the connection between the two periods of Lukács' *oeuvre* cannot adequately be described by reference to concepts such as discontinuity or hiatus. 'Yes' and 'no' are diametrical opposites, but where two points of view so clearly contradict each other they must, by the very nature of this relationship, be intimately linked in some way. Where the answers can be polar opposites, the question must be the same. And, indeed, a more thorough analysis of Lukács' 'early' works not only reveals the presence, right from the beginning, of a series of subjective motifs of radical change (as he himself pointed out in his later writings on his intellectual development),[5] but also discovers parallels, both in content and in ideas, with the later Marxist writings. These parallels are irrefutable evidence of the existence of these deeper-level links. Of particular importance in this regard are the *Heidelberg Manuscripts on Aesthetics*, written between 1912 and early 1918. There is no space here for detailed discussion of these still unpublished works,[6] but it should be mentioned that some of the most fundamental ideas and categories contained in the great late work of synthesis, *The Specificity of the Aesthetic*, can be found here, often expressed in the same terms: the concept of objectivation, the distinction between 'the whole man' and 'man as a whole', the category of the homogeneous medium, the conception of the work of art as a self-enclosed totality, and so on. Also to be found there is Lukács' characterization of the world of the work of art as the Utopian reality appropriate to man's needs – the fundamental idea in his late,

Marxist aesthetics concerned with the defetishizing mission of art.

In pointing out these parallels, the intention is not to replace the generally accepted picture of a discontinuity in the development of Lukács' thought[7] with an equally one-sided – indeed, even more misleading – stress on its 'continuity'. There is simply no doubt that the conversion of 1918 had a profound effect on Lukács' view of the world and influenced the way in which he solved individual theoretical problems. Precisely because the theoretical premises shared by the two works on aesthetics are embedded in different theoretical and ideological contexts, a more detailed analysis could show clearly that even they are given radically differing interpretations and functions and, in some cases, contradict each other outright. A single example must suffice here too: the Utopian function of art in creating a reality appropriate to man's needs is interpreted by the young Lukács (in some of his writings, at least) as the 'Satanism' of art. The work of art creates harmony and fulfilment in advance of, or without, man's true redemption.

In view of – indeed, because of – the existence of this strange web of parallels and contradictions, the parallels between individual motifs, however significant, shed very little light on what actually links the two great periods of Lukács' career. To understand the road taken by Lukács as a thinker, and its individual stages, it is far more important to examine what underlies both positions, to look at the identical ways in which the problems are framed. The real link between the *Heidelberg Manuscripts* and the late *Aesthetics* is that both works, although they were separated by almost half a century, use completely different conceptual tools and frequently come to opposite conclusions, are nevertheless devoted to solving one and the same theoretical problem. Both are attempts to establish the place and function of art within the system of human activities and to explain its relationship with everyday life (in the terminology employed by the young Lukács, its relationship with 'experienced reality') and with the 'generic' forms of human activity and objectivation (in early terminology, the fundamental forms of the 'transcendental constitution') that shape and appropriate reality. But behind the fact that the two works set themselves identical philosophical objectives lies a problem that always presented itself as more than just a theoretical challenge to Lukács (indeed, it was one that embraced his entire life and work): the question of *the possibility of culture*. This essay attempts to examine the early period of his work, if only in broad outline, from this point of view.

Culture was the 'single' thought of Lukács' life. Is culture possible today? To answer this question and at the same time to contribute, through his own activity, to the creation or realization of this possibility remained one of the central concerns of his life. But right from the start, this concept of culture embraced far more than high art or philosophy, extended far beyond the bounds of 'high culture'. For Lukács, the question of culture was synonymous with the question of *life*, with the 'immanence of meaning in life'. For

culture . . . is the unity of life, the life-enhancing, life-enriching power of
unity . . . All culture is the conquest of life, the unifying of all life's
phenomena with a single force . . . so that whatever part of the totality of
life you look at, you always see, in its innermost depths, the same thing.
In an authentic culture, everything becomes symbolic. . . .[8]

Through culture, men and events become part of a meaningful totality.[9] It
invests the most diverse and unrelated facts with living meaning that is
perceived in the same way by everybody and so guarantees that they are
interpreted and evaluated consistently within a view of the world founded on
the concerns of real life. Unity of subject and object, individual and society,
one's innermost convictions and external institutions, becomes possible only
within an authentic culture – not in the sense that conflicts are abolished or
excluded, but in the sense that the culture traces the path along which they can
be resolved and so ensures that 'development is no longer subject to the vagaries
of chance'.[10] Only in an authentic culture can the forms of 'high culture' –
art, philosophy and so on – cease to be alienated from life and life from them,
for in it these forms are only 'the emergence into consciousness of what had lain
dormant as a vague longing in all that had yet to be given form'.[11]

In other words, from the beginning of his development as a thinker the
question of culture meant for Lukács the question of *whether it is possible to live a
life free from alienation*. But behind this question lay his passionate diagnosis of
the hostility to culture, the 'crisis of culture', that characterized modern
bourgeois existence, and his own determined rejection of it. This awareness of
crisis was by no means unique to Lukács. One can point also to Dilthey,
Simmel and Weber (to mention only thinkers whose influence on the formation
of Lukács' views can be demonstrated directly). What set Lukács apart was his
sensitivity to the extent of the contradictions, the tragic power of his struggle
against them, the 'pathos' of his philosophy that characterized his writings in
the first decade of the century, that 'happy time of peace'. The whole of
Lukács' pre-Marxist period was a constant struggle to arrive at a precise
conceptual diagnosis of these contradictions, this 'crisis', and to discover, by
theoretical means, ways out of them, or at least the norms of proper human
conduct appropriate to dealing with them.

In Lukács' diagnosis during this period one can detect two parallel forms of
analysis, one metaphysical and existential, the other historical. The two
processes, or levels of analysis, change from work to work, often merging
within one and the same essay to such an extent that any sharp distinction or
opposition can, in a certain sense, only be a construct imposed for the purposes
of interpretation. With almost periodic regularity Lukács himself tried to
clarify their relationship, both in principle and methodologically.[12] However,

between these two types of analysis there remain, at least implicitly, unresolved yet fruitful contradictions, relating not only to questions of methodology. (This failure to achieve a resolution may perhaps have been the reason for the frequency of Lukács' 'attempts at unification'.) For underlying this problem of methodological 'parallelism' is a deeper problem, a philosophical dilemma (although the two are not identical, nor can one be reduced to the other). The issue is whether the condition of the age in which he lived was an expression of the existential and ontological tragedy of culture or of an historical crisis from which recovery was possible.

It is this unremitting and unrewarded theoretical struggle that distinguishes Lukács' works from those of his contemporaries during this early period and makes the whole course of the development of his ideas so strange and unique. The reason why the development of his thought early on is difficult to trace is that the positive answers and solutions he offers change kaleidoscopically from work to work. Each is an intellectual experiment, usually pushed to its limits, exploring a position that often becomes the object of ruthless criticism in the next work. To give just one example, *The Metaphysics of Tragedy* is one of the best-known and most frequently analysed of Lukács' early essays. Several critics, among them Lucien Goldmann, have pointed out quite correctly that it testifies to links with the later world of existentialist thought. It is, however, much less well-known that at almost exactly the same time as he formulated this position he also wrote a passionate critique of it in the essay 'Aesthetic Culture'. In this critique 'life before the Last Judgement'[13] is branded 'the greatest frivolity':

> anything is permissible when everybody is living in expectation of a great final accounting, which, however, never arrives; for on the day of the Last Judgement all things will in any case be found to be easy, and the communal feeling of tragedy will grant absolution for every frivolity.[14]

The essay, as he himself understood the term, can therefore be regarded as the 'representative' genre of Lukács' early period. According to the introductory study in *Soul and Form*, the essay as a form mediates between art and philosophy. It uses facts drawn from life, or representations of those facts, to express conceptually a view of the world as *experience*, as a question of *life*. But it does not offer clear-cut, conceptual answers. 'The essay is a court, but (unlike in the legal system) it is not the verdict that is important, that sets standards and creates precedents, but the process of examining and judging.'[15] At times the dialectic of polemic and counter-polemic even becomes a structural element of the essay itself, determining its form. It is no accident that some of the essays that are most central to an understanding of his philosophy (the essay on Sterne in *Soul and Form* or *On Spiritual Poverty*, for instance) are written in the form of dialogues.

The fundamental categories of Lukács' 'philosophical', metaphysical and existential, analysis are – in the terminology of the 'representative' essays, with which we shall be primarily concerned here – the concepts of 'life' ('ordinary' life), the 'soul' (and, closely linked with it, 'real' or 'living life') and 'form'. *Life* is, above all, the world of 'impersonal, mechanical forces',[16] a world of rigid forms (conventions and institutions) alien to man. These were once created by the *soul*, guided by reason and by clear goals, but they have inevitably turned into external forces that merely exist but are no longer alive. They have become second nature, 'which can only be described, by analogy with first nature, as the sum total of known but meaningless necessities'. This world of 'ordinary life' is 'something frozen, alien, a complex of sense-expressions (*Sinngebilde*) that no longer elicits a response from the inner, spiritual life of man. It is a Golgotha of decayed spiritual lives,'[17] a tight web of inescapable necessities, yet one that 'is fundamentally contingent and meaningless': the necessity 'of being trapped and held fast in a web of a thousand threads, a thousand contingent connections and relationships'.[18]

The concept of life, however, designates phenomena not only on the level of 'interpersonal' objectivity but also on the subjective level. The empirical individual of ordinary life is lonely and isolated; he searches blindly for a way of making contact with other individuals. But the conventions governing these forms of social interaction make it impossible for him to find a way and mean that he can experience himself only peripherally as well.[19] Only two basic types of behaviour are possible in this life: either man immerses himself completely in the world of conventions, and so loses his real personality, or he escapes from the pressure of irrational, external necessity into pure introversion. However, this second response, complete abandonment to (indeed, dissolution in) a stream of transitory moods and sense experiences, also means giving up the self:

> since everything comes from within, nothing can really come from within: only things in the outside world can induce moods, and enjoyment of one's own soul as an aesthetic experience amounts only to passive observation of something that chance happens to put in one's way. Complete freedom is the most terrible form of bondage.[20]

In the end, this division of life into inside and outside, subjectivity and objectivity, never actually develops into an outright conflict in which one principle or the other could come to dominate.

> To speak of dissonance would be to overestimate [ordinary life]. Dissonance is possible only in a system of notes, that is, in a world that is already a unified whole: frustration, inhibition and chaos are not even dissonant.[21]

Life is an anarchy of light and shadow. Nothing in it ever reaches its full potential and nothing ever reaches an end; new, bewildering voices constantly join in the chaos of earlier sounds. Everything flows and flows together, wildly, in an impure mixture; everything is frustrated and destroyed. Nothing ever blooms into real life. Life means being able to live things to the full. In *this* life nothing is ever lived completely to the full. Life is the most unreal and lifeless form of being it is possible to imagine.[22]

'Ordinary life' is the sphere of 'mere existence', of *inauthentic being*.

Authentic being means the *soul*, and it means it in two ways. On the one hand, in a metaphysical sense, the soul is the substance of man's world, the creative and founding principle of every social institution and work of culture. On the other hand, in an existential sense, the soul means authentic individuality, the 'nucleus' that makes every personality fundamentally unique and irreplaceable and gives it its intrinsic value. This aspect of the Lukácsian conception has unmistakably polemical overtones, at least during his 'essay period' (1908 – 11). The polemic is directed against classical German philosophy, above all against the Hegelian conception of spirit:

it is quite certain that subjectivity is truth; the individual thing is all there is; the individual human being is the reality behind the idea of 'man'.[23]

only the individual, only individuality pushed to its furthest limits, really exists. Whatever is general is colourless, formless and all-embracing, too weak in its openness to any and every interpretation, too empty in its homogeneity, ever to be real.[24]

And the only life that is 'real', authentic, is

that which can be reached in the experience of full and genuine selfhood, in the soul's experience of itself.[25]

This sharpened dualism of life and soul, authentic and inauthentic being, forms what is perhaps the most characteristic feature of the philosophy of the young Lukács. We are using 'dualism' in an avowedly metaphysical sense of the word, for in asserting the substantial nature of the subject, which shapes the human world and its history, Lukács certainly does not claim that the objective world, created by the subjects and then abandoned as inhuman and mechanical, is merely a distorted illusion. Inauthentic being, the world of the structures of ordinary life, stands opposed to the soul as a principle that has equal status, though not equal value. And it has a power of its own, the often crushing power of inertia:

every individual thing, once it has entered life, has a life of its own that is independent of its originator and of any intended goal, independent of its usefulness or harmfulness, of whether it is good or bad. . . . What is important here is the category of existence, mere existence as a force, a value, a category which plays a crucial role in shaping the whole of life. . . . Its own life [the life of every product of human creation] is separate from that of its creator and from any intended goal; it has a life of its own. It begins to grow, perhaps in other ways and in different directions from those which had been intended. It might perhaps turn against its creator and destroy what it had been intended to strengthen and support. The means becomes the end, and no one can know either in advance or in retrospect what great power to influence situations and events is stored in objects, in things. [26]

Thus the category of 'ordinary' life, inauthentic life, becomes for Lukács a synonym for alienation; this alienation is passionately rejected, but it is recognized as an unavoidable *metaphysical* feature of human existence.

It should not be necessary to establish and document the links between Lukács' views under discussion here and the various currents within contemporary *Lebensphilosophie* (above all, of course, his relationship with Simmel). The fact that these links obviously existed should not, however, be allowed to obscure the no less significant differences and even outright conflicts. These emerge straightaway from the various interpretations of the concept of the soul. In general, consistent proponents of *Lebensphilosophie* identified creative subjectivity, which they opposed to the mechanical world of things and material relations, with the irrational and incommunicable stream of psychical experience, purified of all traces of the conceptual. This view was alien to Lukács, and not merely as a consequence of the sharp and explicit anti-psychologism that is evident in his writings from the very beginning. [27] He was also opposed to it for other, deeper, philosophical reasons. We have seen that he always conceived of the world of 'pure introversion' as a typical manifestation of inauthentic being, of 'ordinary life'. (His firmly dismissive attitude towards all forms of impressionism also stemmed from this conception. It was not just artistic impressionism that he rejected.) [28] The 'soul' is experience or, more accurately, it can become experience, but it is not in any way identical with the sum total or stream of one's experiences. 'Soul' means, in fact, the maximum development, the highest possible intensification, of the powers of an individual's *will*, [29] his capabilities and his 'psychical energies', those unique potentialities that every human being is capable of developing, and ought to develop, in order to become a real personality. The 'soul' is, as it were, the 'vocation' of an individual. And this 'vocation' is directed outwards, towards the outside world and other human beings. For authenticity is nothing other than actively using one's abilities to the full, shaping everything that happens to one into a personal destiny that expresses one's innermost nature.

It is not for nothing that we have been flirting with Fichte's terminology in this discussion. For even ignoring the evidence for direct influence,[30] there is no doubt that right from the start the philosophy of the young Lukács had many points of contact with Fichte's (and Hegel's) dialectic. In Lukács' eyes too, man is not what he *is* but what he *could be*. The dualism in his philosophy mentioned above always meant a dialectical struggle between opposing forces. It was not only alienation that seemed to him to be a 'metaphysical' necessity, but also the *active struggle against it*.

At the same time, and in a way that is obviously correlated with it, this interpretation of the concept of 'soul' is also an expression of Lukács' ceaseless efforts to overcome the fundamental subjectivism of *Lebensphilosophie* and its consequent relativism. If authenticity means the narcissistic self-enjoyment of the individual and his acceptance of his isolation as an immutable fact, then the stream of fundamentally incommunicable experiences, each unique and equally valid, destroys all values and value distinctions.

> The self has flowed out into the world and, through its moods and sensations, has absorbed the world into itself. But since this means that the world has also flowed into the self, all barriers between the two have been removed. . . . If things are no longer solid, stable entities, then neither is the self. And when facts disappear, so do values. Nothing is left within or between individuals except moods and sensations, none of which is more justified or more meaningful than any other.[31]

If, on the other hand, authentic life, as an active manifestation of the soul, means the development to its full potential of a unique personality that expresses itself in actions and welds all of life into a single unity, then this development simultaneously transcends what is purely individual. This process of self-realization is the transformation into action, into fact, of a way of living, a possibility of human life, that cannot be duplicated but can be normative and can serve as a model for everyone.

> The way of the soul is: to strip away everything that is not truly part of oneself; to make the soul truly individual; yet what results transcends the purely individual. That is why such a life can serve as a model. It is because the self-realization of a single human being means that self-realization is possible for all.[32]

Only through this intensified struggle of the soul with life can the individual attain that which will remain forever interpersonal and absolute, and hence truly universal – what Lukács calls the *work*: 'from out of our poverty and limitation redemption is born.'[33]

The 'work' means for Lukács the type of objectivity, of 'what is', that does not simply *remain in being* through the inertia of 'mere existence' but *remains valid* as a source of meaning and value. It means the objectivations that have arisen historically but have become timeless by constantly assuming new life and meaning: consummate works of art, the great philosophical and religious systems, science taken as a whole, in its unbroken development. (Lukács' attention, of course, was focused primarily on the work of art.)

This, however, is the point where the philosophy of the young Lukács clearly diverges from the various currents within *Lebensphilosophie* and makes contact with the traditions of classical German philosophy. As he himself stated unambiguously in the article on Croce that appeared in 1915, this point concerns the question of 'absolute spirit' and, more broadly, the question of objectivations.[34] For whereas, according to *Lebensphilosophie*, it is in principle impossible to transcend the purely individual and pointless to try, Lukács always recognizes cultural objectivations of 'absolute spirit' as irrefutable evidence that this transcendence is, in fact, possible. The 'work' (and the 'form' without which it could not exist) provides a guarantee that the struggle against the meaningless, mechanical and isolating empiricism of 'life', the striving towards a meaningful order and real interpersonal communication, is not only something that is necessary but is also not inevitably doomed to fail.

> The resolution – the redeeming power of form – will not be reached until the end of all paths and all sufferings, in the faith, beyond any possibility of proof, that the diverging paths of the soul will come together again at some distant time and place, that they must come together again, since they all started from one central point. Form, however, is the only proof that this faith is justified, for it is its living realization, more truly alive than all of life.[35]

Yet the work or, more accurately, the work of art, regarded by Lukács as of utmost importance, grows out of life, not simply in the sense that as an objectivation produced by a real individual it inevitably displays all the characteristics of its age, but also because it is in essence nothing other than a representation of life, the imposition of a specific form on life. But how is it possible that out of this transient and meaningless chaos something can emerge that is generally valid and has universal significance? If there is *within* life no way in which one soul can communicate with another, how can one build *out of* life a bridge that will last for ever and that all men can use? That is the ultimate philosophical meaning of the question that forms the starting-point of the young Lukács' two systematic works on aesthetics, *Philosophy of Art* (1912 – 14) and *Aesthetics* (1916 – 18), written in Heidelberg: 'Works of art exist – how are they possible?'

The question is to be answered, according to Lukács, by reference to the concept of form. The concept of form is more all-embracing than that of the 'work'. For Lukács, form designates all the functions connected with the creation of meaning. It enables the multiplicity of facts, events and all the other elements of life to be arranged into *meaningful* structures, *organized patterns of meaning*. (Accordingly, form is related not only to the sphere of 'absolute spirit' but also to that of 'objective spirit'.) Each separate form is a particular way in which the soul responds to life. Through these forms, on the one hand, the soul becomes pure and homogeneous, since it is centred upon a single value; on the other hand, using this single value, the soul can bring order to the chaos of life, of 'mere existence', and can invest it with meaning. As the principle of objectivation, the principle of the validity of objectivation, form is also the principle of mediation between life and the soul, although it can never finally resolve the antagonism, the dualism, between them.

The work of art is only one of these ways of 'giving form' to life.[36] From the threads in the fabric of life, running in a thousand different directions and reaching out towards infinity, from the endless sea of reasons and motives, the artist must choose just a few, and must do so in such a way that they are intimately connected with each other and form a homogeneous system, self-enclosed and complete in itself, which can be surveyed in its entirety from one point. The work of art as an abstract concept is nothing other than a

system of schemata which mediate experiences. It is so perfectly self-enclosed that it is dependent for its effect only on the immanent relations of its constituent elements.[37]

The schema in accordance with which the material of life is selected, ordered and structured, a schema that will vary depending on genre, style, etc., is the *aesthetic form*:

the form which arranges the material of life into a self-contained whole, and which prescribes its tempo, rhythm, fluctuations, density and fluidity, hardness and softness; it accents what is felt to be important, eliminates what is less important; it places things either in the foreground or the background and organizes them into groups within this pattern.[38]

Through this shaping process the amorphous chaos of life becomes, in the work of art, an ordered cosmos, a new life, but one which, however – by contrast with ordinary life – is now unambiguous and perspicuous. Every work of art embodies a way of perceiving and understanding life; art is, therefore, the process of investing life with meaning and raising it into consciousness, of transcending the chaos of life. It is a 'judgement on life'[39] and gives 'mastery over things'.[40] The existence of art is proof that the alienation of 'ordinary' life can be overcome.

This is true, however, in relation not only to objectivity but also to subjectivity. Each form embodies a vision, an immediate interpretation of life as experienced – not an interpretation in the sense of a subjective response on the part of a self divorced from life but an interpretation within the schema of a creative arrangement of the raw material of life. This schema is inseparable from the concrete material of the work of art and is itself a source of experiences. It is expressed through the objective structure of the work of art. This is the reason why form is also the principle that ensures communion and communication between individuals, between the creator of a work of art and those who experience it: 'Form is the truly social element in literature . . . the connecting link between creator and audience, the only category of literature that is both social and aesthetic.'[41] Those works of art in which truly great forms are realized, which form perfect, integrated wholes, inspire, *by virtue of their structure*, a vision of life, an interpretation and evaluation of life, to all intents and purposes a world view. And they have an irresistibly evocative power that can inspire everyone with this vision. This explains the universality and eternal validity and influence of the work of art.

But this relationship between life and the soul, the soul's power over life and the transcendence of alienation that is represented by art (and by every other valid cultural 'work'), cannot of itself solve the immediate problems of life raised by its dualistic, antagonistic nature. Art transcends the alienation of ordinary life, but it does not abolish it. For although the work of art springs from life, it also inevitably breaks away from it, and breaks away sharply, simply because it is totally self-enclosed, a complete universe in itself. It is a new life, which, as it is self-contained and complete in itself, has (and can have) no point of contact with anything beyond itself from the moment it comes into being.[42] The relationship between the work of art and life (the reception of art), therefore, can never be anything but momentary contact between different spheres, through which 'inauthentic life' can never be redeemed. One can perceive a meaning in life in and through the work, but that does not mean that one can order one's own life accordingly or invest it with meaning.

Equally, art cannot abolish the inadequacies of human communication that isolate the individual – not only because of the inevitably elitist character of artistic communication (the concept of 'genius' is one of the young Lukács' basic categories) but also because of its inherent nature. The work of art forges a universally valid link between creator and audience, since the link is created *exclusively* by the form objectified in the work. For precisely this reason, however, the link can never be adequate as far as content is concerned, partly because the world view objectively embodied and expressed in the form of the work does not necessarily stand in any relationship to the views and intentions of its creator (according to the aesthetics of the young Lukács, intention and completed work are separated by an 'irrational leap') and partly because the experiences evoked by the work are *eo ipso* the receiver's own experiences. The quality of these experiences – that which makes the experiences unique to the receiver and the effect of the work of art immediate and particular – can never correspond in any way to that of the experiences of the artist.

This process of self-discovery through the work, the experience of being affected by it at the innermost and most personal level – whose endless repeatability forms the basis of its eternal influence – precludes any possibility of a sharing of experience between creator and audience. The possibility of misunderstanding, which in empirical reality was only a *vérité de fait*, becomes here a *vérité éternelle*. [43]

The inadequacy of everyday processes of communication, the possibility of 'misunderstanding', is not abolished by art; it is merely eternalized. It is changed from an empirical to a constituitive category.

Thus the mediation between life and the soul, represented by the cultural objectivations of 'absolute spirit', by 'works', itself becomes the starting-point for new and tragic conflicts. One of 'these is the 'tragedy of the artist', which Lukács discusses in great detail. We have already touched on the most important aspect of this tragedy, namely, the 'unredeemed state' of artists, the fact that

all the perfection they give to their works, all the depths of experience which they pour into them, are in vain. They remain more silent, less able to express themselves, than people in ordinary life, who are all locked up in themselves. Their works may be the highest achievement of which man is capable, yet they themselves are the most unfortunate creatures of all and least capable of achieving redemption. [44]

In this way, Lukács establishes philosophically what we simply took for granted at the beginning of this study: that the problem of culture is not identical with the question of 'high culture', and that its crisis cannot be solved in this area alone. The guarantee provided by the great cultural objectivations, that the struggle against the alienation of ordinary life is not in vain, either in human or in historical terms, offers only hope. It does not supply proof that the goal of this struggle can actually be reached. For the great question of whether culture is 'possible', to use the language of the young Lukács' philosophy, cannot simply be reduced to the issue of whether it is possible to create out of the raw material of life eternally valid, objective forms, forms that must necessarily be divorced from life; it turns primarily on whether it is possible to shape *life itself*, if only in ways that, from a historical perspective, may be no more than transitory.

This question constitutes the basic problem of the young Lukács' ethics. Agnes Heller has made a thorough study of it. [45] Obviously, we can touch only on those aspects of this complex of problems that relate directly to the very general question that interests us here.

Broadly, we can say that whenever Lukács broaches the question of the possibility of culture in general terms and in the context of systematic analyses, the answer is negative. One can point to a number of absolutely unambiguous formulations of this answer. The most explicit and decisive is that given in the *Philosophy of Art*: the shaping of life according to ethical principles is impossible, for the self, as the product of the ethical will, is incapable not only of transforming the facts of the outside world but also of penetrating the soul in its entirety. There is no way in which an individual's inner life can be transformed into 'fate', that is, into a meaningful totality determined by the ethical nature of the personality.

In the light of these facts, the idea of stylizing life according to purely ethical criteria is no longer tenable. Such a stylization can neither destroy the raw material which flows in upon it nor inform it with an ethical vision. And if it should presume to claim the status of a form which could be imposed on the totality of life, it would be an inappropriate form, an allegory.[46]

At precisely this point in the manuscript of 1912 – 14, however, Lukács refers – with every justification – to his Kierkegaard essay (from 1909) as a work in which he had already formulated this position, and one can also find similar ideas expressed in his *Metaphysics of Tragedy*. In the essay on Kierkegaard, too, authentic life, 'true life', seems 'always [to be] impossible in the empirical world of everyday experience', for

one cannot live life at its peak of intensity, fulfil one's ultimate potentialities, all of the time. One has to come back down to dull existence. One has to deny life in order to live.[47]

Realization of the unity of fate and life, of the inner world of the self and outer events, of meaning and being, is granted only to the tragic chosen few, and to them only for a moment:

This moment is a beginning and an end. Nothing can follow from it or arise out of it, and it can have no connection with life. It is a moment; it does not mean life; it is life, a life different from ordinary life, and the two are mutually exclusive.[48]

The struggle for culture, the eternal, restless longing of man 'to make the pinnacle of his existence the plane on which he lives his life, to màke its meaning part of everyday reality,'[49] is tragically hopeless. For although this struggle, which must never be abandoned, is not in vain – it is out of this struggle that the great moral examples emerge that, like works of art, although created by man, possess timeless validity, signify the pinnacle of our existence and our potentialities and give them their truly human dimension – it cannot (in principle) achieve its immediate goal. The 'crisis' of culture is only one manifestation of the metaphysical tragedy of human existence.

Alongside this conception, however, Lukács' early works also offer another perspective, namely, that it *is* possible to shape life through culture. It should be said that this solution is generally to be found in less systematic contexts than that discussed above. It occurs either in the course of the analysis of specific historical or sociological contexts of a particular kind or in the Utopias that are usually no more than hinted at, yet in many ways characterize the ideological direction of the early works. (Those analyses that are distinctly historical in their approach will be examined below, but we can point here, by way of example, to the essay on Storm, which provides a kind of counterpoint to the Kierkegaard essay, visualizing the 'shaping' of life by a bourgeois moral system founded on a vocational ethics of duty.) It is also clear that the actual content of these Utopias often changes within the same work.[50] To cite simply the best-known example, in his *The Theory of the Novel* two different Utopias coexist in perfect harmony. On the one hand, there is that of 'Wilhelm Meister', a world in which human beings actively shape, according to their own goals, the object-ive structures of society in a spirit of inner community and harmonious co-operation.[51] On the other hand, Lukács also proclaims the approach of the 'pure reality of the soul' depicted in the works of Dostoevsky, a 'new world' transcending all social determination and social forms and abolishing the duality of self and world in an immediate communion of souls beyond all objectifica-tions.[52] Yet behind all these differences (one might even say contradictions) as far as the actual content is concerned, there is a hidden common factor: a belief in the possibility of a world organized in accordance with man's authentic nature, a world in which the unbridgeable gulf between his deepest needs and desires and the objective structures of 'external' social existence vanishes, and human beings are no longer condemned to a life of infinite loneliness, alienated from each other. It is a belief in the possibility of a culture that embraces and unifies the whole of life, permeating all aspects of man's everyday existence. And if – disregarding explicitly negative answers – the great diversity in con-tent exhibited by these Utopias may itself be taken as a sign that this belief of Lukács' pre-Marxist period was not, in fact, based on a fully worked-out social programme and a concrete historical perspective, then the constant occurrence of these Utopias in contexts in which they function as critiques of philosophical arguments demonstrating the 'metaphysical impossibility' of culture is clear evidence of the existence of another no less characteristic and consistent feature of his thought: his passionate rejection of an alienated, 'cultureless' world. Despite all the convincing, or apparently convincing, arguments that Lukács advances to demonstrate that the state of the world is unalterable, this rejection makes it impossible for him to come to terms with such a possibility.

Up to now we have been concerned with Lukács' metaphysical and existential analysis of the alienated conditions of modern life and its hostility towards culture. As has been pointed out, however, this was accompanied throughout the early period of his work by a different type of analysis, which in part complemented and in part contradicted it: an interpretation and characterization of the same problems and facts as socially determined, temporal–historical phenomena, that is, an interpretation from the point of view of sociology or the philosophy of history, a *historical* interpretation. In this analysis the crisis of culture appears to be an essential characteristic of modern bourgeois society, determined by its economic and class structure.

The conceptual background and framework of this interpretation is the historiosophic distinction drawn between closed, organic societies (exemplified first and foremost by ancient Greek society) on the one hand, and, on the other hand, open yet mechanistic bourgeois society. These concepts appear as explicit terms in *The Theory of the Novel*, but in its logical structure Lukács' *History of the Development of the Modern Drama* also starts from the same historical comparison; the whole basis of this work is the contrast between antique and modern drama, which is explained and interpreted in terms of this distinction. From the beginning, Lukács regarded the Greek *polis* as the historical example of a society in which culture had become everyday reality. In the *polis*, as an organic community, there was 'common agreement on ethical values in relation to the most important questions of life'.[53] It was 'an absolute ideology, which tolerated no debate or even doubt', a unified world view that was no longer perceived as an ideology. It had 'such an exclusively emotional character that it was as if it no longer contained consciously formulated values'.[54] This 'monoethism' of the ancient Greeks, this power of culture to permeate and organize the everyday life and consciousness of men in a way that seemed quite natural and self-evident, made the world in which the individual lived one in which he felt at home. It did so by investing all aspects of the world, individually and collectively, with a clear and consistent meaning and value that was accessible to every individual. This world order was 'based on foundations which are as firm as rock'. It might on occasion be shaken by 'fate', manifest in the unpredictability of external events or in the irrationality of individual characters, but 'its foaming waves will roll back over whatever has disturbed their calm, and the surface will become still and motionless again, as if nothing about it had changed.'[55] This also shows the extent to which this world was 'self-enclosed'. Greek antiquity knew neither the continual development of intellectual and material productivity nor the degree of individuality that have been brought about by modern bourgeois society. It was a self-enclosed world that did not extend beyond the boundaries of society, and it was, to a certain extent, bound by rigid forms. The system of human relationships, which was based on precedence and subordination and the place of the individual within that system, had been established and reinforced by the inertial force of centuries-old traditions.[56] But because these relationships were organic, 'making demands upon the whole personality of the individual' and inseparable from the personality, the individual did not perceive them as in any way restrictive. On the contrary, they provided a stable framework within which his actions could have meaning and importance:

> In short . . . once it was life itself which was individualistic; today it is the people, or rather it is their convictions and the principles according to which they live their lives. Once ideology was one of the bonds which helped people to perceive themselves as fitting into a system of relationships which was part of the natural order of things. On the other hand, every detail of their lives afforded opportunities to express their personality in their actions and in the things around them. That is why this kind of individualism could be spontaneous and unquestioned; today . . . it is conscious and problematic.[57]

Without question, bourgeois society dissolves this personal dimension to relations between individuals and, with it, the bonds characteristic of closed societies. This doubtless creates new values – right from the beginning, Lukács believed that the development of human productivity and the increasing introversion ('subjectivization') of the individual contained elements of value – but these are gained at the price of the creation of new bonds, which are not personal but reified: the individual becomes dependent on a system of impersonal, dead institutions based on commodity and money relations, which become ever more complex and whose function no one any longer understands.

> This new life liberates man from many of the old bonds and makes him perceive every kind of bond, since it is no longer organic, as a fetter. At the same time it creates around him a whole series of more abstract and complex bonds.[58]

While his 'feeling of autonomy in relation to other people' constantly increases,[59] the individual exists

> more and more only in relation to the things outside him, as the sum total of his relationships to them.[60]

This 'problematization' of the individual, however, means that his world also becomes problematic: his life and fate are controlled by a web of things and reified processes that is impenetrable and meaningless, yet has an irresistible logic of its own. In the place of an 'ethical world order' is the 'modern fate'

> that consists of an intimately linked and horrifyingly logical combination of things (institutions, ignorance of others and of life, the conditions of

life, inheritance, etc.), which, looked at in themselves, are relative and contingent. It is no help if people recognize the uselessness or wrongness of individual parts; they are facts which exert their influence with a power all of their own, like links in a chain of cause and effect, regardless of whether they are justified or not. [61]

This world is governed by laws that are irrational in origin, incomprehensible and indifferent to human values. It has ceased to be home for man.

With the decay of organic relations that appear to be part of the natural order, the new principle that governs relations between individuals is that of *competition*. All forms of dependence on others seem intolerable to the individual. He tries to assert himself against them. But if his personality is to assert himself, it must assert itself *against somebody else*. And this other person is just as anxious to preserve his own autonomy.

> One of the greatest antinomies of individualism is . . . that the personality cannot assert itself without suppressing the personality of others, who can defend themselves only by destroying that individual. [62]

This antagonistic relationship inevitably results in the increasing isolation and loneliness of each individual human being.

> It perhaps does not need emphasizing greatly how much more lonely the individual is today than he used to be . . . The real personality of each human being is a lonely island in the middle of a raging sea, and no voice can reach it without being distorted by the sound of the sea. Often the voice is drowned completely, so that all one can do is watch the outstretched arms of the other person. But in the end even his gestures too are misunderstood. [63]

On the other hand, this constant collision of wills, which are not only antagonistic towards each other but also continually misunderstand each other (since, willingly or unwillingly, every intention destroys the other), can lead only to one result, a result that no one wants, which is determined not by the conscious goals and interests of individuals but by the abstract and irresistible logic of the circumstances of their lives.

This does not happen merely to the extent that individuality is constantly colliding with the power of external material circumstances. These circumstances also have the effect of levelling (making uniform) all aspects of an individual's life. It is one of the most important indications of just how 'problematic' the modern individual has become that the steadily growing, ever more extreme process of individualization is closely interwoven with the diametrically opposed movement towards ever greater uniformity. [64] For economic development controlled by competition is based on the increasing fragmentation and division of labour. An individual's work is becoming more abstract, more divorced from his personality, more alien to himself.

From the point of view of the individual, the essential aspect of the modern division of labour is perhaps that it makes work independent of the irrational, and therefore only qualititively definable, abilities of the worker, and makes it dependent on objective factors relating to func- tionality, which lie outside the individual worker and have no connection with his personality. The relationship between work and worker becomes more and more remote. The worker puts less and less of his own per- sonality into his work, and the work demands less and less of the per- sonality of whoever performs it. The work takes on a separate, objective life of its own, distinct from the personality of the individual, who then has to find some other way to express his individuality than in his work.[65]

However, since this increasing individuality can no longer be manifested in real activity, it is constantly repressed and forced back on itself. It becomes pure in- trospection, and no effort is made even to attempt to shape the course of 'out- side' events, of one's own fate.

The crisis of culture is the inevitable product of this historically determined state of affairs in the world. Within the bourgeois world, culture in the true sense of the word is impossible. It is objectively impossible: no general goal, no meaning can be discerned in the abstract and irrational necessity of the condi- tions created by the 'anarchy of production'. Its objective laws, alien to man, can no longer be related to the individual in a unified view of the world. But it is also subjectively impossible: in this world, where individuals recognize no goals beside themselves and their subjective experiences, they can no longer be united in a common view, and common experience, of the world.

Basing our comments on Lukács' first important work, the *History of the Development of the Modern Drama*, completed in 1909, we have attempted here to summarize his views about the historical and social causes of the crisis of culture – without, it must be said, trying in any way to be exhaustive. What we hope to do is simply to demonstrate the existence of a considerable degree of parallelism between the 'philosophical' and the historical analyses. It should not be difficult to recognize in the foregoing discussion a socio-historical explana- tion of the very problems that Lukács characterized by the metaphysical and existential concept of 'ordinary', inauthentic life. This correspondence extends even to details. For example, the problem of the 'tragedy of the artist' is viewed from the standpoint of the historian as the historically paradoxical task of the modern artist, who is forced to create universal cultural values in a world that has neither community nor culture. The possibility of a unified world view that would guarantee the validity and impact of art must now constantly be recreated by the artist, working alone and with the help only of the formal devices of art. But if he succeeds, his work becomes finally and irrevocably divorced from the everyday world (and therefore also from his own life) and stands opposed to it, irreversibly different, transcendent. The 'tragedy of the artist' stems from the fact that 'what had never been a question of art, and should never have become an artistic problem, did become one.'[66]

This discussion is intended merely to illustrate that metaphysical and socio-historical exposition and analysis of the process of alienation as a crisis of culture accompany each other in a complex pattern of parallels and contradictions throughout Lukács' whole pre-Marxist period. (Similarly, lengthy analysis should not be needed to prove that the socio-historical form of analysis indicates right from the beginning the influence of Marx – albeit a Marx viewed through the prism of Simmel's interpretation.) Lukács himself often posed explicitly the question of the relationship between these two methods of investigation and discussion and set himself the task of reconciling them in a logically consistent way. Indeed, this undertaking constitutes the main theme of some of his writings. There is no space here for a detailed analysis of his answers to this question, which differ in detail and sometimes in fundamental respects but all point in the same direction. We must restrict ourselves to the observation that the problem was more profound and more general than the way in which it is formulated in Lukács' early works makes it appear. Those of his works that address this problem that we have mentioned earlier restrict themselves in the main to *methodological* considerations. (The central focus of these investigations is the relationship between the *a priori* – aesthetic and socio-historical concepts of form.) Important as these analyses are, the contradictions between the two methods of investigation imply something a great deal more significant. They are evidence of various (in part, contradictory) attempts to find a solution to the crisis of culture; they imply different historical perspectives. One should not, of course, assume simplistically that the conception of the crisis of culture as a historical phenomenon – by contrast with the 'metaphysical' interpretation – also automatically postulates a historical solution to this crisis. Not only would such an assumption be a logical *non sequitur*, but in regard to the actual, concrete content of the perspective, the socio-historical analyses, where they pose the question at all, do not in any case offer any solution other than the antinomies already discussed in the context of the philosophical analysis. The conclusion of these works is no more 'optimistic' than that of the 'philosophical' essays or the systematic writings. The difference lies in Lukács' approach to the question.

In the 'philosophical' writings the question of whether culture is possible, of whether it is possible to shape life, appears, as we have seen, to be an *ethical problem*, a question of moral conduct – either active or passive behaviour, but in either case behaviour based on free, individual self-determination or, more generally, a question of the way in which the individual leads his life. The form in which the question is posed in the historical analyses, on the other hand, implies by its very nature a concern with the sociologically determined *transformation of society* and its patterns of life, as well as with the mass movements that might bring this about and the possibility of their success, which can at least be defined in sociological terms.

As is apparent from Lukács' incompletely preserved correspondence, at about the beginning of 1918 his interest became focused on the sphere of ethics and, in particular, on the relationship between ethics and politics.[67] We will not go far wrong, however, if we identify the relationship between the 'philosophical' and historical analyses – already formulated as a conscious question by Lukács by this time – as the 'limiting problem' of the whole of his early development. The antinomy between the two irresistible forces, 'one pouring out without reasons from within and the other flowing without meaning in the world',[68] already implicit in his earliest works, gradually became an explicit and conscious theoretical problem. Seen in this light, Lukács' conversion to Marxism in 1918 was not a break, an irrational hiatus in the evolution of his ideas, but an attempt to find both a theoretical answer and a practical solution to the question that had, in the final analysis, fuelled the whole of his early development.[69]

Translated by Michael Clark

NOTES

1 Quotation taken from David Kettler, 'Culture and Revolution. Lukács in the Hungarian Revolution of 1918–19', *Telos*, 10, 1971, p. 69.

2 Letter to the poet Mihály Babits, March 1910 (ms).

3 A more detailed discussion may be found in Mihály Vajda, 'A dialektika nyomában' ('On the Track of the Dialectic') (ms).

4 *Történelem és osztálytudat* (History and Class Consciousness), (Budapest: Magvetö, 1971), p. 17.

5 One thinks in the first instance of the prefaces to various volumes of his *Selected Works* in Hungarian.

6 In the meantime these manuscripts have been published in German by F. Benseler and myself under the title *Heidelberger Philosophie der Kunst (1912–14)* and *Heidelberger Ästhetik (1916–18)*, volumes 16–17 of Lukács' works (Darmstadt–Neuwied: Luchterhand, 1974 and 1975).

7 Of course, this picture of Lukács is not the only one that has been put forward in the literature on the subject. In particular, there are two studies on which I have based my comments to a large extent, both in this connection and in other respects: Ferenc Fehér, 'Balázs Béla és Lukács György szövetsége a forradalomig' ('The Alliance between Béla Balázs and György Lukács up to the Hungarian Revolution of 1918), *Irodalomtörténeti Tanulmányok* (Budapest), 1969, and Andrew Arato, 'Lukács' Path to Marxism (1910–23)', *Telos*, 7, 1971.

8 G. Lukács, 'Esztétikai kultura' ('Aesthetic Culture') in the volume of the same name (Budapest: Atheneum, 1913), pp. 12, 14 (abbreviated here as *AC*). The essay itself is also published in *Müvészet és Társadalom* (Art and Society) (Budapest: Gondolat, 1969), pp. 72 – 84.

9 Cf. *Die Theorie des Romans*, (Neuwied: Luchterhand, 1971), p. 131 (abbreviated hereafter as *ThR*).

10 *Zur romantischen Lebensphilosophie: Novalis*, in *Die Seele und die Formen* (Soul and Form) (Neuwied: Luchterhand, 1971) (abbreviated hereafter as *SuF*).

11 *ThR*, p. 26.

12 To mention just the most important of these attempts: 'Megjegyzések az irodalomtörténet elméletéhez' ('Remarks on the Theory of Literary History'), in *Müvészet és Társadalom* (*Art and Society*) (Budapest: Gondolat, 1968), pp. 31 – 56 (the essay is abbreviated hereafter as *Remarks*); ch. 3 of *Heidelberger Philosophie der Kunst*; the first few chapters of *ThR*.

13 *Die Metaphysik der Tragödie: Paul Ernst*, in *SuF*, p. 128.

14 *AC*, pp. 22 – 3.

15 'Über Wesen und Form des Essays', in *SuF*, p. 31.

16 *Von der Armut am Geiste*, Neue Blätter, II (1912), 5 – 6, p. 73.

17 *ThR*, pp. 53, 55.

18 *Die Metaphysik der Tragödie*, p. 225.

19 ibid., p. 224.

20 *AC*, p. 16.

21 *Von der Armut am Geiste*, p. 86.

22 *Die Metaphysik der Tragödie*, p. 219.

23 *Das Zerschellen der Form am Leben: Sören Kierkegaard und Regine Olsen*, *SuF*, p. 39.

24 *Die Metaphysik der Tragödie*, p. 232.

25 *ThR*, p. 132.

26 *A modern dráma fejlödésének története* (History of the Development of the Modern Drama) (Budapest: Franklin 1911), pp. 100 – 1 (abbreviated hereafter as *Dev. Drama.*) This concept of 'mere existence' later becomes a key term in Lukács' system of thought. See, for example, *Die Metaphysik der Tragödie*, or ch. 3 of *Heidelberger Philosophie der Kunst*.

27 Characteristically, in his *Obituary for Dilthey* (Budapest: Szellem, 1911), p. 253, Lukács names psychologism as the reason for the complete failure of Dilthey's efforts to bring about a philosophical renaissance.

28 This is formulated most clearly in 'Az utak elváltak' ('The Ways have Parted'), in *AC*.

29 Cf., for example, *Dev. Drama*, I, pp. 12 – 13: 'man's whole being can only manifest itself with immediate energy in his will and in his actions initiated by his will. . . . For emotions and thoughts are transient and variable in form, much more elastic in their nature and more exposed to outside influences than the will. The individual does not know how far his emotions and thoughts are really his own (or how far they have become so). He only knows this with complete certainty when they are tested for some reason, that is, when he has to act in accordance with them, when they become part of his will and result in actions.'

30   *Dev. Drama*, vol. 1, p. 153, refers to Fichte as the common source of the philosophy of Stirner and of Marx.

31   'The Ways have Parted', *AC*, p. 33.

32   *AC*, p. 29.

33   *Obituary for Leo Popper, Pester Lloyd*, 19 December 1911.

34   The aim of this study is to outline the basic structural features of the philosophy of the young Lukács. We cannot go into any more detail about the more complicated aspects of his development. In general terms, this development moves in the direction of an increasing rejection of *Lebensphilosophie*. The last substantial systematic work of this pre-Marxist period, *Aesthetics* (written 1916 – 18), is quite clearly Kantian in character, although it is a very idiosyncratic, distinctly *dualistic* form of Kantianism. Lukács makes this point himself in the first chapter of his *Aesthetics*, when he refers explicitly to the connection between his views in general and those of Rickert and Lask.

35   *AC*, p. 28.

36   The *plurality* and the *autonomy* of the various forms are basic themes in the philosophy of the young Lukács. His *Aesthetics* refers to this question as one of the most important theoretical considerations that turned him against Hegelian philosophy (the manuscript contains an elaborated critical confrontation with Hegel). Hegel's monism and panlogism are based on the assumption that all forms of transcendental constitution can be reduced to one single type, namely theoretical logical constitution – more accurately, that they can be deduced logically from its principles. By contrast, Lukács formulates the Kantian 'basic thesis' of his own system as 'the complete independence of all autonomous forms of constitution from each other and the complete impossibility of deriving any one of them from any of the others' (*Aesthetics*, ch. 1).

37   *Philosophie der Kunst*, ch. 2. This fragment of a chapter was recently published in *Arion*, 5, 1972, p. 39.

38   *Remarks*, p. 38.

39   ibid., p. 39.

40   *AC*, p. 17.

41   *Remarks*, p. 36.

42   This is the basic starting-point of the critique of naturalism that recurs throughout Lukács' early writings. See, in particular, *Dev. Drama*, chs. 7 – 10, and *Philosophie der Kunst*, ch. 2, 'Phaenomenologische Skizze des schöpferischen und receptiven Verhaltens'.

43   *Philosophie der Kunst*, ch. 2. The first two chapters of the work treat the problem touched on here most fully and systematically.

44   ibid. See also *Arion*, 5, 1973, p. 46.

45   'Jenseits der Pflicht', *Revue Internationale de Philosophie*, 106 (1973), pp. 439ff.

46   *Philosophie der Kunst*, ch. 2.

47   *SuF*, p. 219.

48   ibid., p. 226.

49   ibid., p. 233.

50   For more on the Utopias of the young Lukács, see the studies by F. Fehér and A. Heller (see notes 7 and 45).

51   Cf. *ThR*, pp. 117 – 19, 128.
52   ibid., pp. 137 – 8. Cf. also 'Halálos fiatalság (Fatal Youth), in *Magyar irodalom,*
     magyar kultura (Hungarian Literature, Hungarian Culture) (Budapest: Gondolat,
     1970), pp. 113 – 16. To understand the role played by the 'Dostoevsky Utopia' in
     the development of Lukacs' thought, one should bear in mind that the outbreak of
     war led to a distinct shift (albeit short-lived) in the direction of irrationalism. This
     accompanied a resurgence of the influence of *Lebensphilosophie*, which had earlier
     faded. The reasons for this shift emerge clearly in his letters to Paul Ernst. On 14
     April 1915, for example, he writes: 'The power of forms seems to be constantly
     increasing, and for most people they seem to be more real than what actually ex-
     ists. But – and this is for me *the* experience of the war – we must not concede to
     it. We must keep on emphasizing that the only really essential things are we
     ourselves, our souls, and even their eternal *a priori* objectivations are (to borrow a
     beautiful image created by Ernst Bloch) only paper money, whose value depends
     on its convertibility into gold. The very real power of forms cannot be denied.
     But German thought ever since Hegel has been guilty of a deadly intellectual sin in
     investing every power with metaphysical significance.' Less than a month later, on
     4 May, he replies to Ernst's comments: 'When you say that the state is part of the
     self, you are correct. When you say that it is part of the soul, you are wrong.
     Everything to which we are in any way related is part of our self (even the subject-
     matter of mathematics), but this self which "creates" these objects (in the sense
     that they are synthesized by our reason), and makes them an inseparable part of
     itself, is an *abstract* methodological concept, and the annexation to the self of ob-
     jects created in this way is a purely methodological relation. The mistake is to treat
     the self as if it were the soul. Since by giving the subject the status of something
     permanent and substantial one automatically accords the same status to the cor-
     responding object, "forms" become real and metaphysical. And *only the soul*
     possesses metaphysical reality. That is not a solipsism. The problem is to find the
     paths which lead from one soul to another.' (A substantial part of this cor-
     respondence was published in *MTA II, Osztályának Közleményei* (Budapest), 20
     (1972), pp. 284, 296.) However, this irrationalist negation of historical objectiva-
     tions is no longer present in the *Aesthetics*, on which Lukács was working from
     1916 onwards. This work is a clear extension of the basic trend of Lukács'
     development, within which his move in the direction of irrationalism (which part-
     ly reflected the direct influence of historico-philosophical mysticism) proved to be
     no more than a short-lived interruption. The biographical material relating to the
     young Lukács in Hungarian (most of it still unpublished), by contrast, highlights
     mainly this mystical, irrational element in his thought or reacts to it in some way.
     (Important sources are passages from the diaries of Béla Balázs, Anna Lesznai and
     others, and the reminiscences of individual members of Lukács' early circle of
     friends.) It seems, however, that the emphasis in this biographical material is at
     least as much a product of the intellectual attitudes of the members of Lukács' cir-
     cle as a reflection of the views of the philosopher himself.
53   *Dev. Drama* I, p. 173;
54   ibid., p. 173.
55   ibid., pp. 195 – 6.

56 Cf. ibid., pp. 160 – 1.
57 ibid., pp. 148 – 9.
58 ibid., p. 152.
59 ibid., p. 160.
60 ibid., p. 105.
61 ibid., p. 453.
62 ibid., p. 161.
63 ibid., pp. 164 – 6.
64 Cf. ibid., pp. 145 – 6.
65 ibid., pp. 146 – 7.
66 ibid., pp. 196 – 7.
67 The first important document relating to this interest is Lukács' contribution to the debate on conservative and progressive idealism in *Társadalomtudományi Társaság* (Society for the Social Sciences). Cf. 'A konzervativ és progressziv idealizmus vitája' ('The Debate between Conservative and Progressive Idealism'), in *Utam Marxhoz* (My Way to Marx), I (Budapest: Gondolat, 1971), pp. 177 – 86.
68 *Die Metaphysik der Tragödie*, p. 241.
69 Since a number of extremely important early works by Lukács still remain unpublished and others are available only in Hungarian, it would seem necessary, finally, to give a brief survey of them and use them to define, at least formally, the most important phases of his pre-Marxist writings.

    From 1906 to 1907, Lukács was working on his first really significant work, *The History of the Development of the Modern Drama*, written as an entry for a competition run by the Kisfaludi Society. He won the prize for the manuscript but revised it substantially in 1908 – 9, as can be seen from several handwritten chapters of the first version. This revised version appeared in 1911. The study 'Remarks on the Theory of Literary History' (see note 12) is in essence an extension of this work, clarifying its most important methodological presuppositions.

    The 'essay period' spans the years 1908 to 1911. All of the essays contained in the volumes *Soul and Form* (in Hungarian, 1910) and *Aesthetic Culture* (1913; see note 8) were written during this period, as well as some of the essays contained in the volume on Béla Balázs (in Hungarian, 1918). In part, the works contained in the earlier volumes are, in accordance with Lukács' principles of selection and editing, 'replies', which supplement each other in a polemical debate. We have already pointed this out in connection with a number of specific problems in the course of this study. In any case, one must examine some of the essays in the much less well-known volume *Aesthetic Culture* (above all, the eponymous essay and 'The Ways have Parted') and the dialogue *On Spiritual Poverty* (see note 16), not printed in any of these volumes, alongside the most important essays in the volume *Soul and Form* in order to get to know the ideas and views of the young Lukács.

    In 1912 Lukács began working on his systematic *Philosophy of Art*. The work was evidently interrupted by the First World War; three chapters (about 450 typescript pages) were completed by 1914.

    At the end of 1914 Lukács planned a substantial monograph on Dostoevsky. As can be seen from the hand-written synopsis, he wanted to touch on a number of questions (such as religion and atheism, the state, revolution, socialism and terror) in connection with his main theme. After completing the first, introductory, theoretical chapter, however, he stopped work on the project in 1915. The first chapter appeared in 1916 under the title *The Theory of the Novel*.

In 1916 Lukács returned to the philosophy of art and wanted to produce a detailed and systematic treatment of the subject. However, on the basis of a substantially revised conception and a new structural outline, he did not continue the work he had started before the war but made a radical new start. Of the earlier *Philosophy of Art* only the second chapter was to be incorporated into the new manuscript, probably in a revised form. By the beginning of 1918, four chapters of this new *Aesthetics* were finished (about the same length in total as the earlier work he had left unfinished). One of these, the third, 'The Subject – Object Relation in Aesthetics', was published in 1917 in *Logos*. In May 1918 Lukács submitted five chapters of the still unfinished book to the University of Heidelberg in order to habilitate. Rickert and H. Meier even wrote their reports on the dissertation, but, of course, it never reached the stage of being discussed.

2

Georg Lukács and Irma Seidler

AGNES HELLER

I

'Kierkegaard created his relationship with Regine Olsen' writes Kassner, quoted by Lukács in his immortal essay on Kierkegaard. And Georg Lukács created his relationship with Irma Seidler.[1] He created it again and again according to the rules of 'Platonic' conduct: through the prism of *others'* fates, *others'* works, *others'* 'forms'. Virtually every one of the pieces in *Soul and Form* reflects such recreation. 'The Philippe essay is maturing strangely,' he notes in his diary on 20 May 1910. 'It seems this will be the most genuine Irma essay, the lyric of the present stage. . . . Thus the true lyrical series will be completed: George, Beer-Hofman, Kierkegaard, Philippe. The interrelation of the others is much looser: Novalis – the mood of the first meeting; Kassner – Florence, Ravenna; Storm – letters from Nagybánya.' And on 29 May he writes: 'the Ernst essay will be an Irma essay as well.'

Georg Lukács recreated his relationship with Irma Seidler. In none of the essays can we discover even a single objective similarity between the real and the fictional Irma. The recreation of the relationship consists of the exploration of its own *possibilities*, which Lukács thought (and lived out) according to the rules of 'Platonic' conduct. They are daydreams or, more accurately, rational visions, the dreams and visions of 'what could be if . . .', 'what could have been if . . .'. In these daydreams and visions, however, the Other is only a vague shape, an amorphous object; *the only real being is the one who dreams.*

These rational visions are addressed to Irma, but Irma is not present in them. Through the prism of his 'Platonic' stance, the author of the essays testifies to his own possibilities. Kierkegaard exists, but Regine Olsen does not. In Storm's life, consecrated to duty, the beloved wife is no more than an anonymous accessory to the ethical conduct of life. The loves of Novalis are mere symbols of the poet's earthly fulfilment. Philippe's Marie Donadieu is no more than 'great love's' drillground for Jean, the actual hero. ('Marie was for him merely a course in self-knowledge, his duty done; he is now free to walk his own paths.') In the George essay no woman is present, only a man 'who does not wear his heart on his sleeve', passing from loneliness, through love, back into loneliness.

Every individual – in so far as he or she is capable of reflection, of making human relationships the objects of his or her thinking – in a certain sense 'creates' relationship with the Other and goes on recreating it. In the light of later events certain incidents in the past acquire specific symbolic meanings; others disappear into the abyss of forgetting. Indifferent gestures are amplified by the joy of mutual recognition, or they are gradually swallowed up by the slough of sorrow and disappointment. And if something is over once and for all, is there anyone who would not scrutinize the facts repeatedly to verify whether they are indeed the facts of necessity? Is there anyone who would not think through the possibilities again and again with the wish-fulfilling logic (or illogic) of daydreams? A base life poetry turns white into black; on its eerie screen the poet alone remains white. A noble life poetry transforms, again and again, not the colours but the composition. Every individual creates and recreates his or her human relationships; but such creation is most often addressed only to self; it is painful or beautiful only for oneself.

'Kierkegaard [writes Kassner] created his relationship with Regine Olsen, and if a Kierkegaard creates his life, he does not do so in order to conceal, but rather to articulate the truth.' If Lukács continually recreated his relationship with Irma Seidler, he did so not in order to conceal but in order better to articulate the truth. For he had a truth, which was not addressed to himself alone, was not painful or beautiful for himself alone.

When he dreamed and thought out the 'Irma possibilities', he was not thinking out the contingencies that derived from the 'accidental' meeting of two 'accidental' entities. Both the I-hero of the essays and their non-objectified object are invested with symbolic, stylized meaning. The I-hero is always the creative man who strives to impose shape and form on a chaotic, prosaic, lifeless, culture-forsaken world. The object of desire is always life or, more accurately, the life to be shaped. 'In life, desire can only be love' – the object of love is the object of desire *in* life and *for* life. But can life be shaped? Or (to ask the same question in reverse) can there be an organic path that leads from life to the created work? Can the creative individual live a *genuine* life? Is it given to the creative individual to experience love and being-with-others, the happiness of human togetherness?

'Last night I felt again: Irma is life' (Diary, 8 May 1910). In his work Lukács stylized the 'Irma possibilities' into symbolic events. During their first correspondence, which began harmoniously, he considered the possibilities of life together, marriage, companionship: the Storm essay saw light, bearing witness to the fact that life can be given form, that creative work can burgeon from a life consecrated to a calling. After their break-up he wrote the Kierkegaard essay, in which the shaping of life proves to be a futile, shipwrecked endeavour. The Philippe essay, a masterpiece of haughty renunciation, was written in the fear and hope of meeting again. Great love must be ascetic – the creative individual must touch life but only in order to transcend it. Each essay is an *attitude* – testimony to various possibilities, various stances. But the question levelled at these possibilities and attitudes is always the same: how can creation take place? How can forms be generated in a chaotic, prosaic, lifeless, culture-forsaken world?

The truth that Lukács wished not to conceal but to articulate is contained in this question. He created his relationship with Irma Seidler so that in the act he might formulate this question, the vital issue for every significant, conscious, creative individual of the bourgeois world, the problem of the viability of the created work in the first decade of the twentieth century.

'Last night I felt again: Irma is life.' Every individual 'creates' his relationship to the Other and continually re-creates it. If the creation of a relationship with the Other is addressed only to oneself, if it is painful or beautiful only for oneself, then the forms of recreation are infinite and its colours and compositions innumerable. But if someone creates his relationship with the Other for the purpose of articulating a truth, which is not painful or beautiful for himself alone, which is not addressed to himself alone, then the forms of recreation and the colours and compositions are finite. From then on, the general problem defines even the private dreams, and everything in the relationship of the two individuals acquires symbolic significance. The boundary lines between the diary and the essays become blurred: what has each drawn from the other? Did Lukács compose his essays in the way that he did because he had composed his relationship with Irma in a certain manner, or was the reverse the case? Did he create his relationship with Irma in a certain way because in his essays he had given certain answers to the vital questions of the ever-present I? What was prior here: forms or life? Which formed which? Did the human relationship form the philosophy, or did the philosophy form the human relationship?

> But as it is now: metaphysically, I am absolutely faithless, homeless, etc.; in reality, however, I am faithful and earthbound. By now – because in the ultimate human interrelations man acts with the metaphysical essence of his being (well named: *ens realissimum*) – everyone treats me as though I were unfaithful, while (in reality!) I am like a faithful and unfortunate lover. – It was with Irma that all this was most evidently so. (Diary, 11 May 1910)

The I is doubled; spontaneity is lost in so far as it remains incognito; the 'metaphysical I', the stance of the essays' I, is the *ens realissimum*; individual/personal possibilities are circumscribed by philosophical possibilities: the conduct of the individual becomes, willingly or unwillingly, the expression of finite, symbolic forms of conduct. Lukács created his relationship with Irma Seidler through his philosophical I; *he aligned his life with the truth of philosophy.* Every philosopher must *live out* his philosophy; the unlived philosophy is philosophy no longer. But this philosophy – the philosophy of contradiction between life and the created work – cannot be lived out without life's being shipwrecked in the process. Life avenges itself on form in general by conforming to the principles of *this* form. In the Philippe essay of 1910 the hero strides past that stage of his fate in which woman – life – still could play a role, in the following manner: 'Desire had made him hard, strong. He, who had permitted the woman to depart sobbing wordlessly, annihilated, trembling in pain, now gained luminous strength for the renunciation. . . . For he had destroyed the woman's life, had he not?' Life avenges itself on philosophy by realizing it hideously.

And Lukács knew that life's revenge was more than revenge: it was *judgement.* In his dialogue *On Spiritual Poverty* he identified sin with the intermingling of castes. The man of forms *must not* attach himself to life. But the unlived philosophy is philosophy no longer. And in *The Theory of the Novel* a motif emerges that has already been implicit in all the questions he has posed for the world: that of the creation of a new, genuine, interpersonal life, a life that overcomes the dualism of the 'empirical' and the 'metaphysical', a life that (as Thomas Mann said) will once again provide an existential basis for art.

The dreams of *Soul and Form* were addressed to Irma, but Irma was not present in them. The author of the essays bore witness to his own possibilities, to the possibilities of his own 'metaphysical I'. But Irma Seidler was not Regine Olsen. Kierkegaard could create his relationship with Regine Olsen, and he could create it in such a way that posterity could only seek – and find – the possibilities of the philosopher's I in this philosophical poetry. Regine Olsen is truly no more than a non-objectified object, a being transformed into symbol, who does not intrude into the story – which is not her story but that of the man who has given her (symbolic) form. Irma Seidler was not Regine Olsen, who lived happily until she died; she was not the heroine of philosophical parables. She put an end to the philosophical parables once and for all with her final gesture of suicide. It was she, and not the philosopher himself, who cast into doubt and rendered equivocal the philosophy of *Soul and Form* with this final gesture. And through her death she earned the right to share this story, not merely as its object but as its subject as well.

II

Act One

Georg first met Irma in December 1907. It was in the midst of noisy company that he noticed a female voice with an unusual timbre. He set out after the voice, moving from room to room in search of its owner – and found her. The unwritten laws of their social class did not permit them to meet frequently; altogether they spent no more than a few hours with one another.

Irma wants to be a painter – on 28 May 1908 she leaves for Florence. Georg follows her with a friend. Among Georg's papers, the following notes:

Two minutes on the train. . . . Two beautiful moments as we cross the Ponte Vecchio. . . . Saturday, 6 June. S. Croce and S. Lorenzo with Irma. We buy pictures. Bargello. Alone in the evening; one kiss in the dark.

They return to Budapest on 1 June. A few meetings. Among Georg's papers, the draft of the Kassner essay, with the following inscription:

I read part of this to Irma on 28 June 1908, on Svab Hill. After that, I saw her only twice. On 1 July I. leaves for Nagybánya,[2] to study painting.

Among Georg's papers, the following notes, dated between 1 and 3 July:

Scruples: (marriage would be impossible). . . . I was prepared for malaise, fear, the mellowing effect of happiness, fear that I might not be able to orient myself in a more broadly based life.

From 1 July through October: correspondence. 25 October: Irma's first letter to suggest breaking off the relationship. 2 November: Irma's second letter on the same topic. Among Georg's papers, a draft of a goodbye letter:

I must write now, now when you will only receive these lines along with the news of my death. . . .

Irma marries R.

Act Two

In March 1910 Georg sends the Hungarian edition of his volume of essays to Irma, accompanied by a letter. The draft of the letter, addressing her as 'Most esteemed Madam', survived among his papers.

This truly cannot obligate you to me in any manner, for it is I who am obliged to thank you, with the most sincere and most deeply felt gratitude and affection, for everything you have done for me, for everything you have been to me, for what you have made of me.

Irma's answer:

Dear Gyuri,[3] my heartfelt thanks for the book. . . . Sincere greetings, Irma Seidler, R.

The diary begins in April 1910.

There's trouble: I am thinking only of her; she could help me. (27 April)

To remember one event with her is more than a life to be spent with another. (8 May)

But: in that most general sense, everything is 'over between us'. Between us, yes. But from me to her: no. And from her to me, who knows? (14 May).

Irma will have something to do with the end. (1 June)

Strange, I knew her for barely a year, and how long it took me to learn what she really meant to me. (21 June)

Georg decides to dedicate the German edition of his essays to Irma. Dedication drafts:

I place this book in your hands, for you have given me more than I could possibly recount in it, everything that I have acquired and won. And even if you do not need, even if you will not suffer this expression of gratitude, it will still fall silently upon your head like faded flowers in autumn. (14 May)

In memory of my first days in Florence.

I entrust this book to the hands that gave it to me.

Autumn 1910. Georg's letter to his friend, L.:

The difficulties, it seems, are still greater for Irma. I saw a sketch of hers for a fresco. . . . it is as though Nagybánya and R. never existed. And with her . . . this is a bad sign – in terms of her marriage. The fact that she is coming to Budapest this winter while her husband is to stay in Nagybánya is only a symptom of this. . . . Lucky for me that by the time she will have arrived, I shall be far away, that by now I look upon this whole affair with simple human compassion – so much so that I could even be her well meaning friend if it were not so dangerous (for her), which, of course, is why it will not be. . . .

Act Three

January 1911: Georg's letter to Irma, in which he asks her to accept the dedication from him.

You know . . . why these writings were written: because I cannot write poems, and you know, too, to whom these 'poems' are addressed and who awakened them in me.

What I wish to accomplish only an unattached man can accomplish.

Irma's answer:

Thank you for preserving so much warmth for me. I am proud that I had something to do with the production of such a book – or that you believe that I had. I am also glad that – as it turns out – I read the Hungarian edition correctly.

March 1911. Georg and Irma meet for the first time for almost three years. Georg's letters to his friend, L.:

Irma is here and we've met a few times, and so far it seems everything is over. But Irma is so immensely unhappy; it's so certain that her marriage is totally, hopelessly bad.

That the harm she did to me turned out well for me in the end – in this she is innocent. That it was even worse for her – this is her misfortune.

I've chattered on about myself too long; perhaps in your eyes, suspiciously long.

Irma's two letters to Georg, sent by messenger in March 1911.

But I must *absolutely* speak with you alone before your trip. . . . and *don't leave before* we've had a chance to speak with one another. Greetings, Irma. Please send an answer to mother.

I would *very much* like to speak with you, yet. . . . And I wish you lovely days. . . . God be with you, Gyuri, your true friend, Irma.

Her letter to Georg in Florence, 19 April 1911:

My dear good friend Gyuri, why don't you ever write me a line? Please write, my dear Gyuri, for I am as alone here as a stray dog.

Georg's reply:

therefore, I beg you please to understand: it was deeply beautiful that we met again in Budapest, and what revived between us, I sense, is but a beginning. . . . But I am happy to be alone. It's not that I wish you both away – but I wish to keep myself to myself.

Georg's letter, written in Florence, to Irma in Budapest:

At times I fear you don't write because things aren't going well. This would pain me deeply. For I know there's little, almost nothing . . . I could do for you now in case of trouble. But still, perhaps. . . .

Irma's last letter to Georg, 28 April: Something must be understood all over again. *In every respect.*

April – May 1911: Irma's brief relationship with Georg's friend, H. In ending the relationship, H. appeals to the sanctity of friendship. Irma commits suicide.

On 24 May Georg makes the following entry in his diary:

'No one is so poor that God cannot make him poorer still.' I did not know this. Every bond is broken – for she was every bond. And now there are only shared goals, and things, and work. For she was everything. Everything. Everything. Every thought I brought to her was a flower, and its joy and value were that it was hers, and that perhaps she'd see it and delight in it. . . . Now it does not matter . . . whether or not she wanted me. If one feels this way about someone, he must always be ready. He must wait by her doorstep, and perhaps once. . . . Only in this way can he become worthy of what he feels. Only in this way can he earn the right to be human. I have lost my right to life. . . .

III

'The gesture is unequivocal only so far as every psychology is conventional,' writes Lukács in his Kierkegaard essay.

In the world of conventions every gesture is unequivocal, clear, transparent, intelligible. We know what a kiss signifies; we know what a love letter signifies, or a warm squeeze of the hand at the gate, or dancing with the same person all night at a ball, or a serenade under the windows; we know what a betrothal or marriage signifies; we also know what marital infidelity signifies. The significance of individual gestures is regulated by institutions and customs. If the gesture is sincere, there can be no misunderstanding; the only source of misunderstanding is deceit, but deceit also presupposes knowledge of the significance of gestures: it is the abuse of these significations. But the significance of gestures remains unequivocal for all that; indeed, deceit confirms their unequivocal meaning.

Subjectively, Kierkegaard did not participate in the world of conventions; his psychology was not conventional. But in his approach to, and estrangement from, another human being he nevertheless utilized this conventional set of customs. He was betrothed: he retracted his promise. Although Regine Olsen may have sensed concealed in the gesture a uniqueness that could not be described in terms of psychological conventions, she could just as well have interpreted it according to the significations of sacrosanct custom. According to conventional signification, the breaking off of an engagement definitively concludes a relationship. This may be painful, but in the last analysis, according to the rules of custom, it also signifies finality and freedom regained. Regine Olsen was a child of convention, therefore she could marry another man and live happily until she died.

But what happens if the customs lose their validity? What happens when neither of the two people has a conventional psychology? Indeed, what if neither of them has access to a system of institutions and customs whose significations could help to interpret both the Other's actions and gestures and, at the same time, his or her own actions and emotions? Can two people meet at all in harmonious mutual understanding if all existing institutions and their significations embody for them a contemptible, unacceptable, quotidien banality, if life turns into pure chaos, from which they rise like two solitary mountain peaks? Can one soul reach out to another if it experiences only itself as genuinely existent?

Yet the fated togetherness of Georg Lukács and Irma Seidler was rooted in their lonely rejection of the conventions. And precisely because of this, their being fated for each other could never become living for each other.

Both Georg Lukács and Irma Seidler came from bourgeois, Jewish Budapest families, the former from a financially buoyant, rising family, the latter from a waning one. The 'social existence' into which they were born repelled both of them overwhelmingly. They were disgusted by the musty atmosphere of the home contaminated by petty deals, calculations, self-seeking and the conventions of money. This was the life in which they were raised, and they both felt strongly that this life was somehow 'not genuine'. The home, the family, the institutions were all inauthentic. They were both strangers among their own people. Lukács fled into 'pure spirit'; he learned to breathe the heady air of philosophy. To the irrelevant conventions that represented chaos to him he counterposed pure spirit, the created work. Irma's rebellion was rooted in goodness; she could not bear the sight of suffering, and she herself suffered because she was unable to relieve hardship.

> What shall I do? Imagine, a lovely young and talented woman accustomed to hunger: is it not monstrous? What I can do to help her amounts to nil. (26 July 1908)

> I was tremendously delighted with the 10 forints, which I rushed to the L.'s; they immediately bought some paint and food. In the autumn you will receive a small sketch from them . . . because I cannot give them the money like this, without asking for something in return. (2 August)

At the same time this considerate and good person felt uncertain in the atmosphere of 'pure spirit', which for her was not heady but rather too rare. She yearned for palpable, sensual reality, for nature. She writes confidently:

> We have both, I think, passed through in a very healthy way, a perhaps overly theoretical stage. I through nature, and you through positive history, through the study of Marx. (23 August)

In 1919, had she lived, Irma Seidler would certainly have considered her vocation to be the organization of summer holidays for the proletarian children.

This was the root of Georg Lukács' and Irma Seidler's fated-togetherness. And yet, this being-fated-for-each-other could never become living-for-each-other.

Can one soul reach another if it experiences only itself as authentically existent? Can two people understand each other if every word and gesture between them has significance only in and for itself, if the institutions and customs do not offer at least some basis for the *interpretation* of gestures and words? Or, to inquire further: *is pure communication, free of all regulation, created from the void, at all possible?*

Lukács tries incessantly to make himself understood by Irma, to make her understand the being who is *specifically him*, who is no one else but him. 'Love' has no meaning; it is a banal word. 'I miss you' has no meaning; it, too, is a banal expression. What must be made clear to the Other is what it means (for me and only for me) to love, what it means (for me and only for me) to miss someone. But the articulation of the question 'What does it mean to . . . ?' requires an entire system of categories. And Lukács borrows this system of categories from his own philosophy. Personal feelings are not articulated in the conventional significations; they *gain their significance from Lukács' philosophy*, from a philosophy whose essence – and system of categories – is inaccessible to Irma. Every word becomes ambiguous, every sentence equivocal. Desire loses its object; the I becomes a construct; 'making oneself understood' turns into its own opposite. The more Lukács wishes to reveal his I to Irma, the deeper, the more impenetrable, his incognito becomes.

> There are people who understand and do not live, and there are others who live and do not understand. The first kind can never really reach the second even though they understand them, and the second can never understand anything, but then, that cannot be important for them in any case because they love or hate, tolerate or will tolerate, and the category of understanding does not exist for them

writes Lukács in March 1910 to Irma, analysing the failure of their relationship. Lukács created and recreated his relationship with Irma Seidler through the prism of his philosophy, for his analysis is, in fact, philosophical poetry: 'Irma is life.' The man of philosophy understands the man of life; the man of life knows how to live but does not understand the man of philosophy. Thus far the poem. But the reality is this: no man can make himself understood through the prism of his philosophical categories alone; no one can grasp what is intangible. Irma was not 'life' – not in the philosophical sense of the word. She did not merely want to live; she also wanted to understand the Other, but the Other's self-clarification was incomprehensible to her. Lukács did not understand Irma because he wanted to understand her, too, through philosophical categories, and the living person, with his living desires, cannot be understood thus.

You wished to save me – I thank you. You wished to save me, but I cannot be saved. . . . You have ventured upon an impossible task, and you have realized this, have you not? Or, rather, life has made you realize it, life, which loves those who know how to live and hates those of my ilk. (Lukács' goodbye letter to Irma, November – December 1908)

Irma . . . *the* woman, the redeemer. . . . (Diary, 25 April 1910)

But perhaps I could have saved her if I had taken her by the hand and led her. (Diary, 24 May 1911)

Rescue, redemption, grace – these are the categories in terms of which Lukács describes his relationship to Irma, whether in the dialogue of misunderstandings or in his monologues. Irma wished to save him. Irma wished to redeem him. The attempt at redemption failed, and he fell back on solitude. Had Irma truly understood him, he would have partaken of grace, which, in the mystical sense of the word, is merging with the Other. But Irma could not save him. And after the terrible end the roles were – apparently – reversed: it is he who should have saved Irma; it is he who should have redeemed Irma. But he could not save her, could not redeem her, for he had not partaken of the 'grace of goodness' (*On Spiritual Poverty*). But the roles are only *apparently* reversed. Be he saved or saviour, redeemed or redeemer, it amounts to the same thing; *it is he who must partake of grace* in order either to be redeemed or to be capable of redeeming the Other.

'I go to prove my soul' – Lukács was to quote Browning well after the conclusion of our story, when he was researching the conduct of Dostoevsky's heroes – this was the 'challenge' of those living a lifeless life, those who did not wish to live by the norms of custom but still hoped to gain some insight into their own viability. Georg Lukács wished to 'prove' his own soul, his own human viability in his relationship with Irma Seidler. He did not wish to love; instead he sought *certainty*. He did not expect love, but rather this same certainty, proof of his own authenticity, redemption, grace. At that time, this is what the words 'love' and 'I am loved' meant to him.

But they did not mean the same to Irma Seidler. 'Dearest Gyuri, God be with you, write and love me, Irma' (14 August). For Irma wanted neither to save nor redeem the Other, just as she never wanted to be saved or redeemed. She simply wished to love and be loved. But she was loved – or perhaps not? What does it mean, 'to love'?

In the world of conventions every gesture is unequivocal, clear, transparent, intelligible. But, to reiterate the question: what happens when two people meet and neither has access to a system of institutions and customs whose significations could help to interpret the Other's actions and gestures? Can they still invest with the *same* significance the simple phrase that substantiates and resolves everything, that expresses the beginning and the end of everything, that joins soul to soul: 'I love you'?

What did 'to love' mean for Irma?

> You write that the difficult paths (in work) must always be walked alone. . . . But perhaps it is still possible for another to see every step. I see the value of two people's belonging together, in that one is *not alone*, in that all sorts of difficulties, losses, disappointments can be so much better borne if there is another, if someone holds one's hand. (5 August)

For Irma 'to love' meant to accept twofold solitude. To hold someone's hand was, for Irma, the gesture of earthly love.

> Back then she might have felt that I could save her from her troubles, though she did not love me. But perhaps I could have saved her, if I had taken her by the hand and led her. (Diary, 24 May)

The 'receiver' of Lukács' soul did not interpret the offer of holding hands as love ('she did not love me'): for him holding hands was the gesture of rescue, the gesture not of love but of goodness: 'For the union of souls there is no marriage bed.'

For Irma the symbolic holding of hands meant 'to love'; for Lukács redemption meant 'to love'. They both loved, *but neither felt loved* because the words 'I love you' meant something different to each.

Lukács and Irma were both strangers among their own people. For neither of them was ordinary life 'genuine'. The home, the family, the institutions – were all: inauthentic. But what could they counterpose to this?

Lukács posited the unmediated meeting of souls in the state of 'grace'. But the pure, unmediated meeting of souls could only be momentary.

> The possibility – the unique actualization of a possibility, says Eckhart – means its everlasting reality. Metaphysically, time does not exist. The moment when I am I is truly life, full life, and yet the 'moods' that permeate all of life are only 'momentary'. Here too, the same dreadful ambiguity. . . . is this not frivolous as well? In other words: the old problem . . . : at what point does Hjalmar Ekdal become distinguishable from Novalis? (Diary, 11 May)

Lukács does not spare himself the cruelty of the clear-sighted, truly noble individual towards himself; for, indeed, at what point *does* Hjalmar Ekdal become distinguishable from Novalis? At what point does the *conventional egotist* become distinguishable from the poet fearlessly experiencing his death? And how can the Other's 'receiver' not register the very ambiguity of what is problematic/-

ambiguous for the I itself? How can the Other distinguish these two inter-twined possibilities? How can it not see the fear of over-refined but embellished egotism in the stance of 'hours in lieu of life'?

The meeting of souls in the moment, 'hours in lieu of life' – this is what Lukács counterposed to the 'lifeless life' of the everyday world. But was this also Irma's answer? Was this also her choice?

Irma's visit to the Ferenczys:[4] 'They live a lovely life. . . . their life is truly not ordinary, but a noble, warmly simple something built upon immeasurable riches – it is a higher form of existence' (5 August). Irma's choice: life instead of hours, but not the ordinary life – the realization of a 'higher form of ex-istence'. Irma's choice: *habitable institutions.* Not institutions furnished with the banal furniture of custom, but those that provide comfort and warmth, those that create new meaning, those that can be replenished with the authentic life.

But can *privately* inhabited institutions be created? Is there a private language? Are private customs possible? Can two people make a world?

Lukács could not understand Irma's answer, for he necessarily saw illusion in all this; for he knew that no private language and no private customs can exist; for he knew that two people cannot create habitable institutions. Where culture is lacking, there the habitable institution is an 'island' at best. And even if he looked upon these islands with longing and held the authentic life organ-ized on these islands of habitable institutions to be exemplary, he still did not wish to live in Wilhelm Meister's marvellous tower. 'Irma is life' – and Lukács did not want this life.

But 'For the union of souls there is no marriage bed.' Did not the promise of the future lie in Irma's earthly dream after all?

IV

Strindberg – and many others after him – have written of the man and the woman who torture each other until all mutual understanding has been con-sumed by the heat of hate. But has anyone written the anti-Strindberg, the breath-taking drama of two souls in search of one another when all true gestures have become ambiguous, all understanding misunderstanding, when the words that are said cause pain and the unsaid words are even more painful, when we are able to express less and less, when self-revelation has become in-troversion until finally faith is silenced and the two souls are alienated from one another with the finality of fate? Has anyone written this drama yet?

Irma wrote the following letters to Georg from Nagybánya.

Act One: Confidence

I have received your letter, but I am still not frightened by the things you say in it. . . . But then, my dear Gyuri, listen to me: do you believe that two people can grow towards one another genuinely, not superficially but sincerely, without any pain? . . . After we grew so very close to one another, I sensed that something of this sort was bound to come. But I was not afraid. I treat the whole thing as some noble work, something that one does with courageous integrity, with nobility. (3 July 1908)

Act Two: Between Fear and Hope

I am afraid (and at times like this I feel very lonely) that you miss me, and miss me only where thoughts and work are concerned, in that domain which is yours, and mine, but which is not the only domain there is. No, don't be angry about these thoughts, which I can barely express. . . . it should mean no more to you than that there is something I cannot express. . . . I love you very much, you know that – but one should say so again, anyway. (17 July 1908)

As for what you write regarding the two of us, I have only one reply, dear Gyuri – I have been through so much disappointment. There have been men who loved me well, and they were all cowards. They were afraid of me – and now you too are afraid. I want a great love, the love of a noble man. You grant me this. (2 August 1908)

At times . . . it seems as though something has happened with you in relation to me. Something is not quite clear to us. . . . Letter-writing is wretched. . . . Love me and understand everything well. I was unable to say what I thought. I believe we can reach one another – but no, no more talk of this. I love you very much. (5 August 1908)

we so *very badly need* a day together, a lovely, sunny and serious day – with each other. [Georg should visit her; but if it disturbs his work, he should not come.] But if you can, if you are not afraid – then come, for sure. (14 August 1908)

I only know one *single* . . . method for your coming here. And that is: *openly*, with parental permission, with the express purpose of visiting Nagybánya and myself. (29 August 1908)

My last hope is that you might come from Budapest. *Openly*. (2 September 1908)

Act Three: Despair

During the summer you explained somewhat cruelly to me, in long, painful letters, that we cannot make each other happy after all. But at the time, all these things you were saying bounced off me. . . . And now the reaction has set in and it weighs heavily on me. (1 October 1908)

Gyuri, we spent much time together. . . . But we were not together with *every part* of our being. We were not together where I have my ,most wretchedly human core of blood and pulsating flesh which lives in tangible things. . . . And today I will discontinue this combative togetherness because I often feel, to a degree that will brook no argument, that there are things in which the most incisive and deep psychological analysis, as well as the peculiar delight that goes with it, are useless for me, because they cannot substitute for functions of the soul but remain merely intellectual pleasure. . . . You never told me, and I certainly never knew – because I always had ample reason to presume the opposite – I never knew whether or not you *really* considered joining my life to yours. And despite the fact that you have never said you wanted it so, today I ask you to return my freedom, which perhaps you never took from me, which you always hesitated and feared to take. I now reclaim it. You know that I've had to suffer a great deal to gather the strength to write you all this. . . . God be with you, Gyuri. I bid you goodbye because we cannot go on together. (25 October 1908)

My dearest one and only Gyuri, I am packing and coming to Budapest. . . . I want to speak to you, to speak to you and make myself understood. If there is still some way we can reach each other, I want us to do so. And if not, you will still remain in my lasting affection, and I will take my leave in the knowledge that the warmth of all my soul was yours, and I will always watch from afar every step that you take. The only thing that I urgently, deeply desire, if we must part, is that we do so not with bitterness but with magnanimous and tender sentiments – gently. (2 November 1908)

The last rendezvous to which she looked forward did not take place then.

V

There is resigned despair and provocative despair; provocative despair is always prompted by the expectation of miracles. Irma Seidler's despair was prompted by just such an expectation of miracles. Her goodbye letter is ambiguous. Her words speak of breaking up, but the passion that rises from the words with elemental force carries the opposite meaning. Irma wants one thing: the ultimate certainty, the definitive answer. The certainty of breaking up, the certainty of failure – or the miracle. Irma expected a miracle, and when it did not come she challenged it. Perhaps the finality of one certainty would *force* the miracle that the words of togetherness could not force; perhaps the finality of 'no' was the only way to attain the finality of yes'.

Irma's despair was the despair of the expectation of miracles. Perhaps she was not even expecting a big miracle, only a small miracle ('we so very badly need a day together', 'My last hope is that you might come from Budapest') – but the small miracle is as much a miracle as the big one, and it is fruitless to expect miracles; they cannot be forced. He who received the letter had no ear for the secret message; for him, its ambiguity had a single meaning. Georg Lukács was a haughty man, and the haughty man has no feeling for this type of ambiguity. And so the last cry of despair ('If there is still some way we can reach each other, I want us to do so') was in vain; there remained but one alternative, one certainty: the certainty of failure, which was the failure of *two* people.

Irma Seidler loved Georg Lukács – loved him as he was. She loved him for the reason that every lover loves: because he was exactly what he was. Yet Irma very much wanted this man to be different as far as his relationship with her was concerned. She expected a miracle. For the sound of trumpets will cause the walls of Jericho to fall and life-giving manna will fall from Heaven before a significant individual will act contrary to the principles of his own individuality.

'You too are afraid', 'if you are not afraid', 'you always hesitated and feared': Irma expected the biggest miracle of all – she wanted the man she loved to be unafraid.

Georg Lukács wrote in his diary: 'To expect miracles is always the sign of crisis. As long as there is no difficulty, one can have faith in miracles. And they will come. But the expected miracle is always impossible' (6 June 1910). The expected miracle is always impossible. But what does it mean, to 'have faith in miracles'? Could Irma have had faith in miracles?

Faith is always directed at transcendence. To have faith in miracles means that we have no part in the miracle itself. The miracle is external – it is grace. The state of having faith in miracles is timeless. We can have faith in miracles throughout our lives, and we can never say they will not happen; that would constitute lack of faith.

To have faith in another human being means to consider the Other as transcendent, to know from the start that there is no relationship, no reciprocity, that everything proceeds from the Other. The Other is the subject, I the object. I am subject only in so far as I have faith in the Other.

But Irma's relationship with Lukács was anything but religious; for her, a relationship meant reciprocity, the constant dialogue of two human souls. She did not have faith in Georg Lukács, and that is why she had the strength to judge him: 'you always hesitated and feared. . . .'

Irma judged Lukács, yet still wanted to provoke a miracle. But a miracle is just as much a religious category as is faith; the provoked miracle is a paradox. And an appeal to paradox is always the sign of despair: 'to expect miracles is always a sign of crisis', a sign of impotence, a sign of failure. Irma's goodbye letter was ambiguous – but Lukács could have no ear for it because he was what he was. To try to provoke a miracle is, in its own paradoxical fashion, an admission of failure.

And sooner will the sound of trumpets cause the walls of Jericho to fall, and sooner will life-giving manna fall from heaven than will a man who fears, cease to fear.

'Scruples: (marriage would be impossible) . . . I was prepared for malaise: fear, the mellowing effect of happiness, fear that I might not be able to orient myself in a more broadly-based life.' (Georg Lukács' note, 1 – 3 July 1908)

Georg Lukács was afraid of Irma Seidler. It was not for his *life* but for his *work* that he feared:

What I wish to accomplish only an unattached man can accomplish.

I feel more and more strongly that the really important things happen in solitude. . . . I experience solitude as a great 'redeeming' joy – not as resignation to being excluded from life, but as the discovery of life, *my* life, *the* life in which everything is adequate. (Letters to Irma, January and April 1911)

'Last night I felt again: Irma is life' – but Georg Lukács was afraid of this life.

He writes in the Philippe essay:

Great love is always ascetic. There is no difference between elevating the beloved to the height of heights, and so alienating her from oneself as well as herself, and using her simply as a stepping-stone.

In theory, perhaps, there is no difference between these two attitudes, but Lukács was a refined and honourable man: he knew there is, in fact, a difference. And he chose the first course. The figure of Irma became symbolic for him, and he chose this symbolic transformation:

Strange how little I felt the necessity, in Leo's and Irma's case, of their being with me and being for me. . . . Their being here was sufficient. (Diary, 30 November 1911)

He transformed Irma into a mythical figure, into the unobjectified object of his eternal desire. He had faith in her (Irma did not have faith in him), and he could have faith because what was essential for him – for his work – was not being with her but her existence in itself.

Georg Lukács was afraid of Irma Seidler: he feared for his work; and he feared her because he was a refined and honourable man, so, of the two attitudes, he chose the first. *He feared Irma because he feared for Irma*; he did not want to transform her into an instrument. 'Whatever and however Kierkegaard did, he did it in order to rescue Regine Olsen for life.' Regine Olsen was a child of conventions, and she married and lived happily until she died. But Irma Seidler was not a child of conventions, and at the same time, she was unable to have faith in miracles. She tried to provoke a miracle, and simultaneously provoked fate against herself.

Georg Lukács feared Irma Seidler because he feared for his work and he feared for Irma. This fear was of his essence; yet Irma wanted him not to fear but still remain himself. Irma expected a miracle, but the miracle never comes; Irma tried to provoke a miracle, but miracles will not be provoked. Faith knows no time, but miracles can be provoked only *in time* and only with a *gesture of finality*. And Irma – the second time – found the only gesture in which finality becomes indissolubly final, the gesture in which there is no ambiguity.

VI

Lukács tries again and again *to make himself understood* by Irma Seidler, to make her understand the being that is *specifically* him. Everyone who is in love does this. Everyone is a unique entity, and everyone who is in love wants the Other to perceive his or her uniqueness: 'I would love to be loved . . . that I might be seen'[7] – is there a more elementary need than this?

But we know that words are not enough. We know that our vocabulary is poor, and that if it were a thousand times richer, we would still not be able to describe what we are and what the Other means to us because these things are indescribable.

In the world of conventions every gesture is unequivocal, clear, transparent, intelligible. The significance of individual gestures is regulated by institutions and customs. We understand one another – but is it *one another* that we understand? We comprehend the signs, but are we comprehending the *signs of human uniqueness*? In the world of conventions uniqueness is an *obstacle*. There one must *conform*. Individual meanings must dissolve in the universal meaning; they must be integrated with it. In the world of conventions everything is simple and transparent, but is man simple? And can the universal make our *uniqueness* transparent?

Every person is a unique entity, and every person in love wants the Other to perceive this uniqueness, this is what he wants loved, but we know: words are not enough. We need direct sensual encounters, the free play of eyes, the meeting of hands, the embrace. But what does the free play of eyes, the meeting of hands mean? What does an embrace mean? Once we step outside the world of conventions, once nothing has universal meaning any longer, once every gesture exists only for itself – a sign only of our uniqueness – then the direct sensual encounters again *need words*. We circumscribe what we have experienced; we live out what we have circumscribed. 'For the union of souls there is no marriage bed': *even a marriage bed will not unify souls.*

'I would love to be loved . . . that I might be seen.' But the revelation of uniqueness, making oneself known, is no miracle, and even less is it grace. The revelation of uniqueness is an *accomplishment* that develops slowly in the search for one another, and the search for one another is *being together* – if you will, 'holding hands'. This hand-holding is no longer the meeting of two souls in the void, but two people accepting one another. And this acceptance of one another is life, which develops its own customs, of which the gestures will be un-equivocal because they will have *consequences in life*. And uniqueness may still find expression in these unequivocal significations because this being together is itself based on the search for uniqueness. *Habitable institutions*: did not the future's promise lie in Irma's earthly dream after all?

Lukács tries and tries incessantly *to make himself understood* by Irma Seidler, to make her understand the being who is *specifically* him, who is no one else but *him*. He describes himself with words; he articulates himself through categories. He describes his relationship with Irma with words; he articulates that too through categories. These words, these categories are not conventional. They are the categories of his philosophy. Irma does not understand them; the more Lukács reveals himself, the more opaque, the more incomprehensible he becomes for her.

Are these categories 'beyond' Irma? Does she fail to understand what they articulate because she *cannot* understand it?

> Why were Irma and Leo beneficial for me? I think because they were strong enough to understand exactly what I thought, but not strong enough to continue on another plane once they have embarked with me. (Diary, 29 May 1910)

That is, Irma does not consider the Lukácsian categories appropriate for describing her relationship with Georg. She feels that these philosophical categories only alienate them from one another. The articulation of vital problems on a purely philosophical plane is not acceptable to her. She refuses to understand their relationship through the categories of a philosophical system that has nothing but contempt for *life*.

Irma attempts to recover immediacy in the pursuit of mutual understanding, spontaneity, what is *sensually real* from a philosophy that considers sensuality contemptible and excludes spontaneity from the sphere of what it considers to be 'of a higher order'.

> But if you can – for your own sake too – do not analyse this so much in the future. (Irma on the relationship of the Platonist and the poet, the celebrated idea of the Kassner essay.)

> Sometimes one picks a bunch of flowers, then rearranges them – and so far it has always seemed to me that I can never replace their original fresh harmony because I have moved *every single one* of them. In arranging like

this, in seeking harmony like this, one should retain some fixed reference or else one might easily ruin everything. (5 August 1908)

Analysis dissects – and it is not always possible to reassemble things once they have been reduced to their separate elements. . . . the fact that something can be picked to pieces does not prove that it *has to be* picked to pieces, only that the experiment *can be* performed. (30 August 1908)

No, I cannot bear to analyse things; nor do I want to, because it is cruel to place one's own and another's soul on the dissecting table. (1 October 1908)

We are not acquainted with the letters Georg Lukács wrote to Nagybánya, but we can imagine what this analysis might have been like. Lukács was contemptuous of psychoanalysis as an explanatory theory; for him psychological analysis was the analysis of motives and moods. And since motives and moods are ephemeral, constantly changing, their dissection will never reveal to us the *ultimate*, the truly *essential*, the *unconditional*. Yet it was through analysis that Lukács wanted to arrive at the unconditional, ultimate essences. The 'soul', just as it is, in its own essential nature, has *no prior history*. To postulate a prior history would mean losing oneself in the chaos of *contingencies*, would introduce elements into the analysis that were *external* to the 'soul'. And such external elements would be accidental elements. We would have arbitrarily to pick and choose from among an infinity of accidental elements, and what we most wanted to grasp, what we most wanted to know and comprehend in its own *unconditional essence*, in its 'being just so', in its *uniqueness* – pure individuality, the 'intelligible I' – would slip through our fingers. It was this 'intelligible I' that Lukács wished to reveal in his analysis, and it was through analysis that he wanted to arrive at ultimate, unconditional essence. 'The newly self-conscious soul marvels at its entire prior existence like a stranger. . . . These are the dialogues of naked souls with their naked fates.'

This is *existential analysis*. The object of the analysis is not the living individual – for the 'soul' of even the noblest individual carries its own prehistory: he, too, has motives, even motives that are accidental and not decisive in terms of his individuality – but the individual conceived and formalized as *symbol*. Every individual (every significant individual, that is, for only the significant individual is worthy of existential analysis) becomes *the symbol of an attitude*, and the dialogue of two individuals is the meeting of two symbolic attitudes. Every symbolically conceived attitude is a *fate*, and the meeting of two naked souls the search of two fates for one another. Hence Irma is not Irma but 'life', 'goodness', 'the redeemer'. And Georg Lukács is Georg Lukács no longer in his empirical presence but the 'man of the created work', 'solitude', 'unviability'.

It was honest and conscientious of me that I always revealed what there
still was between us, although I did it because I believed . . . that these
things were but the struggles of the past and the future was already on its
way, its first signs were already visible, and that you had saved me, and I
would perhaps be able to reciprocate your saving me. (Lukács' unsent
goodbye letter, November – December 1908)

But Irma Seidler was not 'the saviour'. She wanted to save no one; nor did she
want to be saved. She loved, and she wanted to be loved. But what does it
mean, 'to love'?

It was through *existential analysis*, through the dialogue of two naked souls,
that Georg Lukács wanted to arrive at the ultimate, unconditional essences. He
wanted to provoke redemption with the magic of philosophical analysis, the
magic of *words*. But mere words are the eternity of repetition. Words by
themselves can never reveal fate to us. And if fate is not revealed, then words,
through eternal repetition, only alienate us from one another, and the *vehicle of
communication* becomes the *vehicle of eternal irredeemability*.

'Hic Rhodus, hic salta.' Mere words, analysis, are the eternity of repetition.
For it is only through the *deed* that we gain certainty of what someone means to
us, of what it means to love, of what 'I love you' and 'You love me' mean; it is
only through the deed that we gain certainty of what something means to us.
Only the deed is transformed into fate. Whoever wants to know, whoever wants to
love, whoever wants earthly redemption must always be willing to risk the
'leap' from words into deeds. And this 'leap' cannot be avoided; it cannot be
dispensed with through analysis because analysis is eternal repetition, eternal
repeatability. *Hic Rhodus, hic salta.* The 'leap' from words into deeds is both risk
and the acceptance of risk, for it may turn out that we do not love the one we
love after all; it may turn out that the fate we have chosen is not our fate, that
what was resplendent with symbolism in the analysis may lose its brilliance, and
we may fail to find what we were seeking. Yet without accepting risk, without
the 'leap', we humans can never find one another.

Just one question: is there not something frivolous (the frivolity of empirical laziness deriving from transcendental pessimism) in transforming
every psychological phenomenon into symbols? (Diary, 11 May 1910)

Few men have revealed themselves – even to themselves – with more cruelty,
more relentless honesty. And when Irma Seidler misunderstood Georg Lukács,
she still understood him correctly; she understood what this transcendental
pessimism and this empirical laziness meant *for her*: 'You are afraid of me.'
Lukács symbolically transformed every psychological phenomenon because he
feared the risk of the 'leap'. He feared Irma not for his 'empirical I' but for his
'symbolic I': he feared for his work.

But 'at what point does Hjalmar Ekdal become distinguishable from Novalis?' At the point that Novalis *accomplishes* his work.

VII

Man makes himself the object of his consciousness. Lukács tries and tries incessantly to make himself understood by Irma Seidler. He describes himself with words, he articulates himself through categories, the categories of his own philosophy. Everything becomes theoretical and symbolic. There are no ephemeral motives, no indissoluble sentiments; there is no longer any immediacy, because only what is conceptually mediated and integrated into symbols is real and 'intelligible'. Only those sentiments exist that are part of a conceptually constructed 'fate'.

Man makes himself the object of his consciousness. He is capable of looking at himself through the eyes of the Other; he is capable of judging himself in terms of normative principles; he is capable of consciously socializing his affects; he is capable of *forming* his own moral individuality.

Man makes himself the object of his consciousness. But can a man become 'pure consciousness', 'pure spirit'? The senses may become theoreti*cal*, but can they become theoreti*cians*?

From Irma's letters to Georg:

I too, must frequently think about that evening. . . . it was a part of those few hours when we were still free – free of all self-censure and reflection, free of that small but nonetheless important hobble on that *warmest* life in our innermost depths. (14 August 1908)

write, as spontaneously as possible, whatever comes to mind. Because we need to be more intensely together. . . . (30 August 1908)

the deepest and most incisive psychological analysis . . . is useless to me, because it cannot substitute for functions of the soul, but remains merely intellectual pleasure.

From Lukács' diary:

And as long as communication is not all there is, and all there is is not equally communication, nothing exists. (8 May 1910)

Man's capacity to look at himself through the eyes of the Other, to judge himself in terms of normative principles, *consciously* to socialize his affects, to *form* his own moral individuality: this is the meaning of culture, and this is the conduct of the man of culture. But what happens if one does not see through the eyes of the Other because there are no unequivocal significations, and one cannot comprehend the 'signs'? What happens if the normative principles are nothing more than the skeletons of exhausted conventions? How can man be cultured *without a culture*? How can he make himself the object of his consciousness in the 'era of absolute culpability'?

There is no private language and there are no private customs; the institutions cannot be made privately habitable. In the 'era of absolute culpability', 'the majority of men live without life and remain unconscious of it'. The majority of men do not make themselves the objects of their consciousnesses – not in the noble, the *ethical sense* of the term: 'their fates are concealed by petty "musts".'

But if a man nevertheless wants to make himself the object of his consciousness, he can only do so through theory. No immediacy can remain in the 'soul' because this immediacy only mediates the 'lifeless life'; and the spontaneity of the senses must be renounced because this spontaneity can only be the vehicle of 'absolute culpability'. The man of culture can develop only within a culture, because only in a culture can spontaneity and sensuality themselves become cultured, can a man make himself the object of his consciousness without sacrificing his senses to theory, can the harmony of sensual and intellectual beauty develop. Habitable institutions. *Habitable world*. 'Hic Rhodus, hic salta.'

The man of culture can only develop within a culture. Yet whoever makes himself the object of his consciousness in the 'era of absolute culpability' is over-refined. *Theory absorbs the senses*. 'Poverty in spirit is nothing less than liberation from our own psychological determinants in order to deliver ourselves to those metaphysical and metapsychological necessities that are more properly our own.' But is it liberation to be liberated from our psychological determinants?

In the world of conventions psychology is also conventional. We understand one another, but is it *one another* that we understand; we comprehend the 'signs', but are we comprehending the signs of human uniqueness? We remain strangers to one another, perhaps without even knowing it, because we never arrive at the question 'What are we really?' We know what 'I love you' means, but the other, deeper question never even dawns on us: 'What does it mean that *I* love *you*?'

On the other hand, the fate of the over-refined man who leaves behind the conventional life to rise above it, the fate of the 'naked soul', is poverty in spirit. The senses are absorbed by theory, and there are no more psychological determinants, no past. Immediacy, spontaneity is lost, and only words remain for self-revelation. Articulated words cause pain, and unarticulated words cause pain, and every gesture becomes ambiguous, and every understanding misunderstanding, until at last faith is silenced and the souls are alienated from one another with the finality of fate. 'For the union of souls there is no marriage bed.'

'And as long as communication is not all there is, and all there is is not equally communication, nothing exists.'

Over-refinement is desire: *desire for culture. The over-refined man is the man desirous of culture in a world devoid of culture.* 'In life, desire can only be love.'

'Irma is life.' Habitable institutions. Habitable world. 'Hic Rhodus, hic salta.'

VIII

Don't be angry, though I have ceased to mean something in your life – if I ever was anything – don't be angry if you nevertheless remain the only content in my life. (Georg's unsent goodbye letter to Irma)

Back then she might have felt that I could save her from her troubles; though she did not love me. (Diary, 24 May 1911)

I was never for her what she was for me. (Diary, 27 October 1911)

Irma did not love me – Irma never loved me – I was never anything to her – she always meant more to me than I did to her: Georg Lukács created his relationship with Irma Seidler, and he created it *in this manner.*

I've written with long-distance love

Goodbye, dear Gyuri, I love you very much, Irma.

write, because I love you very much.

but I love you always. . . .

if there is still some way we can reach one another, I want us to do so. And if not, you will still remain in my lasting affection, and I will take my leave in the knowledge that the warmth of all my soul was yours. . . .

Is it possible for someone to read these letters to mean 'She did not love me?'

Why did Georg Lukács create an Irma Seidler who never existed, an Irma who did not love him? He writes in the Philippe essay:

'He who loves is more like unto God than he who is loved, because his love must always remain unrequited, because his love is but a path to self-perfection. He who loves is superior to beloved, and the more he loves, and the less his love is returned, the more loftily he stands.' Lukács created an Irma Seidler who did not love him because it was with the haughtiness of *amor dei intellectualis* that he recreated their history.

The man of conventions, the man 'living the lifeless life', is always *vain.* The men who stand tall and lonely above the world of conventions are always haughty. They are not haughty with respect to anything in particular; the source of their haughtiness is not their socially determined position; haughtiness is their *mode of being*.

The vain man says: I am loved by many. The vain man says: it is me they love more. The haughty man says: I cannot be loved. The haughty man says: it is I who love more strongly. He who loves is more akin to God than he who is loved.

The vain man says: I am attractive. The vain man wants to be attractive. The haughty man says: I am not attractive, and I do not want to be attractive. The vain man says: I am superior. The vain man aims constantly to prove his superiority. The haughty man aims to prove nothing because he is sure of himself.

The vain man compares himself with others: his whole life is a process of 'comparison'. The vain man is envious. The haughty man compares himself with no one: there are no standards that he and others can have in common. The haughty man knows no envy. Even when a superior being crosses his path, he does not make comparisons: he prostrates himself.

For the vain man, to encounter a superior being is a tragedy. For the haughty man, a superior being is the justification for his own life, a joy.

Vanity is self-centred. Haughtiness seeks life's centre in another.

Vanity is jealous: it scents danger in everyone at all times. Haughtiness does not know what jealousy is. Whoever betrays him is dismissed: he is unworthy.

Vanity says to the once-beloved: You deceived me; this is not what you promised. Haughtiness says: You did this, and since I loved you, your deed cannot be wrong.

The vain man says: I was right; I am right. The vain man seeks to be confirmed in his truth. The haughty man wants to be wrong; he seeks a truth higher than himself.

Is it necessary to seek the humiliation of haughtiness? No, because *humility goes hand in hand with haughtiness*. Humility is haughtiness turned 'inside-out' – humility is the manifestation of haughtiness. A superior being is the justification of his life, a joy; if a superior being crosses his path, he prostrates himself; he seeks a truth higher than himself.

The men who stand tall and lonely above the world of conventions are always haughty. Lukács created an Irma Seidler who did not love him, because it was with the pride of *amor dei intellectualis* that he recreated their history. 'If I love you, what business is it of yours?'

I loved you – but you never loved me; he who loves is superior to he who is loved: this is the gesture of haughtiness. But it is not necessary to seek the humiliation of haughtiness because humility goes hand in hand with it. And in the gesture of haughty humility every unconditional essence becomes its opposite: I am not right; the Other is right; the one whom I love is right. *And in the absolute unconditionality of love the beloved rises above the lover.* The lover humiliates himself; haughtiness bows his head because 'before God we are never right'.

> And in this way even this wholly abstract metaphysics of form takes one back to the centre of all things: to Irma . . . because she specifically was the centre of all things, the source of all things, who had to be as she was, who had to do what she did. I must accept that *just as it is*, and I must hold it sacred that I might respect my own life. . . . I used to believe that I should condemn her, but now I don't know. (Diary, 29 May 1910)

Even more unequivocally, and with even more finality:

> People are right or wrong with respect to each other not in terms of deeds and certain events, but in terms of their being: certain people are always right with respect to certain people. And now I feel that she was and always will be right with respect to me. [This is] the self-conscious bow before a superior being; vassalage; Hagen's range of sentiments. (Diary, 2 June 1910)

The haughty man is solitary; humility tempts him terribly. But if haughtiness is to humiliate itself, then the being before whom it humiliates itself must be perfect. Because if the haughty man humiliates himself, then he must accept the being before whom he humiliates himself 'just as he is' so that he may respect his own life. And if haughtiness humiliates itself, it loses its right – and its opportunity – to pass judgement because the being or object before which it humiliates itself can no longer be judged 'in terms of deeds and certain events' – indeed, the 'centre' of life *can no longer be judged at all.*

Lukács brought his philosophy 'down to earth' and transformed it into a myth: 'Irma is life.' And it was this Irma, magically transformed into a philosophical myth, and not the empirical woman, who became the centre of his life. He prostrated himself before her and idolized her, and he denied himself the right to judge her.

But judge, that you may be judged!

For the myth of philosophy will not descend to earth. And the empirical woman is not the Irma of the myth, and she must indeed be judged by her deeds because there is *no essence external to the deeds.* And the lover is not holier than the beloved; neither is the beloved an idol to be worshipped. Let us judge, that we may be judged!

Vanity always judges, but the centre of its judgement is always *itself.* Whatever is right for itself is 'the right'; whatever is beneficial to itself is 'the good'. Vanity also has idols, but they are empirical idols. Vanity *does not abstract from the deed* because it justifies the deed when the deed justifies *it.*

Blessed is haughtiness that seeks greatness. Blessed is haughtiness that can bow down before greatness. Blessed is haughtiness, even in its own self-humiliation.

Haughtiness is solitude's *mode of being* – but what if the haughty man is no longer solitary? Where there is no solitude, where significant substantialities do not need to rise *above* the world to realize themselves, there is no more haughtiness. Haughtiness mellows into *self-respect*. Self-respect is *pride socialized*. Self-respect is the *pride of equals*. The love of self-respecting persons is the love of equals; for the self-respecting individual, the superior being is the object of friendship and alliance. The self-respecting individual also knows no envy; he does not compare himself with others, not because there are no common standards for himself and others, but because *true* equals *are incomparable*, because the uniqueness of individuals is *incomparable*. The self-respecting individual does not say 'I am always right', and he does not say 'Before God I am never right', because *the self-respecting individual does not idolize himself; nor does he idolize anything outside himself*. He judges, that he may be judged.

Blessed is pride, which may mellow into self-respect.

But can one have self-respect in the 'era of absolute culpability'?

Habitable institutions. Habitable world. A world peopled with self-respecting individuals. Culture.

Over-refinement is desire: desire for culture. The over-refined man is the proud man, the man desiring culture in a world devoid of culture.

But can culture be created by the self-humiliation of pride?

IX

'From contingencies to necessity: this is the path of every problematic individual,' writes Georg Lukács in the Kassner essay, the first flower he presented to Irma.

Two problematic individuals in the 'era of absolute culpability'.

Thesis: woman – *the formation of tragedy through death*.

> This self-liberation of the woman does not come about by going to the very end of the most essential necessity, as is the genuine self-liberation of every tragic man. And the end of the drama raises the question posed much earlier by the theorist Ernst: can a woman be tragic in her own right, outside her relationship to the man in her life?

The question contains the answer: woman cannot rise to tragedy; freedom in itself can never be a value to her. In the tragedy's Brünhilde, muses Lukács in his diary, there is something masculine. 'Woman is only woman.'

> I meant shamefully little to her. The only question is: shamefully for me or for her? Mad question: this is tragedy – but she could not rise to where I soared. (Diary, 11 February 1911)

Woman cannot be tragic. 'Woman is only woman.'

> For Irma, yes. Her tragedy lay in life, in a sphere, therefore, in which death is genuinely the dialectical opposite of life. (Diary, 22 October 1911)

The formation of tragedy through death.

> Perhaps there is more in me of the womanly and more of the unwomanly, the artist and the person, than you know – and these two struggle with each other. (Irma's letter to Georg, 20 September 1908)

A girl in a provincial country, early in this century, wished to break with the world of conventions. She wished to break with it as a *human being* and as an *artist*. Because creation, self-realization in creative work, bringing forth the new, was just as indispensable a part of life for Irma, just as much the object of her passion, as it was for Lukács. She was driven by the demon of work. Creative work justified her life; the failure of her work amounted to the failure of her life.

Irma's letters to Georg:

> I break out in a cold sweat when I think that in two short months' time it will be clear whether I can accomplish anything or whether all my effort this year has been simply a sham. (5 July)

> In all my life I have never worked so hard. (19 July)

> I am exhausted from a stretch of over-intensive work, but the results are in no way proportionate to the strenuous efforts involved. . . . things are very far from my goals! the results of the last two months' work amounts to zero. (Early September – date illegible)

In order to break with the world of conventions as a human being, Irma *must become an artist*. If the world of creative work cannot be her home, then the world of men must remain her home, then: 'woman is only woman'. But she not only wanted to be a human being and an artist; she also wanted to be a *woman* – 'And these two struggle with each other.' She did not want to relinquish either. This double fealty, fealty to womanhood and fealty to creative human existence, caused her tragedy because if she could not *be both at once*, then she preferred *not to be*.

A girl in a provincial country, early in this century, wished to break with the world of conventions. And she also wished to be a woman. But she could be a woman only with those who, like her, had broken with the conventional world. But these men were haughty, and in their eyes 'woman was only woman'. She did not want those who knew *a priori* what things *meant*. She wanted neither engagement, nor marriage, nor marital infidelity. She wanted to 'hold hands' with someone who acknowledged her to be an equal in the world of the senses and of the spirit. She had self-respect but the men were haughty, and in their eyes 'woman was only woman'.

Lukács expected her to believe in him. He made a myth of her and wanted her to become this myth; he wanted her personality to conform to the principles of this myth, so that she might rise to the *tragedy of a man*. But she did not want to rise to masculine tragedy because she wanted to create *her own life* and, if necessary – and it was necessary – *her own tragedy*.

The voice of self-respect, the gestures of self-respect:

let both our individual lives grow through our relationship, and vice versa. (5 July 1908)

I think we have both passed through, in a very healthy way, a perhaps overly theoretical stage. . . . (23 August 1908)

These people, from whom I go on receiving and receiving . . . this is lovely and good, for receiving means growing, being supported, carried along. On the other hand, it is not good, for *not being able to give* is such a weightless feeling; one feels so light and airy, like a child, and this can be painful too, very painful. (28 April 1911)

The voice of the recovery of one's own individuality, the gestures of preserving one's substance:

No, I cannot bear to analyse things; nor do I want to. . . . (1 October 1908)

In these letters, I have totally accommodated myself and conformed to you, and I must speak frankly – at the cost of inexpressible sacrifice – I have taken on myself the soul-forms of mutual understanding that you stipulated. And today I will discontinue this combative togetherness. (25 October 1908)

The confrontation of her own creative ego with that of the Other, the voices of judgement, the gestures of the woman-person-creator's world view:

Only those people are good people – and by good I mean something rather grand – whose love of men and range of sentiments in all sorts of human relationships is as spiritual and as '*hellseherisch*' . . . as the attitude of the artist to his work. And those truly devoted to creation and work are those who can relate to their work as to an organic, living entity, which can be warmly loved, which can be killed or saved – but which lives.

A girl wants to break with the world of conventions, but she wants to break

with it as a human being, as an artist – there is no other way for her. And at
the same time she wants to remain a woman, but the men who could be her
companions in solitude are haughty, and for them 'woman is only woman'.

Did Irma not commit a tragic offence by loving the man she happened to
love?

Love can never be an offence. Yet did Irma not commit a tragic offence by
promising something in the ecstatic moments of love, something she could not
deliver in terms of her own individuality?

Irma's first letter to Georg:

> I would like to be able to measure up to the standards you have set for
> me. (30 December 1907)

Eight months later:

> I feel that if I leave my work now, I will leave it on other occasions as
> well. And I also feel that if I cannot sooner or later arrange my life so that
> I shall never again be unable to work full force for the greater part of the
> year, I will leave art behind forever. *With goals such as mine* one cannot get
> anywhere *at this rate.* . . . And still, I might come. Dear God: don't be
> angry with me for this letter – just love me and don't judge me for it.
> . . . I need my work – and I miss you. (30 August 1908)

Should this girl have written, *even this once*: 'I would like to be able to measure
up to the standards you have set for me'?

And here lies Irma Seidler's tragic offence. For she did not keep the promise
she had made. She followed the principles of her own individuality – is there
anything more noble or more justified? *But she should never have made that promise.* The love potion was the potion of death.

'In life, desire can only be love: that is its joy, its tragedy.' Georg was Irma's
everlasting love, the object of her everlasting desire. But she wanted to be a
human being and an artist, and she wanted to live according to the principles of
her own individuality; she was also unable to measure up to the standards her
love had set for her. Yet she had taken it upon herself to do this.

And so, with the gesture of despair, Irma married a painter, renounced love
and decided to live for her art. But this art did not come to fruition; it did not
bring fulfilment.

Irma's last letter to Georg: Today I feel that those ways of seeing and those
perspectives that have sustained me for years – though good and honest – are
miserably poor compared with the intensity of art. . . . Something must be
understood anew. *In every respect.*

Irma could not integrate her love with her art.

'Irma is life.' 'In life, desire can only be love: that is its joy, its tragedy.' Irma could not integrate her tragedy with her life. For her, the love potion was the potion of death.

And through death she formed her tragedy, *her own tragedy. And through her death leap all her deeds became symbolic, and all the contingencies of her life took on the form of necessity.*

Irma expected a miracle. She wanted to provoke a miracle. And behold: the miracle materialized. Lukács never again wrote the words 'Woman is only woman.' The man who had arrogantly stated that a woman's life can never be tragic because freedom is not a value for her wrote this in his diary: 'Ihre Tragödie lag in des Lebens, in einer Sphäre also wo der Tod tatsächlich der dialektische Gegensatz vom Leben ist.' ('Her tragedy lay in the tragedy of life, in a sphere, then, in which death is indeed the dialectical counterpart of life.')

'From contingencies to necessity: this is the path of every problematic individual.'

Two problematic individuals in the 'era of absolute culpability'.

X

'From contingencies to necessity: this is the path of every problematic individual.' Two problematic individuals in the 'era of absolute culpability'. Counterthesis: man – *the integration of tragedy with life.*

I write the word 'man' anxiously. Georg Lukács was 22 years old when he met Irma Seidler, and when the tragedy happened he had just completed his twenty-sixth year.

'With this book I bid my youth goodbye,' writes Georg Lukács in March 1910, in an unsent letter to Irma Seidler, referring to the Hungarian edition of *Soul and Form*. This was the period of *Sturm und Drang*, the time of his *maturing* into manhood. And yet this tragedy is already a man's tragedy, because it is rooted in the stance that Georg Lukács *lived out and took upon himself as the fate of a man*: living and what amounts to the same in this case, thinking through, the conflicts of a man living *in* and *for* his work.

'Kierkegaard created his relationship to Regine Olsen, and if a Kierkegaard creates his life, he does not do so in order to conceal, but rather to articulate the truth.' If Georg Lukács created and continually recreated his relationship with Irma Seidler, he did it in order better to articulate the truth. His questions are not only personal questions; everything is resplendent with symbolic light. His questions are the questions of his great contemporaries, those of Babits,[6] Ady, Bartók and Thomas Mann. Can there be an organic path that leads from life to art? Which life is the authentic life? Can the man of art live an authentic life? Is it given to the creative individual, the one who is at home with creative work, the ambitious man, the one who brings forth the new, to experience love and being with others, the happiness of human fellowship? Is art at all possible in

the 'era of absolute culpability'?
being with others, the happiness of human fellowship? Is art at all possible in
the 'era of absolute culpability'?

Lukács was able to articulate the truth by recreating his relationship with
Irma Seidler. He integrated his love with his work. He accomplished his work.
He built into his work the blood of the mason's wife,[7] so that the fort would
stand and rise above life like a solitary mountain peak.

'In other words: the old problem . . . . : where does Hjalmar Ekdal become
distinguishable from Novalis?'

In the fact that Novalis accomplishes his work. And Georg Lukács also accomplished his work. He built it with the blood of the mason's wife, but the
fort stood: and rose above life like a solitary mountain peak.

> Great love is always ascetic. There is no difference between elevating the
> beloved to the height of heights, and so alienating her from oneself as
> well as herself, and using her simply as a stepping-stone.

In theory, perhaps there is no 'difference' between these two attitudes, but
Georg Lukács was a refined and honourable man: he knew there was a difference. Georg Lukács was afraid of Irma Seidler: he feared for his work, and he
feared for Irma. And because he feared for both he chose the first course. He
transformed Irma's earthly being into a mythical figure, into the myth of 'life',
the object of the creative individual's eternal desire, and he humbled his pride
before this magically mythicized life, before philosophy stylized into life. But
Irma Seidler formed her own life in the death she chose. And with that she integrated her human life blood into the edifice of art, which could stand no other
way, so that it might rise above life like a solitary mountain peak. Irma Seidler
did not want to save anyone, and she did not want to be saved. She did not
want anyone to fear her; nor did she want anyone to fear for her. And so she
became a 'stepping-stone' for the creative individual, even against his will, for
the edifice was erected with her blood.

*It is impossible not to transform life into an instrument if we approach it through
forms.* But the formalized, mythicized, stylized life avenges itself on form and
judges it. Yet is it *truly form* that judgement is passed upon? Life passes judgement on form by realizing it. But is this not indicative of the fact that the form
is, after all, the form of *this* life, that what is reproduced and recreated on the
pure snows of solitary mountain peaks is still the turmoil of this chaotic life?

Life avenged itself on form, but it was not form that it judged; it passed
judgement on the 'era of absolute culpability' in which the majority of men
must live a 'lifeless life', and where the genuinely living, those who give meaning to their lives, must live out the same tragedy whether they erect that edifice
or fall silent through the gesture of chosen death. Habitable institutions.
Habitable world. A world peopled with self-respecting individuals.

He who is ambitious and creative in the 'era of absolute culpability' *must* use
life instrumentally. And Georg Lukács used Irma Seidler as an instrument for
his work – against his will. And the things that happened, and the way they
happened, were all in the cause of the *created work*, for the sake of work. Lukács
writes of Kierkegaard: 'Did he not perchance abandon a potentially successful
struggle against his own great sorrow because he cherished this sorrow,
cherished it more than anything, and could not have lived without it?'
    Georg Lukács' drafted a letter to Irma Seidler in March 1910:

> I thank you for appearing briefly in my life, and I thank you for leaving. I
> thank you for the joys your nearness brought me, and I thank you for the
> pains that nearly destroyed this life: I thank you for them because I could
> not go on without them: they were signs; they were necessary.

His entry in his diary on 27 July 1910:

> Her picture is on my desk for stylistic reasons, for the Philippe essay. But
> I hardly look at it. . . . It has disappeared – although a little desire and
> sorrow for it would not hurt now – for the sake of the Philippe essay.
> . . . The Ernst essay was perhaps ruined (made more pathetic) by her con-
> stant presence; she did not always fit organically into the parameters of
> the essay. But this one may be dry without her.

Lukács' letter to Irma Seidler in January 1911:

> What I want to accomplish only an unattached man can accomplish. . . .
> One who does not know what another human being can be to him, what
> one person can be to another, can only be left to himself but can never be
> firm and free of desire in his scholarly solitude. Only such a man can
> proudly and calmly pass up the false and petty opportunities for
> togetherness that are offered to him; only such a man can chance his en-
> tire life on the perilous fate of his work.

Georg Lukács was afraid of Irma Seidler because he feared for his solitude. He
feared for his solitude because he feared for his work. He constructed his work
in solitude, but as the work cannot be constructed without life, he built this
edifice of his work with the blood of the mason's wife. Irma beame an
instrument of his work, even though Lukács did not want to use her so. It is
impossible not to transform life into an instrument if we approach it through
forms.
    But moral law lives. And moral law commands that human beings must not
use each other as mere instruments. This moral law was alive in Georg Lukács,
which is why he transformed Irma Seidler's flesh-and-blood womanhood into a
myth, why he humbled himself before her, why he said: with respect to her, I
can never be right.

Georg Lukács did not want to use another human being as a mere instrument. He held the greatest commandment of moral law sacred. The frivolity of
'aesthetic culture' was not his path. The day he opened his diary for the last
time, he wrote in it:

> And all this takes me back to the old questions: how can I become a
> philosopher? That is, since as a man I will never be able to pass beyond
> the ethical sphere, how can I create the Sublime?

Here is *Dr Faustus* – in 1911:

> he comforted himself with the possibility, with the object of desire that
> could always be present, yet is not present. It is not present now.

And on 23 November of that year:

> I am being punished for my pride and for the hope I have invested in
> work and the effort expended upon it.

Fate gave him his solitude – but he no longer wanted it. He integrated Irma
Seidler, his love, his life, with his work, but moral law was alive in him: human
beings should not treat one another as mere instruments. This was his tragedy.
Irma Seidler could not integrate her love with her Art, and that is why she
formed her own tragedy through death. Georg Lukács integrated his love into
his Work, and this was his tragedy. *But he integrated this tragedy with his life.*

'Permanent tragedy . . . is the greatest frivolity. . . . the sentiment of eternal
tragedy gives absolution for all idleness,' he writes in 'Aesthetic Culture'. 'For
the union of souls there is no marriage bed.' Perhaps there is – or at least there
ought to be

> by virtue of the fact that everything belongs to us, that everything
> belongs to the soul and every tragic event must be played out within it.
> . . . And the absolution, the redeeming power of form, comes only at the
> very end of all paths and sufferings, in that faith that cannot be proved
> and lives beyond all proof, in the faith that the divergent paths of the soul
> shall meet in the end: They must meet, for they have their source in the
> same centre.

But for the over-refined man all understanding is misunderstanding. The
senses are absorbed by theory. Spontaneity is lost. Only words remain for self-
revelation, and every gesture remains ambiguous. The over-refined man lives
out his tragedy and thinks it through – these two activities are one and the
same for him. And he judges it; *he judges irrevocably the 'era of absolute culpability',
the source of his over-refinement*, passes irrevocable judgement on a world in which
the created work can be built only with the blood of the Other.

The humility of haughtiness is the obeisance of the over-refined man to *bar-*

barism. The hope that 'the barbarians will come and, with rough hands, tear asunder all over-refinement'. *Allegro barbaro*.

Pride mellows into self-respect, the desire of the over-refined man, desire for culture. Habitable institutions. Habitable world. A world peopled with self-respecting individuals. *The promise of Karl Marx*.

Georg Lukács integrated his love with his work, and this was his tragedy. But he integrated this tragedy with his life.

Georg Lukács' 'holding hands' with another Other; pride bowing down before the New God; but that is another story.

Life avenged itself on form by realizing it. And with that, it passed judgement on the 'era of absolute culpability'. But can form also avenge itself on life? And, if so, on what is the judgement passed?

'Kierkegaard created his relationship to Regine Olsen.' And Georg Lukács created his relationship with Irma Seidler. In a certain sense, everyone creates and continually recreates his relationship to an Other. But few – very few – people can create their relationships with the Other in such a way that others after them can also create it and recreate it. Only the *paradigmatic* can become *parabolic*.

Translated by E. Làczay

NOTES

1 In this article I have relied on the following manuscripts, recovered from a Heidelberg bank safe in 1973: the diary of Georg Lukács (5 April 1910 – 16 December 1911); notes and the draft of a letter written by Lukács in 1908; drafts of two letters written by Lukács in the spring of 1910; letters sent by Lukács to Irma Seidler in 1911; letters written by Irma Seidler to Lukács between July and November 1908 and between January and May 1911; the correspondence of Lukács and Leo Popper, 1910 – 11.

   The Lukács quotations are taken from the following essays: 'Rudolph Kassner', 'Sören Kierkegaard and Regine Olsen', 'Stefan George', 'Charles-Louis Philippe', in *Soul and Form, The Metaphysics of Tragedy*, 'Aesthetic Culture' in *Aesthetic Culture* and *On Spiritual Poverty*.

2 Nagybánya is a small town in Hungary that housed an artists' colony from 1896 onwards. By contrast with contemporary academic painting, the colony developed a distinctive naturalistic style that borrowed much from Impressionism in its treatment of light but stopped short of the atmospheric fragmentation of form. The colony hosted many students, as well as accomplished artists from all over Europe, between 1910 and 1920.

3 Affectionate diminutive for Georg. After Irma's marriage their correspondence takes on an appropriate formality, which is not reflected in the undifferentiated use of 'you' in English.

4   Karl Ferenczy (1862 – 1917) was one of the principals and teachers at the
    ' Nagybánya artists' colony and, after 1906, a professor at the Hungarian Academy
    of Fine Arts.
5   The lines are from a poem by the Hungarian poet Endre Ady (1877 – 1919).
6   Mihály Babits (1883 – 1941) was a Hungarian poet.
7   In the Hungarian folk ballad *Kömives Kelemenné* (Mason Kelemen's Wife) a
    mason's wife is immured to guarantee the strength of a fortress.

3

Lukács and Bloch

SÁNDOR RADNÓTI

The subject of the following short essay is the disclosure of the great philosophical friendship between the young Georg Lukács and the young Ernst Bloch, a friendship which is in its details still completely unexplored.[1] Closer examination shows it to be a question of a representative confrontation – the conflict between their respective world views and conduct – which evidently developed mostly in the unconscious thought of the two men. The only explicit proof of this is, at the moment, the critique of Lukács in Bloch's *Geist der Utopie*. That is why the following remarks cannot undertake to present a coherent picture of Lukács' fantastically rich and antinomially composed youthful writings. I would like to stress what Bloch himself stressed: the problem of the 'world abandoned by God', the identical term used by Bloch and Lukács but not with the same meaning.

We can initially formulate the controversy as: ethics or religion? But as soon as this alternative is stated, we must qualify it extensively. For while Bloch's revolutionary philosophy of religion presupposes a whole series of moral expectations and decisions, Lukács neither can nor wants to eliminate faith and God from the horizon of his thinking. Nor can religion detach itself from ethics in the sense that it can be conveyed unconventionally only by some ethic or other, or by mystical 'meta-ethics'. But if we do contrast faith and ethics, we must, of course, mean by the latter an *immanent* ethics. Yet even Bloch does not relegate the desire for celestial bliss beyond earthly existence: 'the soul must become guilty in order to eliminate the stupid *status quo*, in order not to become even more guilty by a withdrawal into the idyllic, or by hypocritical toleration of wrong. . . .'[2] 'Categorical imperative with revolver in hand' is the appropriate ethical standpoint for the present world situation or, as added even more sharply in the revised work: 'guided tactically by Jesus with the whip and only teleologically by the Jesus who loves mankind'.[3] This statement is akin to Lukács' moral-philosophical pronouncement of the year 1919. The words of Hebbel's

63

Judith 'And if God had set sin between me and the deed I must do – who am I
to shirk from it?' are as valid for Bloch as they are a summary of the ethical
content of Lukács' *Tactics and Ethics*.[4] The judgement passed in his *Theory of the
Novel* upon the world that has, in Fichte's words, entered 'the age of absolute
sinfulness'[5] is considered valid by Lukács in his entire early period. One of the
possible conclusions that follow from this, as formulated by Lukács, is that only
the individual person who does not merely live but lives his life through to the
end, identifying with its essence – but only with it – and transcending
everything individual, chooses a 'way' that rises above the commonplace; 'their
ethic must establish perseverance-unto-death as a categorical imperative.'[6] So
he sees it in *The Metaphysics of Tragedy*, his theory of tragedy, which is at the
same time the theory of tragic ethics: 'The deepest longing of the human soul is
the metaphysical basis of tragedy: man's longing for his selfhood, his longing to
transform the apex of his existence to the plane of his way of life, its meaning
into a daily reality.'[7] The paradox of tragic ethics is that it cannot be achieved.
By nature this is a lonesome way; it cannot be striven for; 'the miracle of
chance' lets man fly up and it begins at the point where the 'mysterious powers
drive the essence out of man'.[8] Lukács establishes the immanence of the tragic
form and also of tragic ethics – God is left out of this entire area, reduced to a
mere observer. But man himself becomes God – his solitude, his chosenness,
his crossing of the waters of life with dry feet reintroduces numerous elements
of religious consciousness. Reintroduces them, for he creates an innerworldly
ethics, but one that is unachievable. He creates an innerworldly ethics which,
from the first, fatefully includes the destruction of everything innerworldly –
death. Thus the great work written a few years later, *The Theory of the Novel*,
gives central position no longer to selfhood, the 'assertion' of life, but to 'the
supporting positive meaning of life, totality',[9] summing up, from the vantage-
point of life, the content of *The Metaphysics of Tragedy* in a single categorical
statement: 'The ought kills life.'[10] *The Theory of the Novel* seeks the perspective
of the transformation of the entire life, of the building of a new totality, and the
last sentence of the book leaves the undecidable question undecided: 'whether
we are really about to leave the age of absolute sinfulness or whether the new
has no other herald but our hopes: those hopes which are signs of a world to
come, still so weak that it can easily be crushed by the sterile power of the
merely existent.'[11] When a man registers hope instead of a historical force, the
idea of redemption inevitably returns. Therefore Lukács defends the immanence
of his ethics-closer-to-life as follows:

> The normative man has achieved freedom from God, because the high
> norms of works and of substantial ethics are rooted in the existence of the
> all-perfecting God and in the idea of redemption; for in their innermost
> nature they remain unaffected by the ruler of the present, be it God or

demon. But the realization of the normative in the soul or in the world cannot detach itself from its substratum, from the present (in the historico-philosophical sense) without endangering its most specific strength, its constitutive appropriateness to its object.[12]

Thus man's freedom lies ultimately in redemption, in the perfecting God, but since man acts in actual life, this remains unexpressed. God must stand behind every action, behind every work, otherwise action and work disintegrate, but this must remain unexpressed, for its disclosure would be a hopeless detachment from the God-forsaken world. The most fatalistic desiccation of action and work on the one hand, and the Utopian insubstantiality of action and work on the other.

God-mythology and religious consciousness are thus not as far apart as one might think in the young Lukács' trend of thought. Yet he seeks the other pole, and it is depth of thinking that compels him to sum up the religio-transcendental elements that must necessarily creep in, in given circumstances, into the mythology of the demon *or* of the redeeming God.[13] The fact that in both of Lukács' above-mentioned works the hero is counterposed to the mystic shows the nearness of religion and, simultaneously, of the opposite direction of quest.

This is the other relevant way of life. Loss of self in contrast with selfhood, the suffering of the universe in contrast with its creation, surrender instead of struggle. 'These are the two poles of the possibilities of life. . . . each is the only true overcoming of the other.'[14] So says *The Metaphysics of Tragedy*: 'The mystic is free when he has surrendered himself and been dissolved in God; the hero is free when he has, in Luciferian spite, perfected himself in himself and by his own power, when he – for the deed of his soul – has banished every half-measure out of the world dominated by his destruction.'[15] These are the words of *The Theory of the Novel*. The change of view from one work to the other naturally also transformed the mystic. While in the first piece he is timeless, formless and softly contoured, in the second his experience can be perfected in a work, and if that is the case, it is perfected in him too, 'in the categories prescribed by the historico-philosophical position of the world-clock'.[16] For a more comprehensive description of the mystic by Lukács we must go back a little further in time. In an article from the year 1909 he distinguishes contemplative mysticism – that of Béla Balázs – from the militant mysticism of Ady.[17] He associates the mysticism of the great poet Ady with socialism[18] and sees the socio-psychological bases of religiosity – in a manner enlightening for our whole discussion – in a revolutionary spirit deprived of revolution. 'Endre Ady's socialism is religion (in lesser men, a narcotic), the voice of a preacher in the desert, the call for help of a drowning man, the desperate clinging to the only possibility that is left (worshipping and sometimes cursing it), feeling it to be unknown, mysterious and yet close by, the only true reality.'[19] Herewith the conflict between religion and ethics already fathoms deeper regions. It is evident from the above remarks that the problem of religion and of God is neither for Bloch nor for Lukács a sterile question of the mere existence or non-existence of God. It is always a question of man and man's destiny, and if of God, then not of predestination but of man's needs. How can the existing world be radically changed? This question can perhaps be answered only in practice, by pointing to the subject, to the radical community by which it is changed. But what if such a community cannot be discovered empirically? Necessity is no answer, for two reasons: because while destroying the old it cannot build up the new, and because – this is a point of knowledge today – there is no such necessity. The answer can be only a practical one, but still an answer *must* be given, even if there is no possibility for this sole answer. Thus the 'ought' enters the picture, though – as we already know – it 'kills life'. The (radical) religious necessity and (radical) religious consciousness reacts to this threat: hypostasizes a community where there is no real community. It seeks truth, as Bloch says, contrary to the empirical.[20] Religious consciousness *presupposes* this quest in the empirically given masses of men: without proof it is sure that the terrible temptation to goodness exists *equally* in the masses of men, to use Brecht's beautiful expression. In one passage of his book Bloch expresses the foundation of the compulsion of religion with deep pathos:

> What has us here in its clumsy and then vengeful hand: hampering, persecuting, blinding, the spider, the eating and being eaten, the poisonous scorpion, the angel of destruction, the demon of chance, accident, death, the homelessness of everything meaningful, the fat, banal, hardly penetrable mountain of separation from all providence, the magician of 'pious' panlogism – all that cannot be the same principle that will once hold judgement. . . .

This antithesis necessarily implies twofold principles, 'duality in God, our depth'.[21] Of the twentieth-century God-seekers, with the exception of Ady, none expressed the earthly basis with such sharp definition as Bloch.

> God, as the problem of the radically new, absolute solution, as the phenomenality of our freedom, of our true content, is self-aware in us only as a shadowy occurrence, objectively not happening, only as a combination of the darkness of the experienced moment and the inconclusive self-symbol of the absolute question. That means: the last, genuine, unknown, ultradivine God, the revelation of us all, lives even now, although he is not 'crowned,' not 'objectified'. . . .

> The subjects are the only thing that cannot be extinguished in all external and higher darkness; and that the Saviour lives and *wills* to come again is

evidenced intangibly now as always: but He and God himself have, like everything objective, lost their own power to come and be visibly effective. . . . Thus there is here only one single salvation, and that is the rebellious alliance between the moral self, which alone can still burn in the night of external and higher light, an alliance, sought above everything extraneous, between this self and the silent God who forsakes us and hesitates to be transformed into the Holy Spirit, as the cries, prayers and the deep naming power of heroic-mystical atheism itself.[22]

After the long quotations we have before our eyes the interesting metamorphosis of the critique of practical reason, precisely what Bloch misses as companion piece to a Marxist work approximating a critique of pure reason.[23] The metamorphosis consists in the determination of the thing-in-itself (which in Kant, as is well-known, remained undetermined), in what-is-not-yet, in the still spiritual longing 'and in the perspective existing in music.

It is not my goal to engage in an extensive critique of Bloch, since I am examining the mutual effect of two, in my opinion, representative alternative theories and attitudes. So I allow myself only two remarks. Bloch has nothing in common with the usual correctors and completers of Marxism. Lukács himself fails to understand Bloch on this problem, when in his *History and Class Consciousness* he makes an accusation of this sort against him.[24] For others, to protect the *status quo*, degrade Marx into a specialist who expresses partial truths, while Bloch's every idea and every emotion is aimed against the existing world. From the viewpoint of the demands of the day, he is an orthodox Marxist, and the political morality of his book – as is shown unmistakably by the quotations at the beginning of this article – is identical with the political morality of the greatest personalities of radically leftist-oriented parties and factions of this epoch. But the pre-revolutionary character of his presentation co-operates with the post-revolutionary day of debris removal; the first inspires the second, and the questions that in the fever heat of revolutionary action would perhaps be cowardly questions, harmful to action, 'What will happen tomorrow? How does man change "after the change of his conditions"?' become the most important in the context of involuntary inactivity and the lack of the longed-for but barely even germinating revolution. Here it means the 'completion' of Marx, as opposed to the slogan of the morons: 'Marx says it all.' No doubt in Bloch's Kantianization there is hidden a fundamental problem of the Marxist theories of the period, namely, that 'what is to come in the economy is certain.'[25] But this results in an extremely practical consequence of dualism for today: 'to think purely in economic terms like the merchant but against the merchant implies the homogeneity of the detective and the criminal.'[26] The readers of *Tactics and Ethics* do not have to be reminded of the obvious affinity – I would like merely to note that Bloch is more open, for his conception, not

focusing on moral borderline situations, also shapes more openly the inner prob-
lematics of the vantage point. This is natural, since in Bloch it is only a
precondition: a precondition to his philosophical theory. We must also note
that we are here dealing not with an identity but with an affinity of Lukács' and
Bloch's thinking, since the extreme readiness for self-sacrifice necessary for
orientation in the labyrinth of tactics and ethics, this aristocracy of Lukács'
ideas heated by revolutionary pathos, does of course provide a line of demarcation.[27] And the second remark: the fecundity, beauty and immortality of
Bloch's book is ascribable to the fact that it is a book on the philosophy of
religion. This revolutionary theology gives a coherent answer to Bloch's real
formulation of the question under the conditions of the revolutionary spirit
deprived of revolution.

For, to repeat the point, the question is contained in the paradox of revolutionary spirit without revolution. And when Bloch − in the revised edition of
the book, where he explicates his polemics with Lukács − exaggeratedly and
unjustly, though not without cause, accuses *The Metaphysics of Tragedy* of the
following: that 'Lukács' immanence of tragedy in just this apparently self-
perfective form somehow amounts to a transcendental philosophy of the
friendliness and godliness of existence that is completely incongruent with
it',[28] the basis of the accusation − and also the cause for their parting of the
ways − is that Lukács in this work sees that the unbearableness of the given
empirical existence can be recognized at all only at the pinnacles of tragic ethics,
and only by the chosen few. Therefore in *On Spiritual Poverty* he speaks of
'castes', and therefore, too, in the second part of *The Metaphysics of Tragedy*, he
says:

> The all-decisive word has been said about a man and his fate when it has
> been determined what form his life-expressions bear and what their peaks
> require. . . . Our democratic age has sought in vain to promulgate equal
> rights to tragedy; every attempt to open this heavenly kingdom to the
> poor in spirit has been in vain. And democrats who have thought through
> to the end their demand for equal rights for all men have always contested
> tragedy's equal right to exist.[29]

But on this basis, redemption is inconceivable. Just this distinguishes *spiritual*
aristocracy from base, narrow-minded, decadent aristocracy, that it is privileged
not by a separate future, a separate solution but by a view of essences, suffering
and death. The only humane sense of perspective even today is a perspective
that embraces all mankind. 'The very stones will be redeemed,' answers Lukács
− in accord with his *Theory of the Novel*, to a naively beautiful question by
Anna Lesznai.[30] But however much the quest for perspective forces Lukács in
the direction of religion, he is unwilling to follow Bloch's route. His quest goes
in other directions. In part − on the model of Wilhelm Meister in *The Theory*

of the Novel – he seeks the existing or, at any rate, conceivably possible ideal community, which is no naive enrootedness and no mystical experience.[31] In part he speaks, after Fichte's example, of the progressive ethical idealism that subordinates politics to itself and thus at the same time includes it, and that now extends to every single human being.[32] But these are episodal solutions, and the real insolubility is confirmed by the decision made at the end of 1918. For a historical moment the problem of perspective found its practical solution, the real possibility of a transformation of society, as soon as its subject seemed to draw himself up out of hardship and catastrophe, as soon as the revolutionary proletariat went into motion. Lukács' development – from then on always presupposing the existence of a real community and movement – was first a thinking through of the antinomic moral change, the dialectical abolition of the entire moral problem. In *History and Class Consciousness* 'Class consciousness is the ethics of the proletariat.'[33]

To emphasize development we have digressed from our actual problem, i.e., the early theoretical contrast between Bloch and Lukács. The question of whether the precondition of this philosophy of class-consciousness is still tenable *after* the abolition of the movement cannot be further discussed in this context. Thus we return to the Bloch – Lukács controversy, which can be reformulated in terms of what has been said above.

On the second attempt, the question is worded as follows: spiritual aristocracy or democracy? – but on a religious foundation. In his book Bloch polemicizes with *The Metaphysics of Tragedy* and *The Theory of the Novel*. And, as we saw in one of the remarks above and will see below, the alternative thus formulated is the heart of the controversy. It develops in the sphere of the judgement of works and art. Decisive for the young Lukács and later, though somewhat modified, for his whole life work, are the objectifications: the completed work as such signifies the struggle against the baseness of life, and the great objectifications, as well as their fate, describe the historico-philosophical course and possibilities of man. Our quotations showed that Bloch's central category is the subject. In his thinking objectifications – God and art – have the role of giving a basis to the spiritual community of isolated subjects, to the existence and the identity of radical hopes and desires, and thus to their perspective. This is not the place to consider how far and with what qualifications Bloch's God and his concept of art are to be regarded as objectifications, nor to address the very interesting comparison that results from the fact that for Lukács the form-transformation of the long epic became the medium for his philosophy of history, while for Bloch this came to be the history of music. At any rate one could in Bloch's case prove that he adopted and reversed the musico-philosophical heritage of Kierkegaard, Schopenhauer and Nietzsche. But we must, on the contrary, speak of why, precisely, art is this medium. In Lukács art has a function similar to that which it has in German classical philosophy.[34] 'The visionary reality of the world appropriate to us, art, has become dependent: it is no longer a depiction, for all models have vanished; it is a created totality, for the natural unity of the metaphysical spheres is shattered for ever.'[35] The idea of created totality is identical, but its place in theory is different. For the principle of art can no longer have analogous meaning, and the philosopher who looks around him at the world, which has ceased to be a totality, perceives with resignation the only totality's insignificant role in life as it is. He knows that art also cannot be active in the transformation of the world. 'But this change can never be carried out by art. . . . every attempt to shape the Utopian as something existent, ends in destruction rather than creation of form.'[36] Bloch draws from this limitedness of art practically the opposite conclusions:

> to honour the colourfully darkened visionary clarity of expressionistic art with its radical orientation toward objective content as the last stage before the Second Coming. Yet it must be said in closing that the artist, including the one who wants to be artistically the most eruptive in preaching, knowledge and content, always stands in the realm of appearance. Aesthetic constructs in their islandlike existence are exciting but at first only virtually glowing glass paintings which men interpret, allude to, reinterpret, but then again dismiss. And such is therefore the criterion of the aesthetic clarification seen from the viewpoint of its ultimate category: how could things be perfected without coming to an apocalyptic end?[37]

This especially interesting part of Bloch's book, which incidentally – like *The Theory of the Novel* – begins with the times of blissful proximity to God and similarly arrives at Dostoevsky as an emergent perspective, shows precisely by the astonishing correspondences – in all probability, influences – the greatness of the contradistinctions. In Lukács Dostoevsky goes beyond the limits of the novel as genre, in Bloch beyond the limits of art: 'so that it is no longer art, a still immanent, virtual perfection, but it is I, an internal, imageless, indeed actually workless quest for God, in which objectivity occurs as little more than an auxiliary construct, so that only I myself, the rebirth, the adjustment of the heart appear as work. . . .'[38] For Bloch art is important in that it does not belong to this world – in that it discovers the first signs of the transcendent in the works, in their gift of prophecy. In Lukács a man's work outgrows him; Bloch crowns man, the true man who has been released from his duality. Therefore the problem of form, which for Lukács is decisive, plays no role in Bloch. And if at this point of our analysis we look back at what has been said, the justification of the problem formulation 'ethics or religion?' is again confirmed. 'Ethics, or – as we now say of art – form, is at every moment and in every mood an ideal outside the self,' writes Lukács in one of his very earliest essays.[39] Lukács always sought a standard *outside* the self, Bloch *in* the self. Only a standard outside the self can give a basis to an ethics, but with this statement we have still said nothing about whether this ethics is appropriate for the current generation of men. Bloch asks about these men and can assure their future revolutionizing of society only through the religious doubling of their self, through the theological construction of good and evil.

And now on the art-theoretical side of this antithesis: Bloch is one of the first to give a philosophical basis to avantgardism. The general determination that precisely a theory of this sort has found a place for the avantgarde must suffice us. At that time Bloch's criteria, as concerns the masterpieces, do not yet deviate essentially from Lukács'. Only – and that is the point – they differ as to the function of the work of art. Bloch's functional subordination of art assigns a place to the avantgarde, but Habermas at times, and quite rightly, contrasts Bloch with Walter Benjamin, since in Bloch the symbolic remains the central category of aesthetics.[40] The pre-established harmony of the vision and form remains the specific characteristic of artistic creation; however, the specification loses its significance and the entire question is reduced to a merely technical problem. Art as art interests Bloch very little in the philosophical context of *The Spirit of Utopia*. 'More important than that the outsiders hear song when a man screams in the hot belly of the Pharsalian bull, and still more important than the mechanism by which his screams, transformed into song, are transmitted, are the screams themselves, their undiverted genuineness and depth.'[41] So Bloch summarizes his views of art.

And not only of art. For when he raises a dismayed protest against the form-centred conception of *The Theory of the Novel*, what crops up is not the academic discussion of the priority of form and content, and his dismay is not the result of not understanding Lukács. Our last proof – a critical remark on *The Metaphysics of Tragedy* – sums up the basis of the antithesis paradigmatically:

> Thus one can well admit that great tragedy can most genuinely ensue in this age of remoteness from God and of the heroic atheism active in it; but that does not at the same time mean, as in Lukács, that the emptiness of external life must be powerless, and so that misanthropy or at least the murky, gelatinous, unpredictable, arbitrarily retarded, falsely conceived, moody, maliciously fortuitous and intermittent element of the causal nexus can merely be disregarded as simply and randomly alogical.[42]

We can safely disregard the somewhat exaggerated accusatory accent relating to Lukács' indifference toward empirical life because of the picture we have formed of the young Lukács *post festum* after his revolutionary turn. The debate which was formed in the period before the revolution, and greatly exaggerated in the period after, now stands before us.

The final basis of the two philosophies – the rejection of the existing world (and not in an indirect apologetic manner) and the necessity to transcend this world – is the same.

Does hope (which sees itself as justified and philosophically perhaps also is – though not in a positivistic, verifiable sense) in a future essentially and radically different from this present, which men must create by their actions, have the negative character of ideology and false consciousness or rather the positive character of a historically creative Utopia?[43]

So Lucien Goldmann formulates the contrast. The basis of this seminal Utopia is religious need. Therefore the contrast between transcendence and immanence in the philosophy of history, in ethics and aesthetics, develops on a common foundation. In a late interpretation Lukács speaks about what Bloch and, in the twenties, Benjamin and Adorno have in common with *The Theory of the Novel*, but his interpretation – rightist epistemological theory, leftist ethics, as the basis of this common ground – is problematic.[44] In my opinion, the terminological pair *right – left* can deal *only* with the practical – ethical and political – effects of a theory. The possibility exists that someone, despite the practical consequences of his theoretical viewpoint, is still leftist-oriented in practice. But the practical consequences of the theory formulated in *The Theory of the Novel* and in *The Spirit of Utopia* are themselves leftist-oriented. And yet they are antinomical: each is the only true overcoming of the other.

Translated by David J. Parent

NOTES

1 Part of a chapter of a longer essay on Walter Benjamin, entitled *Credo und Resignation*.

2 *Geist der Utopie* (Berlin: Cassirer, 1923), p. 324. Cf. also *Geist der Utopie*, first version (1918; reprinted 1971), pp. 403ff. Where the ideas are essentially the same, I usually quote the early version (1918) and refer to the other (1923).

3 Bloch, *Geist der Utopie* (1923), pp. 325, 324. Cf. ibid. (1918).

4 Georg Lukács, *Geschichte und Klassenbewusstein* (Berlin – Neuwied: Luchterhand, 1968) [*History and Class Consciousness*], p. 53.

5 *The Theory of the Novel*, trs. Anna Bostock (Cambridge, Mass.: MIT Press, 1971), p. 153.

6 Georg Lukács, *Metaphysik der Tragödie: Paul Ernst*, in *Die Seele und die Formen* (Berlin – Neuwied: Luchterhand, 1971), p. 231.

7 Lukács, *Die Seele und die Formen*, p. 233.

8 ibid., p. 223.

9 *Die Theorie des Romans* (Berlin – Neuwied: Luchterhand, 1963), p. 27.

10 *The Theory of the Novel*, trs. Anna Bostock, p. 35.
11 ibid., p. 153.
12 ibid., p. 91.
13 In Bloch too the lord of the world of today is the dark demiurge, the unilluminated Jehovah. Cf. *Geist der Utopie* (1923), p. 324; (1918), p. 405.
14 *Metaphysik der Tragödie*, p. 230.
15 *Die Theorie des Romans*, pp. 90ff.
16 ibid., p. 91.
17 'Ady Endre', in 'Uj magyar lira' ('New Hungarian Lyrics'), *Magyar irodalom, magyar kultura* (Hungarian Literature, Hungarian Culture) (Budapest: Gondolat, 1970), p. 53.
18 ibid., p. 46.
19 ibid.
20 Cf. *Geist der Utopie* (1923) p. 251.
21 ibid., p. 360; (1918), p. 441.
22 ibid., pp. 246, 189ff.; (1918), pp. 372, 341ff.
23 ibid. (1923), pp. 322ff.; (1918), p. 408. Although this statement is doubtful even as concerns the works of Marx that were known to Bloch at that time, it is absolutely inaccurate for the Marxism of Bloch's contemporaries, whose social democratic theory had moved from Utopia towards objective science.
24 'Reification and the Proletarian Consciousness', in *Geschichte und Klassenbewusstein*, pp. 379ff.
25 *Geist der Utopie* (1918), p. 406; cf. (1923), p. 325.
26 ibid.
27 It would be impossible, in this brief comparison, to elaborate on every detail of the relationship between Bloch and Lukács; anyway, it is philologically unclear on many points. Even extensive analysis of the differences between the two versions of *Geist der Utopie* is impossible. It is at any rate characteristic that the turn of destiny to which Lukács reacted with a radical break with his entire early period prompted Bloch merely to revise his original conception and to stress its secularizing tendency, and deepened his knowledge of Marx. From our viewpoint, it is important that in the rewritten parts we repeatedly discover an open polemic against the ideas of Lukács' early period. In my opinion, this does not contradict the conception of the first version at all. In 1915 – 16 Lukács and Bloch thought that their philosophical standpoints were so close that the individual antitheses would have to be collected in a separate booklet. In reality the profound disagreements, which at first were hidden behind aesthetic 'sub-questions', were made conscious only in the second version.
28 *Geist der Utopie* (1923), p. 282.
29 *Metaphysik der Tragödie*, pp. 248ff.
30 *Gespräch mit Anna Lesznai – Irodalmi Muzeum I. Emlékezések* (Budapest: Petöfi – Múzeum, 1967), p. 13.
31 *Die Theorie des Romans*, p. 136.
32 Cf. 'A konzervativ és a progresszív idealizmus vitája' ('The debate between Conservative and Progressive Idealism'), in *Utam Marxhoz* (My Way to Marx), I, (Budapest: Magvetö, 1971), pp. 177 – 86.

33 'Rosa Luxemburg as a Marxist', in *Geschichte und Klassenbewusstein*, p. 215. Mihály Vajda, in his study entitled 'In Search of Dialectics – Lukács 1918 to August 1919', analyses the decisive significance of the change and the manner in which Hegel replaces the influence of Fichte. Likewise the essay by Ferenc Fehér: 'The Alliance between Béla Balázs and Georg Lukács until the Revolution'. The first-mentioned study repeatedly provides proof of experimentation with the idea of socialism in Lukács' early works. The letters written by Lukács to Paul Ernst offer further proof of this. These findings should remind the future historian of Lukács' development that the philosopher's rejection of his splendid early work – a gesture that he sustained virtually throughout his life – should be taken as symptomatic rather than as an objectively considered break.

34 This philosophical role of art was proven by Lukács himself in his essay 'Reification and Proletarian Consciousness', in *Geschichte und Klassenbewusstein*, pp. 317ff.

35 *Die Theorie des Romans*, p. 31.

36 ibid., p. 157.

37 *Geist der Utopie*, p. 141. I am convinced that the insertion of the contrasting views of art between *Die Theorie des Romans* and *Der Geist der Utopie* would cast a new light on the Expressionism debate that was conducted between Bloch and Lukács in the 1930s.

38 *Geist der Utopie* (1923), p. 142.

39 *Reichtum, Chaos und Form: Ein Zwiegespräch über Lawrence Stern*, in *Die Seele und die Formen*, p. 214.

40 'Zwischen Philosophie und Wissenschaft: Marxismus als Kritik', in Jürgen Habermas, *Theorie und Praxis* (Berlin – Neuwied: Luchterhand, 1967), p. 207.

41 *Geist der Utopie* (1923), p. 133.

42 ibid., p. 284.

43 Lucien Goldmann, *Das Denken Herbert Marcuses. Kritik und Interpretation der kritischen Theorie* (Munich: TWA Reprint Editions, 1970), p. 194.

44 Cf. *Die Theorie des Romans*, Foreword, pp. 16ff.

4

Lukács in Weimar

FERENC FEHÉR

The classic or classicist (let us suspend the distinction between them for the time being) is the personality who creates or reveals a new canon for his age and imposes himself upon it as a paradigm by virtue of his own qualities and the force of his objectivation. Despite his disguise as a humble interpreter of Marx, Georg Lukács was already a classic in the 1920s. Friends and foes alike admit nowadays that *History and Class Consciousness* was the most important event in the history of Marxist philosophy since the death of Karl Marx.

But the conception postulated in *History and Class Consciousness* collapsed at the end of the 1920s. By 'collapsed' I do not mean only (or even primarily) that it subsided under the pressure of the Comintern against heretical works. Resolute, influential opposition to the interdict would have been readily conceivable then, in that era of still virulent heresy. But the hopes of an immediate *parusia*, the radical and instant redemption of the world through the voluntary action of the international proletariat, underlying and nurturing the conception of the book, vanished without trace in the late 1920s. On the other hand, Lukács, the romantic anti-capitalist rebel, did not for a moment want to leave the promised land of revolution, whatever it turned out to be in reality, precisely because it was the only realm in which the 'redeeming deed' could be perpetrated. In particular, the socialist parties held out no such lofty hopes; they represented for him only pseudo-radical surrogates for conventional liberal parliamentary opposition. For him it was an hour of decision: with a dialectical *salto mortale*, he renounced his radical philosophy, his radical attitude, in order to remain in the realm of (alleged) radicalism and, in the wake of the Hegelian pattern, realized his own 'reconciliation with reality'. This was, of course, to an ever-increasing extent, Stalin's reality, which is why it is justifiable to characterize *The Young Hegel* as his own philosophical autobiography up to the point of his reconciliation with the given world. This adjustment to the 'real' had increasingly profound ramifications as the rightist dictatorships became more and more expansive after Hitler's ascent to power. Much as he described it only in terms of a political vocabulary (Popular Front as against old-time 'sectarianism'), in fact it was a philosophically founded attitude towards the world – one full of resignation, conceived of *faute de mieux*, typified by no more than latent energy. Its content was identical with the mobilization of traditional Enlightenment and humanism against a world that broke off all relations with reason and humanism. It also implied the acceptance of what was known as socialism, again with a fair amount of historical resignation and with the critical intention of transforming its 'crudeness', of penetrating its 'barbaric crust' and, step by step, of permeating it with the spirit of humanism and Enlightenment.

His magnificent essays and books on the Weimar period of German classic culture exemplify his 'existential choice' to the fullest extent. Apart from the obvious (namely, the analyses of Goethe), it is important to point out here that these works contain a whole gallery of cultural protagonists who could not represent the mainstream of German cultural dynamics in their own times precisely because they were, in one sense or another, too radical. It was Michael Löwy who first pointed out the symbolic significance of the Hölderlin tragedy in Lukács' conception and its marked resemblance to the Trotsky tragedy. But the verdict is similar in the case of Georg Forster, that rigorous classicist critic of German culture and its servile acquiescence to the degrading powers of feudalism. Lukács unhesitatingly recognizes the moral greatness and the most un-German (that is, insubordinate) spirit of the great radicals from the period of the French Revolution, particularly its Jacobin period, but they are discarded as moral paragons and political leaders for Germany precisely because of their uncompromising nature, their lack of flexibility and their incapacity to adjust to the ever more 'prosaic' turns of reality. One of them ends his life in the mystical cult of heroic death and the lonely night of madness, the other in complete political isolation. Sometimes Lukács positively slanders the young radicals. He not only notes Friedrich Schlegel's converstion to a hysterical Roman Catholicism and the service of Metternich (which are undeniable facts) but even 'spots' and 'uncovers' their alleged source in an over-exalted *Jugendstil* in the early radical writings of Schlegel, then a persecuted *enfant terrible* and a convinced Francophile in German literary life.

The way in which Lukács describes Heinrich Kleist, the rightist radical, the opponent of moderate Prussian conservatism (or half-hearted liberalism) is equally typical. Kleist is not only condemned by Lukács for his rightist fanaticism; Lukács does not only write of Kleist that his 'reactionary instincts' crippled the unparalleled theatrical genius in him. Lukács also counterposes Kleist to more moderate conservative writers (Eichendorff among others) who allegedly all prove to be superior to him precisely by virtue of their being *less* radical. Rightist or leftist, radicalism seems to be a bad omen for the Lukács of the 1930s and 1940s. The runners-up in this historical race for superiority are, of course, the Olympians: Goethe and Hegel. They both had their *Sturm und Drang* youth, their early republican or at least irreverent, rebellious vehemence, but they both paid allegiance eventually to the increasingly prosaic character of bourgeois life, a reified outcome of a frozen revolution. The new type of dialectic that Lukács elaborates here in historical disguise is the offspring of resignation, sometimes of self-deception. An example of the latter is the Lukácsian characterization of the Hegelian ethic as one that had allegedly overcome the Kantian antinomies by the theoretical reproduction of the totality of bourgeois society – as if any ethic departing from, and landing in, bourgeois society could overcome Kant at all. On the other hand, the new version of Lukácsian dialectic continues to be critical reason. It is important to stress this preserved critical dimension of his reconciliation with reality because several important socialist critics (among them Isaac Deutscher), turning Lukács' own terminology against him, labelled him the advocate *sui generis* of the Stalin era, its indirect apologist. For my part, I am convinced that Lukács was totally justified when he characterized his position during this period as that of an irregular and irreverent 'partisan', not a rank-and-file member who observes strict military discipline. Beyond any doubt, it was a most contradictory position. He incessantly tried to reveal the 'ideal type' of the system as opposed to its empirical reality, a procedure barely tolerated by the system itself (hence the constant conflicts between Lukács and the cultural bureaucracy), but this same procedure also entailed acceptance of the final principles of the regime. This critical distance was necessary, and at the same time sufficient, for Lukács to elaborate his classicism, to build up his personal Weimar, an island of culture in a world of power relations that were unambiguously hostile towards the outspokenness of any democractic culture.

Whenever one mentions Lukács' turn to Weimar, one has inevitably to speak in terms of evaluation. Here is the place to mention that Lukács himself radically rejected the metaphor of Weimar, together with its opposite, Potsdam, as a valid and principal contradiction of German culture. It was consistent with the self-deceptions of his position that he should believe that he had transcended both poles of German misery, that of a defenceless cultural opposition and that of the harsh reality of a half-way militarized bureaucracy. Was this turn progress or regress, measured by the yardstick of the 1920s? I think there is no unequivocal answer to this question. If we want to catalogue what Lukács had lost, the first dimension to be mentioned is precisely the reproduction of the above-mentioned antinomy in his position. The dichotomy of a socially impotent cultural opposition and a socially omnipotent, culturally sterile, undemocractic power structure – an antinomy that for Marx and Lukács, at both poles, testified to the prevalence of social misery – re-emerges unmistakably in his work. Secondly, the situation involved for Lukács (and this has been recently analysed by Agnes Heller in detail) an imperative to renounce every kind of positive philosophy, to accept the official dialectical materialism, an increasingly meaningless metaphysics, a type of philosophical thinking that had been so vehemently rejected, even as an enterprise, by the author of *History and Class Consciousness*. Finally, Lukács literally lost his sensitivity to the new radical cultural possibilities. This development can best be symbolized by his famous incapacity to grasp Brecht's significance. Instead of recycling a discussion that exhausted its own potentialities, I state simply that this lack of sensitivity was a direct result of his abandoned radicalism. On the other hand, his equally vehement rejection of the *Proletkult* writers (both in the Soviet Union and in the German Communist movement) was wholly consistent with the positive aspects of his new position. It meant opposition to a bureaucratic Party literature, the pompous servant of an apparatus with over-developed aggression and little talent, which pretended to be 'the voice of masses'.

The first positive aspect of Lukács' turn to Weimar is his abandonment of the myth of the proletariat. The romantic anti-capitalist philosopher who elaborated (in the fragments of an unfinished book on Dostoevsky) an anti-capitalist mythology in the very first moment of the outbreak of the First World War, with the 'Russian idea' of a redeeming, mystical-revolutionary-religious community at its pinnacle, hoped to find a concrete social *topos* of synthesis after the Hungarian revolution of 1919. Lukács thought out one of Marx's most important intellectual experiments to the end and elaborated a consistent Marxist philosophy of fetishism that conferred on the proletariat the distinguished role of the implementor of synthesis. According to this philosophy, it is the proletarian *existence* that solves the riddle of the *essence* of bourgeois world. Here my aim is merely to point out the *sociological* factors that prompted the collapse of the theory. First, of necessity, the conception had to be a short-term dream of a turbulent revolutionary period. When it turned out (and this happened very soon) that the proletariat behaved simply as one class among others (even if a centrally important one) in the ensemble of the social forces fighting for a socialist transformation that had separate interests – including conflicts of interest and various parties representing the same class – the proletarian mythology had either to be abandoned or to be transformed into an insincere, deliberately manipulative ideology. It is a sign of Lukács' absolute theoretical honesty that he chose the first option. Secondly, the proletarian mythology had very soon been transformed into a semi-religious idea (actually in *History and Class Consciousness* itself). This idea was the *cult of the élite*, advocacy of allegedly the only non-fetishized social group that had the prerogative to direct the social process of defetishization on the grounds of its 'correct' viewpoints and intentions. But apart from the lamentable consequence of comparing theory with reality, immanent theoretical considerations as well forced Lukács to renounce his favourite idea. The conception was clearly aristocratic, and it was impossible to found the democratic cultural idea of a socialist Weimar on an aristocratic basis. It was equally impossible to depart from a semi-religious premise in advocating critical rationalism. As a result, the élite remained for Lukács a kind of social precondition but no longer the guarantor of cultural fulfilment. It is only from these premises that he could discover for himself the Marx of *The Paris Manuscripts*, the universal philosopher of alienation. It was only in departing from these grounds that he could gradually elaborate his own theory of 'species character' (*Gattungsmässigkeit*), his own aesthetic and literary theory (which was a facade, a disguise for his philosophy in the 1930s and the 1940s). It was only on this methodological basis that he could reject the central role of *class reduction*, until then the key concept of Marxist understanding of culture.

But why classicism precisely? Was it the only possible *tour de force* in this twilight (in which illumination, as we know, Minerva's owls would fly) that promised at least a certain way out of the impasse? Lukács, irresistibly drawn to a monolithic theory of truth, would have unhesitatingly answered in the affirmative, but I doubt the validity of such an answer. In my view, it was not the only option, at best merely one of the good and correctly chosen ones, in the hardly tolerable climate of the period. Here are some parallel alternatives picked nearly at random. Brecht insisted, defying in good Fichtean manner all factual evidence to the contrary, on the *existing* and *general* validity of the language of revolution and revolutionary movements. This is indeed an instructive example of the fertilizing role of ideological self-deception. It was precisely this vulnerable standpoint that helped Brecht towards his lasting achievement: the new non-tragic drama, the immortal, symbolic portrayal of the ultimate dilemmas of capitalist society beyond prescriptions of class action and organization and the narrowly normative ethic of movements. (Of course, an additional factor was needed: his preserved distance from 'real socialism', an anxiously guarded and protected 'separate status' with a large amount of *mauvaise foi*.) The prophetic personality of Ernst Bloch occurs here. His stylistic *mélange*, concocted from nearly equal portions of Jewish-frivolous expressionist irony and the highest pathos resembling not so much the Gospel or the Torah as the most remarkable pages of ancient and medieval rebellious mysticism, is an accurate mirror of his message. It reflects the *nihil* of an unredeemed and insignificant present and, at the same time, the promise of, or at least the urgent need for, an imminent *parusia*. Such ambivalence alone was sufficient grounds for Marxist *Lebensphilosophie*, in his case distanced from, later rebelling against, that which had arrogated to itself the name of socialism. His was an optimistic rival to Heidegger's tragic fundamental ontology under the auspices of the principle of hope. When he espoused socialism in the late 1940s and early 1950s Jean-Paul Sartre invented a further representative solution: the technique and ethic of *radicalisation du mal*, accepting all distortions of personality caused by alienation and at the same time fomenting them in order to provoke an explosion: the revolt or a revolution.

All these courses made it natural, as it were, for their respective representatives to become leading symbols or theoretical supporters of the avantgarde. At the same time, none of them was open to Lukács. Brecht, a disciple of Karl Korsch, was identified by Lukács with his own theoretical past, the period of *History and Class Consciousness*, which he believed himself to have transcended and which he at least publicly recanted. Following Bloch would have been for him a relapse into the religious interlude of the Dostoevsky fragments, the 'radicalism in a God-forsaken world', in a period in which he surmised that he had found at least a foothold from which the Fichtean 'complete sinfulness' of the world could be surpassed. As far as all the early attempts at *radicalisation du mal* are concerned, from his youth on he regarded all such escapism from capitalist alienation with the greatest suspicion. For him, they were mostly paths leading to the self-destruction, not the emancipation, of personality.

Here are the roots of his classicism. Even in his youth, as a vehement opponent of officially accepted bourgeois culture, as an early 'modernist', Lukács was the zealot of a *new constructivism*, of a monumental and tragic art of order, measure, proportionate dimensions, an art of palpable and visible essence, instead of impressionism and naturalism, mere collections of experiences from the surface. In his youth he projected that the repositories of such an art would be small spiritual communities to come (this was the meaning of the 'Dostoevsky perspective' from an aesthetic viewpoint). After the Revolution he expected its realization in the anonymous, collective world of the fighting proletariat. This is true, even though Lukács always had a *negative* relation to the idea of 'proletarian culture' *sensu stricto*. In his debate with Paul Ernst, once his favourite playwright, in the 1920s a militant ultra-conservative, Lukács does not deny *ex principio* the possibility of the emergence of a proletarian culture, as Ernst did, but he is just as sceptical about it as Trotsky was. Surprisingly, he even makes a reference to Trotsky, who was already living in exile. But the absence (if not the outright impossibility) of a full-blooded proletarian counter-culture means by the same token *the absence of solid cultural measures and standards*, a cultural gap, particularly as the rejection of bourgeois standards is commonplace for the radical. The absence of solid standards on the one hand, the quest, even the yearning for a new harmony on the other, is precisely the definition (and the precarious position) of the classicist (but, of course, not the classic) author. The distinction is made for obvious reasons: the latter simply gives voice to what exists and needs only to be formulated; he shapes what exists anyhow. The classicist, for his own part, the sentimental *organon* (to use Schiller's terminology), confronts Being with an Ought, with the intention of transforming Ought into Being. He confronts existing 'nature', already degraded into a mere convention, with a new cultural pattern that is destined to be transformed into new nature, a new functioning world of consensus. It is precisely in this sense that Lukács can be termed a classicist, the advocate of a new, universal canon. He formulated its programme when he was the People's Commissar of the Hungarian Soviet Republic in the following way. Capitalism separated culture from life and thereby contaminated both. Real socialism would be a way of life becoming culture and culture will become a way of life. But what is this if not the well-known programme of classicism, that of a plebeian Weimar? Should the (well founded) objection arise that Lukács was sometimes sentimental in a problematically naive way – in other words, that he actually imputed norms and canons while maintaining that he was simply 'deciphering' them in the face of an already redeemed cultural cosmos – I would reply that his self-deception was a trait shared by nearly every classicist. Winckelmann considered himself the simple 'archaeologist' of a still existing ancient harmony, while in fact he was a zealot and an engineer of a radical turn, a break with 'nature' deeply degraded into convention.

The first dimension of Lukács' classicism is the postulate of *ethical democracy*. The term 'postulate' needs some further qualification. Lukács' theoretical activity in the 1930s and 1940s focuses on historical studies (because of his renunciation of a positive philosophy) in the classic era of bourgeois art and philosophy, roughly from the time of the joint Weimar efforts of Goethe and Schiller to the 1848 Revolution. Whenever he leaves this garden of classicism, and in whatever direction, it happens either to preserve the continuity of an analysed national culture (predominantly the German and the Russian) or to wage war against 'decadence', which, in his conception, is characteristic only of *the post-1848 period*. (The exception to this is Romanticism, treated by Lukács as a forerunner of decadence.) The essays are small moral biographies, constituting as a whole a compendium of typical personality distortions that should be overcome or paradigmatic attitudes that should be generalized in an emancipated future. (This is why so many 'pure aestheticians' are deeply dissatisfied with their *sensu stricto* aesthetic output. In fact, these essays should be regarded as preludes to an ethic that was never completed by Lukács.) The attention is always focused on what is regarded as paradigmatic, and the author's text always suggests that the discovery of the emancipatory message of classic bourgeois culture has been prompted only by an already existing order that has generalized all fruitful types of behaviour elaborated by its forerunner, the so-called progressive bourgeoisie. It is very difficult, generally futile even, to decide how far this simulated methodological precondition stems from the tactic of paying lip-service to an almighty and not particularly tolerant bureaucracy and how far from genuine self-deception. It is important that, departing from a vague ideal of a socialist-humanist classicism in the early 1930s, which takes on more and more flesh and blood *en route*, Lukács selects precisely the paradigmatic types of attitude that *ought to be* generalized in the socialist future. Hence the postulate is just that – in fact an Ought confronted with reality, however much this is denied by the author himself.

What is the meaning of ethical democracy, of this category that at first glance seems so far removed from social struggles, so Utopian, so very academic? It has a very serious and very concrete meaning indeed. Following in Marx's footsteps, Lukács' writings are full of invective against mere formal democracy. From the early 1930s onwards he often enlists the concept of 'new democracy', later that of 'people's democracy'. Whenever he tries to define the concept in terms of actual politics, the result is lamentable. It amounts to no more than a proposal to realize the old pattern (dictatorship as a 'maximum of democracy') only 'slowly', 'gradually', 'peacefully', so that the democracy suggested by him is not new, and it has always been questionable to what extent it is democracy at all. This is the price that the 'partisan' has to pay for the acceptance of military discipline. But behind this crust, a real and dynamic content palpitates; a genuine philosophical project is at work that is aimed at overcoming formal democracy while preserving (not abolishing through a fraudulent dialectic) the democratic framework of life. Time and again the Lukácsian quest for 'genuine' democracy seems to be a simple relapse into the romanticism of *The Theory of the Novel*. It will suffice to consider to what extent he emphasizes the moral superiority of the Scottish clans in Walter Scott's novel, the background presence of a peasant community in Russian literature (which is his real motive for elevating Russian development as a whole to the rank of a classic culture). In other instances 'genuine' democracy is merely a small island of refined and sophisticated persons, as in the analysis of Goethe's *Wilhelm Meister*. But when we read attentively his masterly analysis of 'genuine' democracy, the essay on Gottfried Keller, we begin to understand his intentions fully. Keller's Switzerland can be a model of 'genuine' democracy because it is *not yet* affected by the wave of capitalization. But this is no romantic nostalgia, since Lukács expressly states that this type of democracy can and should be projected into a free future. Thus he arrives at his first, very important result: the separation of what Hegel (and that radical critic of Hegel, the young Marx) called *bürgerliche Gesellschaft* (in the sense of 'civil society') and capitalism. Democracy in its 'genuine' form is not the offspring of capitalism; it is only 'formal' democracy that is given birth in industrial capitalism. 'Genuine' democracy is historically prior to capitalism and can be projected *beyond* it as well.

What are the characteristic features of 'genuine' democracy? It is *direct* democracy in the sense that it tolerates no more than the relative separation of men and institutions. Of course, this is the age-old dream that has inspired every attempt to revive ancient Greece. It was 'put on the agenda' by the most extreme wing of the *Montagne* in 1793 – 4 (with whose success posterity is only too familiar). True, Lukács does not bother to analyse the pertinent

Rousseauean dilemma in a sociologically relevant way, the question of whether or not a huge social body can be governed by direct democracy at all and, if so, to what extent. But the free atmosphere in which the Kellerian heroes communicate speaks for itself. It radiates the concept of self-governed mankind, a regulative theoretical idea without which socialism cannot be realized. In this world there are indeed state, institutions, public affairs; the mystical dream about an unmediated world vanishes from Lukács' horizon. But there is no state repression, no fear of institutions, no feeling that institutions could be alien to the average citizen's will. There is even a palpable certainty among the protagonists that every institution is a free creation of man, subject as a consequence to charges triggered by new social initiatives. In a word, there are no reified structures in the small universe of Kellerian Swiss democracy, the harbinger of a self-managed mankind.

Further, the separation of the private from the public sphere becomes most relative in this cosmos. The Lukácsian essays are, in this respect, forerunners of what was accorded special importance and lastingly valid formulation by Habermas: *Öffentlichkeit*, the free public sphere. Lukács in this essay points to the education of a genuine citizen as one of the major tasks of 'normal' family life. This is one of Keller's most serious and favourite themes, and in its Lukácsian interpretation it is equivalent to the abolition of the unbridgeable gap between *citoyen* and bourgeois. In his treatise Habermas discloses the only worthy substitute for *Öffentlichkeit* in the so-called intimate sphere of bourgeois family life. Both together represent very vigorous and healthy opposition to the Hegelian dictum according to which the individual is the offspring not of the family but of bourgeois society in the narrower sense of the word (that is to say, the legal system, state and moral regulations). While Hegel merely reverses the normal hierarchy of individual and 'objective spirit' that is predominant in capitalism, both Lukács and Habermas, in their respective theories, seek the elimination of this alienation. Moreover, the Lukácsian conception of education for public life, an absolutely general feature of Keller's world, is not simply identical with the ensemble of civic liberties, which is, of course, a necessary precondition of every real *Öffentlichkeit*. The Lukácsian idea points beyond this and develops into a general social dynamic of domination-free communication, to use Habermas' terminology again, a constitutive principle of the (socialist) ethical democracy where equals talk the language of freedom and equality to equals. The famous scene so frequently quoted by Lukács, in which Keller's beloved hero, the 'green' (i.e. immature) Heinrich, is reprimanded by his lover for his 'plebeian haughtiness' towards a girl whom he believes to be a countess but who is actually a poor relative, reveals the deepest intentions of this world. In it domination-free communication is incompatible with class prejudices of any kind.

'Genuine' democracy is also a communal world, moreover: a world of communal, collective ethics, *Sittlichkeit* (this is why he termed it 'ethical democracy'). The opposition of subjective morality (whose greatest advocate is Kant, with his formula of the categorical imperative) to collective ethic is the constant subject of Lukács' unresolved struggle for a new moral theory. The basic dilemma inherent in the theory can be formulated roughly in the following way: how can the moral bipolarity of the capitalist world be transcended? This bipolarity means lifeless convention, the 'moral of national economy' – to use Marx's formulation – at one pole, the Ought, a nearly suprahuman demand, at the other. In the various phases of his long life and philosophical development Lukács experimented with three attempts at a solution. In his pre-revolutionary youth, when, despite being a convinced neo-Kantian, he was on very bad terms with Kant's ethics and failed to understand the deeply democratic character of the categorical imperative, that litany of non-specified commandments for Everyman, he proposed two contradictory solutions. One of them was a Kierkegaardian meta-ethic, an aristocratic undertaking; the other (during the revolutionary upheaval of the First World War) the democratic, but mystical idea of the 'Russian spiritual community'. The latter was a world of (non-sentimental) love in which there were collective moral principles but no alienated Ought. It scarcely needs to be pointed out that after the Revolution the first had to be renounced because of its aristocratic character, the second because of its patent mysticism.

As far as his position in the 1920s is concerned, the best summary of it can be found in his famous *Tactic and Ethic*. An objective-collective basis of ethic as *something already existing* (not only postulated) was smuggled into his conception. This basis seemed to be provided by the 'correct' philosophy of history (which is tacitly identified here with an allegedly existing 'proletarian consensus'). Only one subjective principle was added to it: conscience (the sense of responsibility for our violent actions). But apart from the fact that once the presence of a 'correct' measure for all deeds is granted, the root and function of the subjective principle remain unexplained, the whole position, bearing all the hallmarks of a Hegelian conception, stands or falls with the existence or non-existence of the hypothetical proletarian consensus. (It is Hegelian in the sense that it implies the actual elimination of all ethic while it claims only its reformulation.) Once Lukács had abandoned the hopes (or the illusions) of such consensus, and since he never gave up the postulate that Kantian moral rigour should be transcended, the quest for a new solution was binding on him. It is precisely this that had been provided by the idea of 'genuine' or 'ethical' democracy, in two senses. On the one hand, the functioning of a democracy with a free public sphere (*Öffentlichkeit*), based on domination-free communication, requires collective morality, the abolition of the moral dichotomy of the public and private sphere, the existence of well defined and valid – more precisely, generally internalized – norms. On the other hand, domination-free communication itself is a process of education in collective morality. This is why a pedagogical principle (with collision and catharsis at its summit) played such a large role in Lukács' thinking of that time. This is why the *Erziehungsroman* (*Tom Jones*, *Wilhelm Meister*, *Der grüne Heinrich*, Mann's Joseph tetralogy) and the idea of 'moral apprenticeship' are accorded such a distinguished role in his moral – literary essays. A deep and unassailable optimism underlies the whole conception, increasing certainty that tragedy as a phenomenon of life can be overcome. His most anti-Heideggerian *Faust* study stresses that the leading principle of the historical dynamic of humankind is of an 'epic', not a 'tragic', character. The essays on Goethe and Keller (and, at the end of his life, the magnificent study on Lessing's *Minna von Barnhelm*) emphasize the importance of 'moral wisdom'. Basically, this category covers a way of life that does not evade collisions; it is even ready resolutely to undergo tests, but only those that no longer provoke the tragic crowning of life so highly exalted in the early essays. In other words, this is a rupture not only with the Kierkegaardian haughtiness of his youth but also with the moral Jacobinism of the 1920s, which recognized only so-called 'borderline situations' as worthy of moral consideration.

We may observe an inherent contradiction in the conception of the collective morality of ethical democracy in Lukács. It has been pointed out by Agnes Heller that Lukács' central moral category is the moral personality 'beyond duty', a moral personality that has internalized norms to such an extent that there is no need for independently existing, external, alien moral demands. This is a revival of the age-old dream of the free agent of moral action, who accepts no authority imposed from above but looks rationally at his fellow creatures and the world and is in turn rationally scrutinized by them. Needless to say, this was a highly heretical idea in Stalin's era. But it is, at the same time, an ambiguous position. According to the methodological preconditions, the free agent acts 'as if' norms no longer existed in the form of merely external forces, since they have been wholly internalized by him. But how can we establish not so much their existence prior to the process of internalization but rather their exact content? This issue explains why a much too polyphonic category, decency (*Tüchtigkeit*), plays such an extraordinary role in the characterization of the protagonists of the literary essays. Anyone who is morally 'in order', anyone who is normal, anyone who knows 'instinctively' how to behave in a precarious situation, is decent. Of course, it is easy to discern a deeply Aristotelian quality in such a conception. The concept of decency is the nearest thing to one of the old-fashioned virtues of the city-state but, needless to say, without Aristotle's detailed inventory of particular virtues. This testifies to the fact that Lukács could not overcome (even with the 'auxiliary construction' of ethical democracy) the central dilemma of modern morality. The question remained a question: can the formal principle of morality (the unspecified moral demand) be unified with a material ethic and, if so, to what extent?

The last dimension of an ethical democracy is its *pluralistic structure*. No doubt, in this world the great paradigmatic personalities – first of all Goethe – are always present. In true classicist spirit they shape the actual structure of this world. But Goethe is the mentor of *modern* times, who himself pronounced the verdict so often quoted by Lukács: all men *together* constitute humanity. Thus the correct moral decision is a modified version of the Aristotelian *mesotes*, the medium value: not a point that can be filled by a single correct deed but a whole field of various, equally approvable, acts. The Lukácsian ethic does not acknowledge the inflexible rigour of his own epistemology. (It is here that we can study for the first time the extent to which his *aesthetic* conception is shaped after the fashion of his ethical conception; I am convinced that his theory of the fruitful aesthetic medium, that of particularity, grows out of the ethical medium.) Irrespective of whether we have in mind the analyses of the writers or their protagonists, we constantly observe this ethical pluralism. Although Goethe is the paragon, the demi-god of the classicist Olympia, Pushkin (whose portrait is painted, by the way, with a considerable amount of politically motivated partiality) appears as his equal, sometimes his superior, because of his more resolute social commitment. Although for Lukács political commitment is a virtue in itself, it may be the source of a narrow-minded bias as well (as in the case of Börne), or, should the writer's politics be badly chosen, it may become the cause of the collapse of the whole work (as in the case of Gogol, in his last creative period). The ideal is, of course, the writer who courageously defends his artistic principles and political priorities, who is active in the public sphere – a Lessing (Lukács' favourite model of the 'partisan' under the 'enlightened' tyranny of Frederick the Great), a Keller, a Tolstoy, the prophetic spokesman of the coming 'peasant revolution', an Anatole France, a Thomas Mann. But Lukács is not only indulgent toward the constant compromises of the idolized Goethe; he also shows exceptional tolerance towards the petty weaknesses of Heine, even the overtly anti-revolutionary ideology of Dostoevsky, that is to say, in all cases in which an intact emancipatory will is demonstrated by the objective body of the work which, in Lukács' philosophy of art, is a corrective principle overruling personalities and ideologies.

I can further document my thesis by pointing to the Lukácsian analysis of the protagonists of literary works. Novels about education are of primary importance here, the ones in which educator and educated have no fixed roles, in which people freely exchange social roles. This is how Philine, a charming and irresponsible young tramp in *Wilhelm Meister*, is elevated by Lukács (it is doubtful whether Goethe intended this as well) to the rank of a bearer of *amor dei intellectualis*, Spinoza's fundamental principle; this is how in the analysis of Keller's novels and short stories illiterate housewives, artisans and especially women become the embodiment of the morality of decency, by contrast with the over-refined protagonists who are badly in need of 'criticism from below'. Is it really necessary to point out that all this is but the realization of the Marxian maxim that the educator too should be educated, that all this is the democratic, pluralistic abolition of the rigid dichotomy of the Enlightenment? Further, Lukácsian moral analysis constantly relativizes the greatness of the Superman. It is not only the petty individualist who has donned fancy dress and hides behind the histrionics of self-proclaimed greatness that is being ruthlessly exposed here (although one of the reasons for Lukács' unwavering preference for Ibsen is the latter's magnificent and uncompromising critique of Hjalmar Ekdal, who becomes the scourge of his family because of his egotistic prerogatives, which are based on an unrealized but much vaunted 'great invention'). Genuinely great protagonists (Faust above all), if their life strategy is based on egoistic self-realization, are just as mercilessly unmasked and hounded through the purgatorial fire of education as long as they cannot find their way to a programme of collective emancipation. Sometimes they are unconditionally rejected by Lukács as Byronic Supermen of Romanticism. While he never denies that they are extraordinary by comparison with humbler men, their greatness does not persuade Lukács to place them on higher rungs of the moral ladder than those whose capacities are inferior and whose passions are less tempestuous. Finally, even among those who resist the increasing capitalization of the world, who are 'partisans' in their own ways, just as Lukács is in his own, there is no single 'correct' stratagem for resistance. Apart from those who withdraw into the recesses of their studies and private lives to preserve their integrity, whose tacit opposition is entirely (sometimes enthusiastically) approved of by Lukács, even among the militants there is no single course to resistance. Of Balzac's protagonists, the life of the lonely literary guerrilla (D'Arthez) is ranked just as highly as the heroic self-sacrifice of a Michel Chrétien on the barricades of the cloister of St Mary.

It is legitimate, then, to state that the idea of the 'genuine' 'ethical' democracy did mean radicalization, despite Lukács' renunciation of his merely political radicalism of the 1920s. True, Lukács shared some of the weaknesses of his idol, Goethe, when he paid lip-service to a power structure that has less taste for cultural development than did some of Goethe's masters. Equally true, Ought was constantly confounded by him with Being, and the price he has had to pay for his role as an unwitting, indirect apologist is that he is now open to bitter criticism, sometimes unjust, sometimes justified. But the ethical Ought was radically conceived. It demanded that a world commensurate with the free-collective ethic should come into being, a non-authoritarian, pluralistic world of ethical democracy that knew no moral tyranny (or tyranny of any other kind), a world with a domination-free public sphere.

The second dimension of Lukács' classicism consists in the *supremacy of* reason. To take a stand on behalf of rationalism was an absolute imperative of the 1930s and 1940s, that triumphant age of irrationalism *par excellence*. To resort again to a sketchy typology, neither Adorno or Horkheimer nor Popper could avoid this confrontation. Their respective proposals are well-known. To an ever-increasing extent, the founding fathers of the Frankfurt School had been characterized by a negative dialectic, which reached its climax in the period in question in *The Dialectic of Enlightenment*. Here the famous Lukácsian *Leitmotiv* of the 1920s, the exposure of rationalism as 'the spirit of capitalism' (a point of departure for the whole *Kulturkritik* of the Frankfurt School, which they constantly exploited but actually never acknowledged as their major stimulus) had been transformed into a real philosophical perversion. It is precisely reason at its summit that is on trial here for having given birth to its counterpart, *irratio*. In the genuine spirit of negativity it is not only the self-deceptions of the bourgeois era of rationalism that are criticized (a parallel to this is Sartre's brilliant, though somewhat exaggerated, attack on 'analytical reason'). The whole campaign to make the human universe rational is declared futile from the very beginning, and although criticism of cultural fetishism is maintained (and reaches its magnificent apotheosis in Adorno's philosophy of music), it is the voice partly of an impotent and partly of an aristocratic opposition – as is the case with every theory of fetishism. On the other hand, Popper is resolute in advocating the claims of critical reason. The 'irrational' choice of the leading values of theory, cumulative knowledge (a choice that cannot be accounted for rationally, which is why the theory is critical even of its own foundations) defends the rights of rationalism against both *any* mythologically legitimized totalitarianism and reason's own overdeveloped ambitions. But Popper's oversimplistic sociology (of 'open society and its enemies'), as well as his reduction of once all-powerful reason to the restricted formula of the cumulation of knowledge (all else is regarded by him either as a nonsensical project or as a deliberately manipulative totalitarian ideology), display a resignation about the chances of reason in history that is similar to the conception of negative dialectic

From the 1930s up until his death, Lukács' rationalism, in flagrant contrast to that of both Adorno and Popper, was characterized by an expansive spirit (not surprising in a classicist). Every period in which European classicism has flourished has developed under the aegis of a particular type of rationalism. Seventeenth-century French classicism soared to remarkable heights under the influence of Descartes and Gassendi, and Lucien Goldmann has identified Pascal as the first great forerunner of dialectic reason. Early eighteenth-century British classicism, the age of Swift, Pope and Addison, was influenced directly by the majestic upsurge of English rationalism from Hobbes to Locke, however critical particular writers may have been of particular thinkers. And Weimar was an heir to Enlightenment and a disciple of Kant, even if it sometimes engaged in bitter polemic with the master. Lukács, then, was not without precedent when he nominated Karl Marx, as the rationalist *par excellence*, as the focal point of the epic battle between *ratio* and *irratio*, as portrayed in *The Destruction of Reason*.

For Lukács another important reason for embracing an expansive universal rationalism was the fact that every theory of action that is not based on a consciously selected faith or mythology must be based on the premises of some rationalist principle. The fact that in a certain sense Lukács always remained a philosopher of praxis, despite the collapse of his philosophy from the 1920s onwards, is undeniable. What I am referring to here is not only his diatribes against the separation of *vita contemplativa* from *vita activa*, the hereditary sin of ancient humanists, not only the opposition of the 'narrating' realist to the merely 'descriptive' naturalist, but also the very core of his classicist ideal: ethical democracy. Ethical democracy as a concept had to be defended against the menacing waves of various tyrannical and irrationalist mythologies, and it had to be generalized in order for a world commensurate with ethic to emerge. But both gestures, that of defence and that of generalization, are principles of action.

However, if we take a closer look at the rationalism of Lukács in the 1930s and 1940s, we are aware of a peculiarity. His cherished principle, always at the centre of his literary and philosophical debates, in the name of which he pronounced a crushing verdict on nearly the whole of German culture in the last two centuries, is a postulate for him rather than a coherent theory. It is certainly not a *type of dialectical reason*, by contrast with his thinking in the 1920s, when he had a positive philosophy, a complete and coherent conception of the abolition of reification, when the subject – object dichotomy had been counterposed to the arid rationalism of antinomies. Elements of the previous conception were maintained, such as the very conception of alienation (primarily in *The Young Hegel*), that of unequal development, the increasingly meaningless category of totality that in the period of *History and Class Consciousness* had had a clear-cut content, since it was the offspring of the labour of totalizing reason, a state of equilibrium that had to be upheld by constant totalizing efforts. But these categories remained only fragmented pieces of former cohesion. Until the *Ontology* he never even attempted to synthesize them.

But the most problematic element in Lukács' rationalism is perhaps his 'bad naivety' in establishing the very principle. He thematizes reason as such, establishes 'laws' and general developmental tendencies of 'reason', unperturbed by the fact (so familiar to him both in his neo-Kantian youth and in the 1920s) that at least two generations of thinkers, from Dilthey to Husserl and the beginnings of neo-positivism, made enormous efforts which were tragically futile in the light of the failure of the majority to resolve the dilemmas of the Cartesian world epoch of rationalism and its Kantian renewal. Moreover, for Lukács the fact that a thinker should devote his energy to the clarification of the categorical preconditions of thinking remained until his dying day an absolute signal of the thinker's intellectual inferiority. For him this was a clear indication that such thinkers regarded reason not as something *given* but as something to be *construed*. It is easy to localize the source of this unacceptable naivety: in the mental operation analysed above, in his positing that a new consensus of ethical democracy actually existed. For Lukács this was the prevalent medium from which the synthetic principles of a new rationality were supposed to be easily deduced. That was self-deception for two reasons. First, ethical democracy was, in point of fact, an Ought; it was a concept that ought to have been established theoretically in a 'sentimental' way, instead of being naively taken for granted. Second, ethical democracy in its Lukácsian conception was a world without synthetic rules *sui generis*, a very fluid (or, rather, airy) medium based exclusively on moral personality.

The categories of this very vague conception of rationalism (deciphered from rather than revealed by the text) are the following. Its epistemology is a firmly upheld but barely underpinned conviction regarding the unlimited possibility of knowledge of the world ('external reality'); its critique of ideology is a theory of fetishism; its philosophy of history is a universal conception of progress. There is no need to waste many words on this epistemology, which is a strange mixture of certain elements of the Hegelian logic (especially the highly problematic dialectic of the concept from its abstract beginnings up to the moment of its being 'filled' with concrete content, actually a pseudo-logical abbreviation of the World Spirit's Odyssey towards the goal of history) and some elements of a Plekhanovian materialism, with Lenin as a mediator. Not the content of this *mélange* but its function is to be taken seriously. This was a *declaration* of the chances of knowledge, a polemical invective against relativism and agnosticism. But a peculiar contradiction emerges here, far-reaching in its theoretical consequences. Precisely because of the vagueness of epistemology, of its obvious vulnerability, it assumes an authoritarian posture. A social science with general laws does exist, Lukács states with the imperturbability of supreme arbiters, and it is only incorrigible relativists who question it. He brushes aside with one gesture not only the lessons of the neo-Kantian fiasco so well-known to him but also *his own* criticism of such a science as reification dating from the 1920s. Truth exists 'in history', 'in the things', he states with equal ease, unaware even of his own panlogistic position, and it is a 'single' truth in regard to each epistemological constellation. When he spelt out the principle in the form of a maxim ('There is an infinite number of ways all leading to falsity, but there is only one leading to truth'), the roots of this epistemological authoritarianism became visible. Again, it is the Hegelian homebound World Spirit, the bearer of the puzzle of world history, that we are confronted with. A deep chasm opens up here in the heart of the theory, an irreconcilable contrast between the pluralism of ethical democracy and the monolithism of its epistemology.

A detailed analysis of the further two components of Lukácsian rationalism, its theory of fetishism and its evolutionism, would be pointless, since they are actually nothing but auxiliary constructions to bolster his *classicist anthropology*, the last dimension of his classicism to be mentioned here. The general principles of his rationalism are clearly constituents of his classicist anthropology. Epistemological optimism is needed because man is indestructibly a rational being, a *Vernunftswesen*, as Kant put it, a being that can attain to knowledge of himself and of his world. Causality is needed (with adequate laws), because man is *causa sui*, a free agent. The theory of fetishism is needed as well to account for the factors as a result of which man has partially lost this clear self-knowledge: fetishism is, in fact, a 'diagnostical category' in Lukács' rationalism. And, finally, evolutionism is needed because man, ontologically and 'under healthy social conditions', is a being in constant development, equipped with an inexhaustible reservoir of developmental potentialities. At this point I cannot hide my admiration for Lukács' obstinate resistance to his own epoch. It was an irrevocable philosophical act to defend the primogeniture of free personality as *causa sui*, as a product of his own activity within the framework of a genuine democracy, in the age of Hitler's and Stalin's witches' sabbath, to defend the unity of personality against its disintegration *en masse*, to advocate the principles of harmony and substantiality as those of social sanity, in terms of a theory of personality, in an age in which laments about the shallowness, the amorphous quality of personality were widespread and in which the statement of its being a fact was transformed into various techniques of the *radicalisation du mal*. Old-fashioned as it was at certain crucial points, classicist anthropology advocated the principle of hope to the same extent as Bloch's prophecies.

But old-fashioned it was indeed in its proclamation of the unquestionable and unproblematic supremacy of reason over our whole personality structure. Sometimes it bore the unmistakable hallmarks of the most overconfident periods of Enlightenment. In a certain sense it is justified to term Lukács the Anti-Freud, a theorist of the pure 'ego' by whom the whole problematic of the *id* (it may be called a 'psychological' as opposed to a 'moral' character) is dismissed with a gesture of a negative evaluation, a theorist for whom everything that is not reason is regarded as mere 'obstacle'. One of Lukács' fundamental character traits returns here, a feature that originated from his pre-Marxist youth: his hatred for psychology, the rejection of this empirical branch of learning, which explains nothing because the 'soul' (which is later on called 'substantial personality') is a result of free action; it is not determined by any external factors, nor has it a genesis in any explicable sense. A methodology adequate to cope with this negative attitude is pursued by Lukács consistently up to the end of his active life. With him writers have no biographies, in sharp contrast to Sartre's method, by which Flaubert's *oeuvre* is derived from Flaubert's personality, which entails interplay of a psychological character and the objectivations of his age shaping his moral and intellectual character. Lukács makes a further move: he describes in appreciative terms the importance of

Makarenko's pedagogical principle of 'forgetting one's past'. It was a strict precondition in the Soviet writer's and pedagogue's quite exceptionally 'humanistic re-education camp' that the problematic past of those being detained there should not be analysed in any way but should be strictly forgotten. The problematic chapter of one's past sealed off and guarded from the interference of the analyst – this is perhaps the most symbolic gesture of rejection of psychology in our psychology-ridden age.

It is also worth investigating briefly how Lukács conceives of the counterpart of reason. He often mentions 'instincts' in a very vague and logically inexact manner. With respect to writers we have 'degenerating reactionary instincts', as with Kleist; with respect to protagonists of literary works, obsession with 'Fascist instincts' (as in the case of Petepre's wife in Mann's Joseph tetralogy). These are only two examples among many. Obviously, the term 'instinct' here means nothing that can be identified with, or is even akin to, a genetically given psychological framework; it is, rather, something rational in substrate but irrational in content. In the pages of *The Destruction of Reason* the same mythological battle is waged over personality structure as over the history of ideas: that between *ratio* and *irratio*. In fact, both protagonists are 'products of reason', but only one of them may claim that rank. *Irratio*, then, is not identical in Lukács with what is simply non-reason; it is not a relatively and justifiably separate domain but the duplication of the same sphere. Anything that is rational in substrate but not in its ideological function is degraded to the level of the 'merely instinctive'.

However, this means not simply the supremacy but the tyranny of reason in Lukácsian classicism. An enlightened and liberal tyranny it is indeed: the right to emotionality is not only granted by the classicist – rationalist; it is placed at the centre of his doctrine. The 'culture of feelings' is one of his key concepts. Moreover, all those acquainted with his *oeuvre* know that one of the central issues of his vehement anti-Kant polemic (which was, on the whole, very unjust) was directed, among other things, against the devaluation of emotionality by Kant and his ensuing inhumane rigour. *In principle*, then, there was sufficient room in Lukács' theory to give shelter to what was termed by him 'non-rationality' (emotions, efforts and the like). But the means by which to articulate this programme was missing from his conceptual framework. The body – mind dualism had been resolved by Lukács in such a way that mind *(ratio)* does not simply rule 'body' (whatever may be covered by this wide concept of 'non-reason'): the whole field of the 'non-mental' is absorbed outright by the 'mental'. Hence his quasi-Victorian conception of sexuality and the erotic. He constantly praises the 'tact' of his favourite great realists for having depicted the scenes *avant* and *après* – that is to say, for having described the intellectual preliminaries of, and retrospective comments on the sexual act, but never the act itself. It is no accident that one of Lukács' recurring ideas is the democratization (generalization) of the Stoic, a sublime but aristocratic type whose attitude towards his own corporeality is at best tolerantly condescending. In Lukács there is only one positive counter-example, a series of emotionally cultivated women (Minna von Barnhelm, Goethe's Philine, Keller's Judith) who are intellectually no match for the male protagonists but who can 'instinctively' fulfil the role of moral censor at times of conflict. Men are generally at a loss when faced with potential and actual collisions, partly because of their rigid morality (in this case, the women's emotional culture represents a more dynamic type of rationality, without any need for overt ideological formulations), partly because men generally lack emotional culture. But the most striking instance of reason's over-confidence, even arrogance, in Lukács, is his conception of our confrontation with our own mortality. Apart from certain absurd statements, simply dragged into the sublime atmosphere of his classicist essays from the worst of propaganda literature ('It is only the decadent bourgeoisie that dreads death', etc.), one can find in his work a unilinear rationalist conception. Death is a simple continuation of the style chosen and realized earlier by the dying person. Undoubtedly, the theory contains a grain of truth, even an important particle of it, namely, the anti-Heideggerian aspect of the Lukácsian thesis. It is life that dominates us, not death; we live in and for our lives, not in anticipation of our inevitable death. Lukács, himself an incarnation of the wise man, adherent of a renewed and updated Stoicism, was certainly not an anxious man. But there must be a limit to even the most determined rationalism. In my opinion, Sartre was perfectly right when he challenged Heidegger with these words: *La mort n'est pas ma dernière possibilité, mais la néantisation de mes possibilités.*

The most fertile and, at the same time, the most problematic feature of the anthropology of Lukácsian classicism is its dichotomy of *health and disease*. Its audibly evaluative tone jars with one of the dominating tendencies of our age: the substitution of psychology (and the explanation of general behaviour by reference to the pathological) for morality (and moral judgement). In the general darkness, where everyone seems to be neurotic, in which one hardly can tell good from bad because it is 'not done' to make judgements of that kind, the age-old principle of moral judgement is an uninvited guest. In Lukács there is a long catalogue of the social maladies – fanaticism, the bureaucratic spirit, ego mania – and these are literally diseases, since in Lukács both oppressors and oppressed *suffer* from alienation, and suffering appears here as disease, as a distortion of the personality. But there is a counter-catalogue as well, that of the 'virtues' or, to use a simpler and less obsolete word, the traits of the healthy (or at least of the ones who have recovered from various social illnesses). The problematic feature is that the line of demarcation is too sharply drawn. Such an uncompromising counterposition of the healthy with the ill leaves no room for communication between them. We observe here a contrast wholly characteristic of our age. While in Lukács' classicist rigour one can always find the measure of sanity, we never find an unmoralizing conception of illness (if some-one's health, in a social sense of the word, is 'undermined', he or she no longer 'deserves' to belong to the healthy) or any chances for recovery of the ill. Health and illness are hostile, mutually exclusive principles. I think Sartre pro-poses a much more democratic theory in his existential hermeneutic specifically devised for the neurotic (which in him is identical with the man of our epoch). On the other hand, Sartre never provides explicit measures of sanity.

Lukács' famous theory of realism, constantly the focus of aesthetic debate during the last forty years, can be understood only in terms of his rationalism, particularly since it is, in fact, a theory and a searing criticism of fetishism. The protagonist of the theory is the realist artist, the man of defetishization, who penetrates the surface of an enchanted world of capitalist reification in order to proceed from 'crust' to 'core'. As far as intentions are concerned, this theory was aimed at the defence of order and coherence as against general social chaos and the disintegration of personality, at the defence of the free rational agent, the *Vernunftswesen*, by contrast with the morality and personality structure of the subjects of various dictatorships. In a certain sense, the theory of realism in-volves the (partial) recurrence of the conception of totality of the 1920s. Defetishization is not a mere epistemological act, not simply equivalent to 'understanding the whole' instead of being held captive by the partial. Totality is labour and the result of labour. The 'substantial' individual, the man of essence, elaborates the whole raw material of the 'crust', of mere appearance, and not only is he 'grasping the whole' but he is also the embodiment, and a positive result, of the totalizing efforts themselves.

In spite of all emancipatory intent, the Lukácsian theory of realism could not become the leading and fertilizing value idea of a radically new art. On the con-trary, it had been vehemently rejected not only by conservative artists but by the overwhelming majority of the radical avantgarde as well. The content of these discussions is so well documented – from the early debate about Expres-sionism between Lukács at one pole and Bloch, Eisler and others on the other, to the irritated reactions of many a leading figure among exiled German literati (for example Döblin), to the more recent attacks of Adorno and Enzensberger and the most famous debate, the Lukács–Brecht polemic itself – that there is no reason to enter into philological detail. The main issue was Lukács' hotly contested concept of decadence. It is perhaps needless to mention that 'decadence' (together with its logical counter-concept, progress through con-tradiction) is a legitimate part of the Marxian heritage. Marx himself declared the whole era of capitalism to be hostile to poetry and art in general. He stated that after the revolution (of 1830, but specifically the June 1848 battle between the Paris proletariat and the French bourgeoisie) in proportion to the pro-letariat's emergence as a self-conscious factor *les capacités de la bourgeoisie s'en vont.* But all sterile questions of orthodoxy aside, it is a strange thing to observe that nearly all those who attacked Lukács mercilessly because of his 'conservative' theory of decadence (accusing him either of ignorance with respect to modern art or of a 'professorial' spirit), actually developed their own theories of decadence as well. Sartre, in his *L'Idiot de la famille*, locates the negative turn of bourgeois literature precisely where Marx and Lukács did: in the June uprising of the French proletariat and its bloody aftermath. From this time onwards all artists who were 'normally', not neurotically, bourgeois joined in the decline. Adorno is no more tolerant than Lukács either of practically all of modern music (with the gratifying exception of the New Vienna School) or of the present-day listener, whom he simply labels as 'regressive'. A close look at Adorno's analysis of Stravinsky or Sartre's of Leconte de Lisle (that 'typically bourgeois' prince of new lyric poetry) – not to mention the conservative modernists – reveals that the differences in rigour are fairly relative. For Ortega or Huizinga, as for Berdaiev, the whole age is a vulgar period of 'massification' (*Vermassung*) of culture, and in a posthumously published interview Heidegger terms modern art in its totality 'destructive'.

Clearly, our age is too deeply problematic not to be judged. Lukács' unique position among his contemporaries consisted not in his being a judge of his age (he was only one among many) but rather in the fact that while the judgement of his contemporaries was selective, the Lukácsian verdict was all-embracing. All modern artists (with the exception of Thomas Mann, that guiding star in his firmament, who was later joined by Béla Bartók), were weighed and found wanting: they were not to be included in the realm of the 'great realists'. (Of course, this is not literally true; a whole catalogue of those who were realists can be found in the works of Lukács, but such instances are either clear-cut lapses of aesthetic taste or unmistakable gestures of political concession.) In this sense, certain autobiographical elements may be found in the Lukácsian portrait of Georg Forster, the German radical who in his ardent moral contempt for his own age labelled the whole of contemporary art inferior to that of ancient Greece. The stress is on the word 'radical'. The Lukácsian conception of decadence was not an academic position adopted by a scholar brought up in the literary *salons* of the nineteenth century but (and this is said in conscious opposition to the majority of the critics of the Lukácsian *oeuvre*) a vestige and continuation of an earlier problematic radicalism and an aristocratic approach.

The fact of its radicalism needs little proof. A polemic that denies a cultural period the right to existence is by definition radical, particularly as Lukács consistently accepts the Marxian definition of radicalism and grasps cultural malaise at its roots: the social ills of the man of alienation. The question of how a radicalism of leftist – democratic provenance can be regarded as aristocratic seems more problematic. (The aristocratic character of rightist radicalism is an obvious fact.) This peculiar marriage of opposites cannot be explained without returning to the circumstance that Lukács' theory of realism was basically a theory of fetishism. But we know that all theories of fetishism inevitably have aristocratic aspects: the theorist has to occupy a uniquely (and only supposedly) non-fetishistic position in order to see through the fetishized universe of others, to be able to pronounce a verdict on their fetishized consciousness. Lukács was always ready to assume the role of judge, partly because an authoritarian streak was never alien to his intellectual physiognomy and partly because of the monolithic features of his rationalist epistemology, analysed earlier. The principal reason, however, was his positing of the world of ethical democracy as Being, not Ought. This firm belief in the existence of what merely ought to exist granted Lukács (or so, at least, he believed) an Archimedean point, an allegedly non-fetishistic position from which he could survey clearly the whole field of fetishization. This is why the Lukácsian theory of realism, that radical rejection of a whole existing culture, was bound to assume aristocratic dimensions.

The first dimension is *essentialism*. As is well-known, the Lukácsian criterion of the realistic or anti-realistic character of a work of art depends on whether the latter is rooted to the surface of the world or is able to break through to the realm of essence. Of course, a whole set of dilemmas immediately arises when attempts are made to regard the ontologization of appearance and essence as two spheres, as the contrasts of 'surface' and 'depth'. This is a type of ontologization that implies evaluation in Christian hieratic thinking, and appropriately so, but it is out of place in any immanent thinking. This approach raises a specific problem in the case of works of art. Any attempt to determine what is 'essential' and what is merely 'apparent' in a novel, a painting, a symphony, entails the introduction of an alien non-aesthetic principle into the assessment of aesthetic formations. (We know already that with Lukács this alien, external principle stemmed from his classicist *anthropology*. Everything was essential that was characteristic, both in structure and in content, of the substantial man of ethical democracy.) In fact, what can be directly 'deciphered' from a work of art is whether it adopts a flat and superficial verisimilitude (and this only in literature and fine arts – the 'artificial language' of music raises its own problems in this regard), whether it has organized its 'own world' (and this question can be answered only with some hesitation as well). The question of whether a work of art is 'beyond' (or 'above') the sphere of the merely apparent' is a matter for arbitration, which cannot be founded on the impersonal, epistemological objectivity that the Lukácsian theory claimed to have.

It will suffice to refer, by way of illustration, to the most striking instance of this: Lukács' view of Kafka. For various (mostly ideological) reasons – because of Kafka's emphatic insistence on a hopeless *condition humaine* and for artistic reasons (Kafka's predilection for the allegoric) – Lukács could not include him among the select band of the 'great realists', not even with the aid of the usual methodological trick of the 'triumph of realism'. Neither could he conceal his admiration for Kafka's manifest genius. As a result, Lukács admits, even emphasizes, Kafka's distance from anything that may be regarded as 'surface', as merely 'apparent', which means that Kafka succeeded in creating a 'sphere of the essential', the absolute criterion of the realistic work of art. But since Kafka's 'sphere of the essential' bears the unmistakable hallmarks of the pseudo-transcendence of modern religious need; it is labelled by Lukács 'pseudo-essential'. This is a classic example of what I earlier called 'arbitration', and it reveals itself as a simple arbitrary principle. The theory of realism is a consistently aristocratic theory of fetishism. At a given non-fetishistic, Archimedean point there must be – allegedly, there is – an élite that decides whether a work has or has not an 'essential' character (whether it is realistic or not) and, further, whether the 'sphere of the essential' in it is genuine or only 'pseudo-essential'. It may safely be stated that if in Walter Benjamin's aesthetic the recipient was a co-constitutive factor in the very existence of the work of art, in the Lukácsian theory of realism the place of the recipient is occupied by the arbiter-critic.

A special epistemological apparatus is added to the essentialist conception of art and literature. (For me the whole problem of to what extent Lukács' standpoint can be regarded as 'orthodox Marxist' has only secondary importance. But since this question has been widely discussed, let me mention that, to my knowledge, Marx never used the term 'reflection' in any epistemologically relevant context.) The whole apparatus of the theory of reflection rests on concepts that fall to pieces as soon as they are subjected to even the most superficial scrutiny. The first question that springs to mind is the following: who is the subject (and what is the organ) of reflection? Were we to consider the brain of any particular recipient to be this organ, irrespective of whether the recipient in question could or could not become a genuine subject of art (for instance, a creative artist), which would be the only straightforward answer, we would be confronted with a number of unresolvable epistemological – methodological dilemmas. There is, first, the insurmountable problem that although every mirror, *sensu stricto*, is a non-selective medium, a non-selective brain is the brain of an imbecile. The second dilemma is that if the central organ (or subject) of reflection ('mirroring') is the brain – in other words, the intellect of the artist – the whole edifice of the theory of realism, which centres on the works of art, not on the artistic personality, would immediately collapse. The third and final dilemma is that if we posit the isolated brain (or the artistic intellect), in its confrontation with the world, as the basic epistemological formula, we relapse into an atomistic, pre-Marxist way of thinking, with all its insoluble *aporias*, which was clearly not the intention of the author of the theory of reflection.

Those who advance this theory would immediately object that from the start the 'reflecting brain' has been conceived of as a selective medium, an organ that accomplishes the transition from appearance to essence (cf. Lukács' constant and ardent polemics against the 'mechanistic' view of art and literature that identifies the reflecting brain with a camera). But a 'selective' mirror is clearly no mirror at all – or, more precisely, the term is a metaphor, that of dialectical reason. Dialectical reason is, however, a collective epistemological entity, an objectivation, which could not be imputed to any mind or brain as its inborn capacity precisely because of its being an objectivation, a collective historical achievement.

Lukács did not use this over-metaphorical concept of a 'dialectical mirror' because he lacked discrimination. Men of philosophical genius, whether well versed in logic or not, never lack that. His dilemma lay deeper. He had only two options: either he worked with an isolated Cartesian subject of knowledge, or he accepted the idea of a collective subject, and he wanted to avoid this latter position. As we know, there was a period in his life during which he yoked dialectical reason ('true knowledge'), without the slightest hesitation, to one exclusive collective subject: the proletariat. (It was for this reason, among several others, that *History and Class Consciousness* rejected the theory of reflection and eliminated all epistemology in the proper sense of the word.) As emphasized above, it was progress on Lukács' part to sever the link between the fate of genuine artistic creation with a class position, to reject the technique of class reductionism that was equally widespread among adherents and opponents of the theory of reflection. (In a peculiar rear-guard battle, it was Lucien Goldmann who created the only aesthetics commensurate with the position of *History and Class Consciousness*: a structuralist sociology of art based on collective subjects with a strict class character.) The only way out of this impasse was to accept the concept of a 'dialectical mirror', metaphorical as it was, and to place at the pinnacle of the theory the artist, with his particular capacity for *Wesensschau*, for breaking through from appearance to essence. (Of course, all this happened without clarification of the methodological duality.) Such a position was in perfect harmony with the general anthropology of Lukácsian classicism: the artist seemed to be the paradigm of man proceeding from the 'crust' to the 'core', from appearance to essence. This solution also allowed for the arbitrariness of a theory of realism. The formal and empty category of essence could be filled with whatever content the theorist desired.

It was a part of the uncompromising theoretical nature of Georg Lukács (he often paid political, never theoretical, lip-service) that he could not leave 'essence' in its empty, formal, contentually undefined state because that would have been 'Kantianism', 'formalism', inventions of the devil. There would have been an easy solution in the 1920s: to posit essence as identical with class content. As a result of this, the only essential art would have been the one that expressed the existence (and the imputed consciousness) of the proletariat. In this phase of his development, in which he had already abandoned this position and all solutions stemming from it, he accepted as the basic moment of his interpretation of realism one of the most contradictory, most problematic ideas of Marxist sociology: that of the duality of base and superstructure. Lukács implanted this duality into his understanding of literature and art in such a way that superstructure became identical with appearance, base with essence. Theoretically this identification had never been unequivocally formulated, but it was constantly practised by him. Anyone who follows Lukács' *modus operandi* closely, the manner in which he slices off layer after layer until he arrives at the 'final determinants', will see my statement fully demonstrated. The identification of essence with base (or economic sphere) rarely led Lukács into such blunders as the case of his essay on Balzac's *Peasants*, in which he eulogized an exceptionally bad novel simply because it was the chronicle of a smallholders' tragedy at the time of the Restoration. But the identification had three inevitable consequences. The first was that Lukács had to confine his literary investigations to the classic bourgeois period, roughly the period between the end of the eighteenth and the beginning of the nineteenth century. Hence not only ancient Greek but also Renaissance art (and Shakespeare himself, so important to the young Lukács) were necessarily excluded from his work – and this was appropriate, for Lukács himself had stated that historical materialism in the strict sense of the term (in other words, the dichotomy of base and superstructure conceived of as a coherent doctrine) was central to an understanding of capitalist society alone, in its pure form. Even if we take into consideration all critical sociological and economic remarks regarding Marxian theory, it was reasonable (if one-sided) to describe the historical period that was Lukács' main period of investigation by reference to reduction of all social phenomena to the economic base. However, after this period, particularly after the First World War, when a considerable and ever-increasing part of 'intellectual production' (of superstructure) resolutely and overtly turned against the capitalist base, when the whole social status of 'intellectual producers' radically changed, the Lukácsian interpretation lost a considerable amount of its original – restricted – relevance. (This is the second inevitable consequence of his position.) Restricted relevance it did have. Where else, if not in a society in which all social phenomena were reduced to the principles and motives of the base, the economic sphere, would a theory of fetishism hold true? When the situation changed structurally, a new interpretation became necessary, and Lukács' incapacity to grasp the structural change was one of the major factors that prevented him from approaching modern art soberly. The third consequence is obvious. If he were to expand his theory of realism into a general aesthetics, the whole reductionism, the identification of 'essence' with 'basis' would have to be abandoned. Whereas within a limited space, and with only relative results, literature could be understood in terms of a reductionist theory, art in general could certainly not be understood thus.

The third aristocratic dimension of the theory of realism was the discarding of the recipient. Lukács' motives were radical again, primarily his life-long contempt for the bourgeois audience, very akin to Brecht's morphology of visitors to theatrical performances for 'entertainment purposes'. In his youth, when he ascribed at least a negative importance to 'audience', Lukács deduced the decline of dramatic forms directly from the existence of an audience of that type. In the 1930s and 1940s, in the heyday of the theory of realism, there was a more deep-rooted philosophical consideration that forced Lukács to ignore the recipient. The recipient as a phenomenological figure in the understanding of art was inextricably bound up with everyday life. Despite the fact that the key Lukácsian categories of the reception of art and literature (the suspension of daily activities, the transformation of 'the whole man' into 'man's whole' and the like) necessarily implied a rise above everyday life, this rise could be only temporary. Both the need for art (ontologically prior to the work of art and a basic function of the recipient, constitutive in the former's existence) and the return of an enriched recipient to everyday life (posterior to aesthetic pleasure) indicate that the recipient belongs with his/her whole 'surface' in the everyday. But for a theory of fetishism the 'sphere' of the everyday had to be, of logical necessity, a sphere to be transcended, the domain of the merely 'apparent'. The great essays of the 1930s, especially those collected in the volume *The Problems of Realism*, are full of invective against the 'naturalist cult of the everyday'; here 'naturalist' is synonymous with modern art in general.

So a contradiction appeared in the theory that Lukács was never able to overcome. On the one hand, everyday life had to be transcended; this was a postulate of the theory itself, as it was the terrain of the fetishized audience whose demands had to be discarded for the realistic work of art to come about at all. On the other hand, Lukács was a zealot of ethical democracy, which he posited as Being, and the elementary requirement of the audience of ethical democracy was an art accessible to Everyman, a 'popular' art in the modern sense of the word. The Lukácsian charges against the 'incomprehensibility' of modern art, the brisk rejection of certain literary and artistic techniques as such, since the 'people' would not be able to digest them, stemmed from the constant, if hidden, presence of the postulate of ethical democracy in the theory. But Lukács could not have it both ways: to demand a monumental 'popular' art and at the same time to reject totally the only soil in which demands of that type could grow meant theoretical deadlock.

The mid-1950s, the period after Stalin's death, prompted a change in Lukács' political and aesthetic position, even if not a 'radical' one. The change in Lukács was slow and gradual (the old reverberations of 'anti-realism' cropped up in his writings in the most unexpected places); it involved no return to the (Jacobin – proletarian – monolithic) radicalism of the 1920s; it did not imply a radical renunciation (either political or aesthetical) of the premises that had guided him since the Hungarian Revolution in 1919. What I would term the growing but ambivalent militancy of Lukács' last theory had three underlying causes. The first was the shock triggered by the Twentieth Congress of the Communist Party of the Soviet Union, by the unexpected confrontation with (at least a part of) the real face of Stalin's legacy, which prevented the 'partisan' from seeking the 'ideal type' of the system. Even if Lukács did not for a moment want to abandon his existential choice, he had to give up his decades-old 'reconciliation with reality'. The demand of the day was not to find the 'ideal type' of Stalin's system but to rebuild the edifice he left to his successors, to mention the very minimum programme that could legitimately claim to be reformist. The second cause was the ever more intense social struggles both in Eastern and in Western Europe. It was at this time, as the anti-Stalinist movement in Eastern Europe was gathering momentum, that the first sign of a new anti-capitalist force appeared, a fairly pluralistic one, since it involved both what we call now the 'New Left' and 'Eurocommunism'. The partisan's feeling of total isolation and concomitant social paralysis was slowly vanishing, and as a result new elements of activity could be built in the theory. Finally, the all-encompassing alternative of rationalism versus irrationalism collapsed. It had to disappear because neither modern capitalism nor Stalinism could be functionally described by it. New categories moved forcibly into the forefront of Lukács' thinking.

All this concluded in contradiction. When the programme of reform that was a reaction to the Twentieth Party Congress was drafted, all illusions about the contrast between Ought and Being evaporated. Socialism as an ethical democracy had perforce to be formulated as a task, not as something existent. This facilitated the inclusion of elements of activity in Lukács' theory. Because of his growing resignation concerning the fruits of political revolution and his rigid inflexibility regarding his own 'ultimate principles', these active elements assumed an exclusively pedagogical – aesthetic character. The summary of the efforts of this period, the crowning work of his classicism, *The Specificity of the Aesthetic*, was unambiguously a revival of the Schillerian 'aesthetic education of humankind'.

No doubt, for Lukács this was a problematic position to adopt, since after Marx he was the most vehement opponent and critic of characteristically German misery: the combination of lofty aesthetic programmes and the absence of realistic social alternatives. Accepting this position, heavily criticized by himself, was clearly the price he had to pay for remaining captive to his own original premises. Lukács' inner contradiction has often been emphasized, and rightly so, but the whole truth about him in the mid 1950s and early 1960s cannot be dismissed with such a curt verdict. The fact that Thomas Mann, in a letter written on the occasion of his seventieth birthday, praised him in enthusiastic terms as the constant advocate of European culture within com-

munism, can, of course, be interpreted by certain ultra-radicals as merely an exchange of compliments between bourgeois *Schöngeister*. But apart from the fact
that Karl Marx and his doctrine had been the result of precisely that same European culture, we have to take account of the more epoch-determined elements
of the Lukácsian mission. This point can perhaps best be clarified by an anecdote
from the 1930s that I heard from Lukács. Johannes Becher, the famous revolutionary – expressionist poet of the 1920s, a leading Comintern functionary in
the 1930s, later Minister of Culture of the German Democratic Republic and a
close friend of Lukács, complained to him bitterly about the barbarian character
of the times. Lukács replied: 'Can you imagine the advent of new Giottos and
Masaccios from a decadent Rome without an interlude of Alarich's Goths?'
This was said, of course, in the spirit of a predeterministic philosophy of
history. One has enough personal and historical experience to know now that
there is no logical or historical necessity for new Giottos to emerge from the
tents of barbarians. But the real question is this: who is the advocate of new
Giottos, who of the barbarians? And if we think of a hysterical cult of barbarism, of over-refined savagery, reaching to Godard or Jean Genet, the 'Saint',
orchestrated and guided from the capitals of culture, if we recall the French
Communist philosopher Politzer, who spoke with exaltation of the 'existential
gesture' of the officer of the Red Guard who extinguished his cigarette on the
tapestries of the Winter Palace, we observe an inauthentic and unholy alliance
between truly Roman over-refinement pretending to be 'simple' and genuine,
'unspoilt', ignorant barbarism. The classicist Lukács demanded complete
sincerity from those living in and producing culture, unreserved acknowledge-
ment of the fact that the renouncing culture is itself the negative cultural product of an over-ripe civilization. He never ceased to propose a programme for
the general cultural education of mankind. I would not conceal that for all its
inner ambivalence, I am still voting for Lukácsian classicism as the most
democratic socialist alternative of the period.

Lukács' *Aesthetics*, his manifesto concerning the aesthetic education of
humankind, is based on the following philosophical consideration: it is only in
the 'aesthetic sphere' that the unity of subject and object is realized. All who
are familiar with Lukács' work, and the distinguished place of subject – object
unity within it, are aware of the import of such a statement. This means, in
other words, that the non-alienated sphere *par excellence* is the sphere of the
'aesthetic'. Two critical remarks are in order here. First of all, we may discover
in the emphatic importance ascribed to a simple ontological constellation, that
there is no object without subject and vice versa, a position that is similar to the
one criticized by Lukács himself, namely, emotional emphasis is laid on the
thing-in-itself. In philosophy style is also decisive, and I believe the source of
this emphatic tone to be the vestiges of an anti-reification mysticism never completely overcome by Lukács. This mystical streak becomes more apparent –

and this is the second critical remark – if we follow the conceptual shift in Lukács. The correlation of subject with object, an elementary ontological constellation, is gradually transformed by Lukács, in nearly all his works, into subject – object unity. But subject – object unity is a highly unstable equilibrium and as such can be characteristic only of moments of 'peak experience' (to use Maslow's terminology). For that reason subject – object unity is an expedient for establishing an 'aesthetic sphere', but it is unsuitable for any ontological distinction between the aesthetic and the non-aesthetic.

This ontological detour constitutes not a refutation but, rather, a further qualification. It clarifies to what end the 'aesthetic sphere' was specifically devised by Lukács, what theoretical advantages this field offers and in what its limitations consist. The sphere of subject – object unity is an island in a sea of other spheres and forms of activities with a simple subject – object correlation and without any value accent. But no romantic despair, not even resignation, is attached to this statement. Aesthetic reception – as subject – object unity – is the highest possible example of the identification of a particular person with the human species, and as such, it is an unstable equilibrium and cannot but be unstable. It is a model as well, a paradigm of types of behaviour needed in everyday life, in the true spirit of Lessing: art is a preparatory school for public virtues.

The first consequence of the new standpoint is obvious: reconciliation with the everyday, a novel feature in Lukács. The 'methodological secret' of the book is the following. Everyday life is a domain ultimately given, beyond which research cannot proceed. It is a specific sphere very much resembling the Husserlian *Lebenswelt* (it is called everyday *thinking* in Lukács). The attitudes pertaining to the everyday involve an adequate personality structure, that of the 'whole man', the particular person being totally absorbed by his daily activities. At the same time, constant 'outflows' and 'refluxes' take place from the 'stock' of the everyday towards higher types of activity, enriching the 'stock' by the continuous 'refluxes'. (The term 'higher types of activity' needs further clarification: the Lukácsian 'aesthetic ontology' is unequivocally hierarchical; in it 'outflows' towards art and science are deemed to be of a higher type.) This is the way of all flesh, as no one can remain for a lifetime entirely within the framework of the everyday (this is the exact and complementary obverse of what was said above about the impossibility of remaining in a state of 'peak experience'). As a result, 'outflows' and 'refluxes' constitute a personality dynamic. This is also a general socio-historical model, in which the progress can clearly be distinguished through which mankind (the 'species') elaborates its higher objectivations from an unarticulated compound of work, magic, pre-science, pre-artistic mimetic elements: the means by which chaos comes to be cosmos. A complete evolutionist philosophy of history is presented to the reader here, the only one that accomplishes the mysterious task formulated by Marx as a general principle of philosophy of history: the fusion of the phylogenetic and the ontogenetic.

The evolutionism inherent in this conception is a demystified version of the Hegelian march of the World Spirit. It is led by a consistent (but immanent) teleology, which results from human actions that drive the route of mankind consistently 'upwards'. The book implies a consistent hierarchical, evaluative position: science stands 'higher' than pre-scientific knowledge, religion than magic cult, art than the primary mimetic structures inextricably bound up with magic. In a certain sense, and very much in keeping with the spirit of Hegel, every stage of development finds its truth in the 'other' (i.e. the 'higher' results from the 'lower'). To crown this view of the overall tendency of evolutionism Lukács operates with a conception that is untenable for any relevant modern linguistic (not to mention psychological) theory: the alleged 'evolution' of the language from the 'abstract' to the 'concrete'. It would be an easy task to enumerate the contradictions of this evolutionism, particularly as it actually eliminates even the Marxian dilemma so central for Lukács himself, namely, the perennial validity of works of art that belong inseparably to epochs left behind by the historical march of the species – in other words, the dilemma formulated by Marx as the famous 'Homer paradox'. (Inserting the concept of 'unequal development' in his train of thought does not resolve this dilemma at all.) Instead of petty objections, the whole construction is better regarded as a problematic derivative of a peculiarly Lukácsian brand of rationalism. But problematic as it may be, one positive aspect of the new theory should be pointed out: the seemingly unbridgeable gulf between reason and the everyday attitude of man, an absolute (and most aristocratic) feature of the earlier Lukácsian theory, disappears. The whole edifice of the aesthetic is built up 'from below', departing from the daily efforts of man, which were condemned in the 1930s and 1940s to being incurably alienated. Every time Lukács inveighs against the Heideggerian conception of *Being and Time* in his *Aesthetics*, he unwittingly takes a stand against the consequences of his own former theory. The distinction between 'below' and 'above', the hierarchical way of constructing the world theoretically, has undoubtedly been preserved here, but this is no longer identical with the differentiation between 'surface' and 'depth'. The essentialism of the theory of realism is eliminated; more precisely, it is replaced by a genuinely democratic conception of the education of personality.

The programme of elevating the particular person to the level of the species retains certain vestiges of essentialism in its terminology: the particular person is still the 'crust', which gradually rises to be the 'core', the 'substantial' man. But we are no longer confronted with two 'spheres', with two separate 'worlds', which are time and again identified with the counterposed realms of 'sanity' and 'disease'. The Manichaean dichotomy of the 1930s and 1940s increasingly gives way to real ethical *alternatives*. In addition, these latter have a solid basis in everyday activity, in this ineluctable fundament of human life, both a springboard for the fixation of the particularist structure and a material basis from which to rise to the level of the species. As a result, this is an educational project, a broader version, a recurrence of the dynamic of ethical democracy, instead of an essentialist ontology. At the same time it offers a social therapy. It is human personality ossified in its particularist structure that comes to be identified with the (actual or potential) diseases of personality, but this is a democratic alternative because Lukács assumes that in principle every human being is capable of rising to the aesthetic or any other 'higher type' of activity. It is perhaps unnecessary to remind the reader that all these characteristic features were constitutive elements of the original classicist conception. *The Specificity of the Aesthetic* is indeed the apex of the Lukácsian efforts in Weimar and the transformation of an essentialist ontology of fetishism into a cosmology of the self-creation of the individual.

Lukács' reconciliation with the everyday inevitably involves the rehabilitation of the recipient. The terminological switch from 'realism' and 'reflection' to 'mimesis' (inconsistent as it is) has a crucial impact on the structure of his whole theory primarily because the 'mimetic formation' gradually rises from a position as mere ingredient in a compound of magic and labour to the level of a separate 'world' through collective activity that does not recognize the dichotomy of creative and receptive personality. Even if with Lukács the measure of assessment in art is invariably provided by the great masterpieces, he has shifted his point of departure. For forty years he has been guided by a transformed version of the original Kantian question, 'There are *a priori* synthetic judgements of taste, but how are they possible?', which reads as follows: 'There are works of art, but how are they possible?' Departing from the unquestionable axiom of the existence of the works of art as something ultimate has been decisively reshaped by the introduction of the principle of mimesis. And the resolution of the (transformed) Kantian dilemma does not pertain only to an 'archaeology of art'. A new sphere (or frame of activities) has been created thereby, in which every participant is a constitutive actor, irrespective of whether he or she is an artist *sui generis* or 'merely' a recipient who incessantly creates in daily activities the very preconditions for the existence of the 'aesthetic sphere'. In this new conception the constant interplay between situations in which the 'whole man' predominates and others in which 'man's whole' prevails – in other words, the dichotomy and confrontation between the personality of daily activities and man suspending these activities to turn with his whole surface towards art – is no longer a state of degradation for Lukács. The tension thus created is stimulating in the *Aesthetics* of the old Lukács: one can see here the extent to which the recipient contributes to the creation of the aesthetic as the proper field of the education of mankind.

It is in these terms that we can understand the importance of the Lukácsian category of 'species character' (*Gattungsmässigkeit*). (Its general philosophical problematic cannot be tackled here.) As we have seen, the greatest merit and accomplishment of the 'aesthetic' is that it elevates man, both in his creative and in his receptive capacities, from the everyday to the level of 'species character'. 'Becoming substantial' in this way occupies the place of penetration to the 'triumph of essence' for the old Lukács. While the capacity to penetrate the essential remains a somewhat mysterious blessing for the select few, especially under generally fetishized conditions (including the equally mystical 'triumph of realism', whose 'perfectly comprehensible and rational' character was stated so vehemently by Lukács), the course of rising to the level of species is, in principle, open to everyone. For the same reason, the 'aesthetic' is not only a democratic but also a pluralistic sphere. *The Specificity of the Aesthetic* provides a universal philosophical foundation for the pluralism of ethical democracy, as delineated in the literary essays of the 1930s and 1940s.

The gods of the gay Epicure lived in *intermundia*, in peaceful asylums in an otherwise harsh world. In the much denser and menacing substrate of his world, Lukács the Olympian took refuge in the Weimar of his classicism, in a self-erected *intermundium*. But while he was an Olympian, he was very much a human and a militant spirit. As a result, his classicist writings find only a temporary abode in such *intermundia*. They haunt the external world of tyranny and oppression with their message of socialism as realized ethical democracy.

5

Lukács and Husserl

MIHÁLY VAJDA

Marxism and phenomenology show striking parallels in their relation to science. But since there are many phenomenologies and Marxisms, this problem cannot be analysed in the abstract. Thus the following analysis will focus on two fundamental works: Lukács' *History and Class Consciousness* and Husserl's *The Crisis of European Science*. This selection is not arbitrary. The two books are representative of their respective schools and decisively influenced further developments. Furthermore, both books are products of the decades between the two world wars and can be considered to be typical expressions of the crisis of bourgeois culture.

Philosophy's relationship with science is not determined exclusively by its character and development but primarily by the intellectual climate in which it is continually reformulated. Marx's relation to science was necessarily much more positive than that of his twentieth-century followers. 'The exclusiveness with which the total world view of modern man, in the second half of the nineteenth century, let itself be determined by the positive sciences and be blinded by the "prosperity" they produced'[1] – to use Husserl's own phrase – also played a decisive role in Marx's thinking. Though he vehemently criticized both the findings and the procedures of bourgeois social science, especially economics, from the viewpoint of a different concept of scientificity, he had no doubts about the value of science as such.

In the twentieth century the sciences and their function have lost this sanctity. Modern phenomenology itself was the product of an age whose unconditional faith in science played a conservative rather than a critical role. This explains phenomenology's unambiguous relationship with science. Marxism's relationship with science is more complicated. One important factor here is the tension between its nineteenth-century origins and its permanent radicalism. Precisely to preserve its radicalism, the so-called philosophy of praxis, or 'Western Marxism', whose main work was Lukács' *History and Class Conscious-*

ness, had to take a very militant stand against the scientism of conservative Marxist schools. This was not only the expression of their political conservatism but also an attachment to orthodoxy in the narrow sense of the word. Lukács, who defined orthodox Marxism as methodology, had to extract the latent critique of science from Marx's own method.

The following article will attempt to outline briefly where the two critiques converge. Neither critique attacks science's claim to be scientific. What phenomenology and Marxism criticize in the exact sciences is their claim to exclusiveness, which does not and cannot meet scientific requirements. Today's sciences fail to justify their existence: they have nothing to do with the meaning of human existence. Husserl formulates the question very sharply from the beginning:

> Merely fact-minded sciences make merely fact-minded people. . . . In our vital need – so we are told – this science has nothing to say to us. It excludes in principle precisely the questions which man, given over in our unhappy times to the most portentious upheavals, finds the most burning: questions of the meaning or meaninglessness of the whole of this human existence. . . . Scientific, objective truth is exclusively a matter of establishing what the world, the physical as well as the spiritual world, is in fact. But can the world, and human existence in it, truthfully have a meaning if the sciences recognize as true only what is objectively established in this fashion, and if history has nothing more to teach us than that all the shapes of the spiritual world, all the conditions of life, ideals, norms upon which man relies, form and dissolve themselves like fleeting waves, that it always was and ever will be so, that again and again reason must turn into nonsense, and well-being into misery?[2]

Lukács emphasized this just as strongly: a science that merely discovers 'facts' and seeks to determine the laws and structures of our world from these facts cannot guide our activities and actions.

> A situation in which the 'facts' speak out unmistakably for or against a definite course of action has never existed, and neither can or will exist. The more conscientiously the facts are explored – in their isolation, i.e., in their unmediate relations – the less compellingly will they point in any one direction. It is self-evident that a merely subjective decision will be shattered by the pressure of uncomprehended facts acting automatically 'according to laws'.[3]

Sciences can do no more than predict events to which we must adapt. In this sense, they are not a means to self-realization; they make us part of the 'objective' world governed by the natural laws they have discovered: they make us objects of transcendence.

This failure of science to carry out the task of human knowledge, i.e., to give meaning to our existence, stems, according to both Husserl and Lukács, from the fact that science is unable to assume the *standpoint of the totality*. Science has *been reduced to technique (technē)*, an art of manipulation that rules out meaningful and really human actioɪ in favour of limited calculation, since it approaches human reality not as a totality but only as the sum of 'particular facts' governed by 'objective' laws. The loss of the totality means at the same time *the abolition of historicity*. 'The unscientific nature of this seemingly so scientific method consists', says Lukács, 'in its failure to see and take account of the *historical character* of the facts on which it is based.'[4]

Husserl formulates the same idea in positive terms.

This we seek to discern not from the outside, from facts, as if the temporal becoming in which we ourselves have evolved were merely an external causal series. Rather, we seek to discern it from the inside. Only in this way can we, who not only have a spiritual heritage but have become what we are thoroughly and exclusively in a historical-spiritual manner, have a task which is truly our own. We obtain it . . . only through a critical understanding of the total unity of history – *our* history.[5]

What science lacks is precisely this critical understanding of the total unity of our history.

The next common point of criticism is the *critique of total quantification*. The sciences have reduced our qualitative world, the world we live in – the *Lebenswelt* in Husserlian terminology – to mere quantitative relations. The loss of a sense of quality is tied to the loss of meaning for the particular time. For modern science time has lost its quality: it has become just another dimension on the same level as space.

There are numerous other points in common between the Husserlian and Lukácsian critiques of science. In fact, it would be difficult to distinguish the two standpoints, since the critique of science in the two works is identical. Not only do they criticize the sciences for not accomplishing the real tasks of human knowledge and for their methodology, but both blame a wrong attitude, a *false rationalism*, for the failure. This crisis of the sciences is also a crisis of man (in Husserl the crisis of European man, the surrender of true teleology; in Lukács the crisis of capitalism – but the two views amount to the same thing: the total reification of man) and has its roots in naturalistic objectivism.

The 'crisis' could then become distinguishable as the *apparent failure of rationalism*. The reason for the failure of a rational culture, however . . . lies not in the essence of rationalism itself but solely in its being rendered superficial, in its entanglement in 'naturalism' and 'objectivism'.[6]

And for Lukács

> the salient characteristic of the whole epoch is the equation which appears
> naive and dogmatic in the most 'critical' philosophers, of formal,
> mathematical, rational knowledge both with knowledge in general and
> also with 'ou.' knowledge.[7]

The corollary of this one-sided, formal, objectivistic and naturalistic rationalism
is necessarily irrationalism: the irrationality of the whole. The rationally
knowable partial systems, 'the principle of rationalization based on what is and
can be calculated',[8] and the world of first and 'second' nature obtain within the
irrationality of the whole world – a world where man walks as a stranger,
homeless and exposed to irrational forces.

   This rationalistic objectivism, combined with an ultimately irrational world
view, characterizes the whole attitude of modern science and is the distinctive
mark of our era. Yet, this dismal failure of the sciences is only a *sign of mankind's
vital crisis*, whose causes and practical solutions both Husserl and Lukács seek to
discover. In attempting to do so, both trace the history of modern European
philosophy; both show how the objectivism of early modern thinking necessarily ended in scepticism; both regard the attempt of classical German idealism
to restore the identity of subject and object in transcendentalism as having only
half-succeeded; and then both show that the solution must be sought in a
transcendentalism carried to its logical conclusion.

   Yet, the conditions under which this goal is attainable seem at first glance to
be diametrically different. The holistic standpoint, which could lead to the
recovery of the sciences and of human existence, is seen by Husserl as the true
philosophical perspective and by Lukács as that of the proletariat. In Husserl the
restoration of true humanity is an individual and purely intellectual project,
while in Lukács it is the practical achievement of a class. For Lukács the mental
reorientation, the recovery of the total standpoint through knowledge, seems
to be only a subordinate, partial factor of the practical upheaval that is shaking
the bourgeois world. One could even say that the following statement by
Lukács also characterizes Husserl's position:

> The specialization of skills leads to the destruction of every image of the
> whole. And as, despite this, the need to grasp the whole – at least
> cognitively – cannot die out, we find that science, which is likewise based
> on specialization and thus caught up in the same immediacy, is criticized
> for having torn the real world into shreds and having lost its vision of the
> whole.[9]

   In description and goals, Lukács' radical brand of Marxism and phenomenology agree. For Lukács, however, the Husserlian approach is only a partial

aspect of what they both criticize and seek to transcend. For Lukács the Husserlian solution would be only a pseudo-solution, since progress in knowledge can occur only as part of progress in social relations. The history of ideas and historical materialism cannot and must not be reconciled. In Husserl it is the mind itself that by itself must rediscover its original path, which emerged in European history, so to eliminate false objectivity, while in Lukács the revolutionary transformation of the bourgeois mode of production is necessary to restructure the human mind.

This simple contraposition of the two conceptions, however, is an unfortunate simplification. The coincidence of critique and goal is unthinkable if the Husserlian conception is reduced to the history of ideas and Lukács' to historical materialism. No doubt, in Husserl the determining factor of human history is spirit (*Geist*). But if this were nothing more than the attitude of a wide variety of men, which in every concrete historical situation determines their respective activities, then his entire phenomenology would be meaningless and internally contradictory. The psychologistic attitude of the so-called history of ideas was the main object of Husserl's critique in his very first works, and even in the *Crisis* it was still considered the other side of objectivistic science.

> Historicism assumes its position in the factual realm and by absolutizing this realm without quite neutralizing it (since the specific meaning is by nature alien to historical thinking or at least does not influence its general determinations), what follows is a relativism closely related to naturalistic psychologism and entangled in similar sceptical difficulties. . . .

he writes as early as 1911, in his famous *Philosophy as a Rigorous Science*.[10] The history-of-ideas standpoint was and remained as alien to Husserl as the naturalistic one.

Could the Husserlian 'spirit' be the same as Hegel's 'Absolute Spirit'? An Hegelian interpretation of phenomenology is not at all absurd. Since Husserl never found the final solution to his transcendental phenomenology, the door was left open even for this interpretation. The solution Husserl sought, however, was altogether different. Hegel's Absolute Spirit, whose development is the totality of human history, reduces every concrete person to a means for the totality. Hegelian philosophy remained the philosophy of human alienation. The Husserlian spirit, on the other hand, is a unity of thought and action whose true development is the real becoming not only of mankind but also of every single human personality. For Husserl the realization of the attitude of transcendental phenomenology is 'the rebirth of Europe from the spirit of philosophy'.[11] It is not just a new conceptual attitude but also a new practical one: a genuinely new spiritual form of life. Of course, he does not explore material preconditions of this new life. Yet, his philosophy does not turn out to be merely a new contemplative attitude. That the unity of theory and practice can and ought to be realized is as much an integral part of Husserlian phenomenology as of Marxism.

For yet a third form of universal attitude is possible (as opposed to both the religious-mythical attitude, which is founded in the natural attitude, and the theoretical attitude), namely, the synthesis of the two interests accomplished in the transition from the theoretical to the practical attitude, such that the *theoria* (universal science), arising within a closed unity and under the *epoche* of all praxis, is called (and, in theoretical insight itself, exhibits its calling) to serve mankind in a new way, mankind which, in its concrete existence, lives first and always in the natural sphere. This occurs in the form of a new sort of praxis, that of the universal critique of all life and all life goals, all cultural products and systems that have already arisen out of the life of man; and thus it also becomes a critique of mankind itself and of the values which guide it explicitly or implicitly. Further, it is a praxis whose aim is to elevate mankind through universal scientific reason, according to norms of truth of all forms, to transform it from the bottom up into a new humanity made capable of an absolute self-responsibility on the basis of absolute theoretical insights. [12]

Similarly, Lukács' position differs sharply from shallow historical materialism. The standpoint of the identity of subject and object is not merely an advance in thought but also the total transformation of earlier forms of association and behaviour. It is not at all a matter of a mindless, quasi-automatic upheaval of social relations (and ultimately of relations of production) brought about by natural laws (or alternatively: by an arbitrary effort of the will) precipitating the attainment of the real standpoint. The social upheaval and the discovery of the true viewpoint are not only inseparable; they are ultimately identical processes. The revolutionary transformation of the world of reification (that is, of the bourgeois, capitalist mode of production), corresponds with the development of the proletarian class-consciousness ascribed to the proletariat (the standpoint of the identical subject-object). This had already been formulated by Lukács in 1919 as follows:

The development of society is a unified process. This means that a certain phase of development cannot take place in any area of social life without exerting an impact on all other areas. Through this unity and coherence of social development it is possible to grasp and achieve an understanding of the same process from the standpoint of one social phenomenon or another. Thus, one can speak of culture in its apparent isolation from other social phenomena, for when we correctly grasp the culture of any period, we grasp with it the root of the whole development of the period, just as we do when we begin with an analysis of economic relations. [13]

If we consider Husserl's and Lukács' critiques of science in these terms, then the fact that Husserl focuses only on the philosophical aspect of the process and concentrates exclusively on the change of spiritual attitude does not affect the similarity of the two conceptions. For the one, the standpoint of the identical subject-object is that of the true philosopher. For the other, it is that of the proletariat. But what prevents the true philosopher's standpoint from also being that of the proletariat, since each standpoint is ultimately formulated as 'the philosopher's'?

The true difference between the two standpoints thus does not reduce to that between the history of ideas and historical materialism. Yet, even if, following Lukács' argument, we accept the premise that the essence of a historical period can just as well be understood by its culture as by its forms of production, because every age constitutes a historical whole, it remains to be seen whether in Husserl the total lack of analysis of social relations, understood in the broadest possible way, indicates that he cannot explain the sequence of various attitudes, or even that he regards this sequence as not needing any explanation. It may be useful here to turn to the individual passages in Husserl's book where he speaks outright of the 'factual' causes of a change in attitude. For instance, in discussing the formation of the Greeks' original theoretical attitude, he writes:

> Naturally the outbreak of the theoretical attitude, like everything that develops historically, has its factual motivation in the concrete framework of historical occurrence. In this respect one must clarify, then, how *thaumazein* could arise and become habitual.

'We shall not go into this in detail,' he adds. Thus for Husserl the 'factual motivation' of 'historical developments' is secondary,[14] as it is for every historical view that does not see the history of mankind objectivistically as a natural event and does not attempt to grasp every detail of this history. If men have made their own history (if it was not determined by transcendent powers), then the factual motivations should not be conceived as the causes of the change of attitude. According to Lukács:

> The idea that we have made reality loses its more or less fictitious character: we have – in the prophetic words of Vico . . . – made our own history, and if we are able to regard the whole of reality as history (i.e., as *our* history, for there is no other), we shall have raised ourself in fact to the position from which reality can be understood as our 'action'.[15]

Unless one wants to explain human history objectivistically in terms of transcendent causes, one need follow only the inner connection of successive attitudes. If this is the case, the true history of mankind can also be grasped by examining the sequence of changes of attitude. Shallow historical materialism saw history as the evolution of forms of physical activity – first as the result of relations of production, then as the development of the means of production (in both cases, transcendentalism). This evolution includes the sequence of mental attitudes as well.

In this regard there is an important difference between the two conceptions. Both Lukács and Husserl stress the element of consciousness in human development; both analyse the development of philosophical conceptions as expressing the spiritual essence of European history. Both seek a solution to the crisis inherent in the domination of positivist science, characterized as objectivistic, naturalistic and rationalistic in a bad sense. Husserl calls this age of *reification* a false turn of European teleology. But has this era taken a false turn for Lukács as well? Lukács also ascribes a negative value to reification, even when he casts aside the Utopian standpoint of a moral imperative.

Whenever the refusal of the subject simply to accept his empirically given existence takes the form of an 'ought', this means that the immediately given empirical reality receives affirmation and consecration at the hands of philosophy: it is philosophically immortalized.[16]

For Lukács the question is only whether reification is a necessary precondition for the unreified, unalienated conditions of subject-object identity, or whether it is just a stage of European history which mankind could avoid. While for Lukács the holistic standpoint can be attained only by abolishing the world of fragmentation, Husserl seems to regard the age of the naturalistic attitude as an accidental, intermediary stage.

Although Husserl and Lukács both depict the course of European history from Descartes to classical German idealism in terms of reification, Husserl attributes the entire false development to a single mental step, that of Descartes. Here the difference between the two is obvious. Lukács concentrates on modern social science. When he criticizes science, he usually means economics, law, etc.; the natural sciences play no specific role in his analysis, although his critique applies to them, too. Husserl likewise condemns the objectivistic, naturalistic attitude of every science. For him, however, this attitude is not a necessary consequence of the scientific method, which he considers one of mankind's most valuable achievements. What is problematic is only the false understanding of the method's meaning. The appropriation of this method by the social sciences (*Geisteswissenschaften*) is a typical example of this aberration. Efforts to construct a world of the mind analogous to the world of nature created by the natural sciences could only take place if the natural sciences falsely interpret the world of nature. They regard it as objective nature, erroneously identifying a technical procedure with an objective description. This false attitude emerges as early as Galileo.

> Galileo, the discoverer . . . of physics, or physical nature, is at once a discovering and a concealing genius.[17]

And further:

> I am of course quite serious in placing and continuing to place Galileo at the top of the list of the greatest discoverers of modern times. Naturally I also admire quite seriously the great discoverers of classic and post-classical physics and their intellectual accomplishment, which, far from being merely mechanical, was in fact astounding in the highest sense. This accomplishment is not at all disparaged by the above elucidation of it as *technē* or by the critique in terms of principle, which shows that the true meaning of these theories – the meaning which is genuine in terms of their origins – remained and had to remain hidden from the physicists, including the great and the greatest.[18]

This 'having to remain hidden' points not to historical limitations – which would follow from Lukács' theory – but to the impossibility of devoting oneself completely to this method and at the same time maintaining a critical distance from it.

> But the mathematician, the natural scientist, at best a highly brilliant technician of the method – to which he owes the discoveries which are his only aim – is normally not at all able to carry out such reflections. In his actual sphere of inquiry and discovery he does not know at all that everything these reflections must clarify is even in *need* of clarification, and this for the sake of that interest which is decisive for a philosophy or a science, i.e., the interest in true knowledge of the *world itself, nature itself*. And this is precisely what has been lost through a science which is given as a tradition and which has become a *technē*, insofar as this interest played a determining role at all in its primal establishment. Every attempt to lead the scientist to such reflections, if it comes from a nonmathematical, nonscientific circle of scholars, is rejected as 'metaphysical'.[19]

The birth of the natural sciences as such did not necessitate the development of naturalistic objectivism. Yet the successes of the natural sciences blinded modern European man: 'The world must, in itself, be a rational world, in the new sense of rationality taken from mathematics, or mathematized nature; correspondingly, philosophy, the universal science of the world, must be built up as a unified rational theory *more geometrico*.'[20] And, of course, 'if scientifically rational nature is a world of bodies existing in itself – which was taken for granted in the given historical situation – then the world-in-itself must, in a sense unknown before, be a peculiarly *split* world, split into nature-in-itself and a mode of being which is different from this: that which exists psychically.'[21]

Thus we have the world view of exact science, of bad rationality and objectivism: the standpoint which has lost the world as a totality. Lukács could also agree with this description of the development of contemporary thought. This world of rational theory *in the geometric manner* is nothing but capitalism's world of 'second' nature, whose essence combines the ever-increasing domination of nature with the loss of the totality. The splitting of the world into nature-as-such and the psychic nature of isolated individuals (understood as 'second' nature) corresponds to the world of capitalist reification as described by Lukács. Here

> a man's own activity, his own labour, becomes something objective and independent of him, something that controls him by virtue of an autonomy alien to man. *Objectively* a world of objects and relations between things springs into being (the world of commodities and their movements on the market). The laws governing these objects are indeed gradually discovered by man, but even so they confront him as invisible forces that generate their own power. . . . *Subjectively* – where the economy has been fully developed – a man's activity becomes estranged from himself; it turns into a commodity which, subject to the non-human objectivity of the natural laws of society, must go its own way independently of man, just like any consumer article.[22]

For Lukács the failure to reflect on the true meaning of scientific method is a necessary consequence of those relations of production that are the other side of the totality, including domination by method. Reification, furthermore, cannot be philosophically transcended until it has been overcome in practice. Lukács must be close to Husserl in thinking that Descartes

> accomplished the primal establishment of ideas which were destined, through their own historical effects (as if following a hidden teleology of history), to explode this very rationalism by uncovering its hidden absurdity. Precisely those ideas which were supposed to ground this rationalism as *aeterna veritas* bear within themselves a *deeply hidden sense*, which, once brought to the surface, completely uproots it.[23]

Bourgeois thought cannot overcome itself. The holistic perspective can be attained only by the proletariat.

Husserl merely explains what happened with Descartes.

> For Descartes, the *Meditations* work themselves out in the portentous form of a substitution of one's own psychic ego for the [absolute] ego, of psychological immanence for egological immanence, of the evidence of psychic, 'inner,' or 'self-perception' for egological self-perception; and this is also their continuing historical effect up to the present day.[24]

Once this psychological misinterpretation was anchored in European thought, total objectification of the subject was necessary to attain subject-object identity. Husserl leaves unanswered the question of whether this misunderstanding could have been avoided.

Husserl believes that transcendental phenomenology is possible only from the vantage point of the disinterested observer which the modern, exact science and rationalistic philosophy have surrendered for their rationalistic attitude. In Lukács the standpoint of the identical subject-object is not at all that of the uninvolved observer. On the contrary, Lukács stresses that only the class which has been most deeply affected by the social conditions of reification and whose fate clearly depends on overcoming the bourgeois attitude can, by a practical and theoretical act, do away with this reification.

To anticipate the result of our analysis: the real difference between Lukács and Husserl lies in their approach to the question of *false consciousness*. For Lukács the holistic perspective is the standpoint of the proletariat, while for Husserl it is that of the true philosopher. This difference has been described here as inconsequential, since the proletariat's standpoint is also formulated theoretically in a philosophy and since Husserl does not discuss the sociological relevance of the philosopher's standpoint. The dissemination of knowledge, however, is for Husserl a political struggle, a question of power:

> Clearly this leads not simply to a homogeneous transformation of the generally satisfactory life of the national state but probably to great internal schisms in which this life and the whole national culture must suffer an upheaval. Those conservatives who are satisfied with the tradition and the philosophical men will fight each other, and the struggle will surely occur in the sphere of political power.[25]

Unlike Lukács, Husserl does not specify the sociological composition of this circle of philosophers.

In the light of this discussion, the most important questions of our time seem to be whether we need a total reorientation to overcome the crisis of our era, and whether such a reorientation – be it total or partial – must represent the standpoint of *one* sociologically and concretely delimitable social group (or whether it is attainable independent of such particularity).

Let us return to Husserl's conception of the development from the natural attitude to transcendental phenomenology.

> Extrascientific culture, culture not yet touched by science, consists in tasks and accomplishments of man in finitude. The openly endless horizon in which he lives is not disclosed; his ends, his activity, his trade and traffic, his personal, social, national, and mythical motivation – all this moves within the sphere of his finitely surveyable surrounding world.

Here there are no infinite tasks, no ideal acquisitions.[26]

> Now natural life can be characterized as a life naively, straightforwardly
> directed at the world, the world being always in a certain sense conscious-
> ly present as a universal horizon, without, however, being thematic as
> such.[27]

This natural attitude, this unity with the socio-cultural world, is the normal
mode of human existence.

> All other attitudes are accordingly related back to this natural attitude as
> reorientations [of it].[28]

On the one hand they have emerged historically from the first, primal attitude;
on the other, they remain anchored in the original attitude even after other
historically determined generations have forged higher and different attitudes.

> The individual men who reorient themselves, as men within their univer-
> sal life-community (their nation), continue to have their natural interests,
> each his individual interests; through no reorientation can they simply
> lose them; this would mean that each would cease to be what he has
> become from birth onwards. In any circumstances, then, the reorienta-
> tion can only be a periodical one.[29]

The original attitude is practical in its connection with its socio-cultural en-
vironment. There are two different possible reorientations towards universality:
the practical and the theoretical. Husserl labels the higher-level practical attitude a religious and mythical one, characterized as consisting in this: 'that the
world as a totality becomes thematic, but in a practical way'.

> But all this speculative knowledge is meant to serve man in his human
> purposes so that he may order his worldly life in the happiest possible way
> and shield it from disease, from every sort of evil fate, from disaster and
> death.[30]

> But in addition to the higher-level practical attitude . . . there exists yet
> another essential possibility for altering the general natural attitude,
> namely, the *theoretical attitude*.[31]

> Man becomes gripped by the passion of a world view and world
> knowledge that turns away from all practical interests and within the
> closed sphere of its cognitive activity, in the times devoted to it, strives
> for and achieves nothing but pure *theoria*. In other words, man becomes a
> non-participating spectator, surveyor of the world; he becomes a
> philosopher. . . .[31]

> [This is] the peculiar universality of his critical stance, his resolve not to

accept unquestioningly any pre-given opinion or tradition so that he can inquire, in respect of the whole traditionally pre-given universe, after what is true in itself, an ideality. But this is not only a new cognitive stance. Because of the requirement to subject all empirical matters to ideal norms (i.e., those of unconditioned truth), there soon results a far-reaching transformation of the whole praxis of human existence (i.e., the whole of cultural life): henceforth it must receive its norms not from the naive experience and tradition of everyday life but from objective truth. [33]

As already indicated, this teleology has gone astray in modern objectivism by regarding technique (*technē*), a mere art, as truth.

Thus both critiques of science have no other goal than to rediscover *truth.* Both maintain that the meaning of our history can be grasped only from a holistic perspective. A mankind that seeks to adapt to its own world as something alien surrenders its human essence and fails to realize its teleology. In Lukács' opinion too, this teleology consists, ultimately, in achieving a mankind which draws its norms from *objective truth*, i.e., which is capable of absolute self-responsibility by virtue of absolute theoretical insights. It is a question of objective knowledge. Lukács says: 'the proletariat is . . . the first subject in history that is (objectively) capable of an adequate social consciousness.' [34] 'It was necessary for the proletariat to be born for social reality to become fully conscious.' [35] Both Lukács and Husserl posit the necessity of total reorientation, the nature of which consists in grasping the totality. This knowledge of the totality is self-knowledge.

Such a radical reorientation means the abolition of the duality of philosophy and science. Lukács:

only by overcoming the – theoretical – duality of philosophy and special discipline, of methodology and factual knowledge can the way be found by which to annul the duality of thought and existence. [36]

Husserl:

A definite ideal of a universal philosophy and its method forms the beginning; this is, so to speak, the primal establishment of the philosophical modern age and all its lines of development. But instead of being able to work itself out in fact, this ideal suffers an inner dissolution. [37]

Along with this falls the faith in 'absolute' reason, through which the world has its meaning, the faith in the meaning of history, of humanity, the faith in man's freedom, that is, his capacity to secure rational meaning for his individual and common human existence. [38]

Both thinkers seek the Archimedean point from which the disintegration of human knowledge and life can be reversed and a unified *teleology* of human existence be established, one marked by self-determination. The critique of fragmentation and false objectivism implies the *emancipation* from external determination. This critique of science owes its vehemence to the disenchantment caused by the failure of science and scientific objectivity's promise of freedom. The bourgeois era replaced tradition preserved by God with a new, possibly much more abject servitude to 'factual' objectivity, to faceless, crude, merciless 'facts'. Man was alone, powerless to control a godless world. Exact science promises to guarantee survival, contingent on understanding and adapting to the discovered facts and their laws. Yet a world ruled by anthropomorphic (albeit unknowable) forces is preferable to this. All radical critiques of science, including phenomenology and Marxism, seek to reveal this scientistic world view as false consciousness.

Does the denial of this world view necessarily result in a holistic perspective? Is it *either* total exposure to *or* total power over our destiny? Is the assumption that man must be either master or slave justified? To answer these questions we must raise another: how is it at all possible to grasp historical reality as a totality? What does that mean? The holistic standpoint cannot reside in the totality of the object alone but presupposes that of the subject as well. Otherwise the objectivistic world view remains intact. The totality is *ab ovo* the unity of *object and subject*. This is for Lukács and Husserl the unified process of human history. Mankind, the subject of knowledge, is also its object, since man has created the objective world he knows, including nature. To conclude from this that man makes alone his own history is to be confined to the Hegelian standpoint. Man remains an *abstract* concept, easily replaceable by the absolute mind. For the flesh-and-blood individual only the knowledge of reality as *his own power* is significant. Prerequisite to this power is the individual's participation in the formation of that reality. *That is what rules out the holistic standpoint.* Both philosophers realize this. Husserl was preoccupied with this problem all his life. He accepted neither the Hegelian solution, in which the individual is sacrificed, nor a solipsistic, and ultimately relativistic one. He tried to show that the intersubjectivity of the transcendental ego satisfies the requirements of a holistic conception.

Lukács, on the other hand, simply casts aside the standpoint of the individual.

> The individual can never become the measure of all things. For when the individual confronts objective reality he is faced by a complex of readymade and unalterable objects which allow him only the subjective responses of recognition or rejection.[39]

For the individual, reification and hence determinism are irremovable.[40]

Lukács finds the subject capable of grasping the totality in the proletariat as a class:

Only the class can relate to the whole of reality in a practical revolutionary way. (The 'species' cannot do this as it is no more than an individual that has been mythologized and stylized in a spirit of contemplation.)[41]

Does this description of an individual having been 'mythologized and stylized in a spirit of contemplation' apply only to the species and not to the class? Lukács' answer is clear. By contrast with mankind, hitherto unable to realize its real historical unity, the proletariat is forced to do so. The individual proletarian is the first individual in history who can identify unconditionally with his class, though not with the whole of mankind. Since the self-knowledge of the proletariat entails the self-knowledge of all of society and history, the class-conscious proletarian, as a representative of his class, becomes the real subject of history. To the extent that the class-conscious proletariat ceases to articulate society in terms of classes, Lukács also posits, ultimately, *the total absorption of the individual into the species*.

Either total submission or total control? The critique of naturalistic objectivism, the critique of a relentless factual world (the scientism of total bureaucratization) is justified: man is not subject to rule by persistent, objective facts. The world view of objectivistic science and of bad rationalistic and irrationalistic philosophies must be transcended, but not from the standpoint of the totality. For that would mean the identity not only of subject and object but also of the subject as it understands itself in the object: the identity of the individual and the species. That identity signifies the total repression – annihilation is impossible – of individuality.

Philosophy's belief in its ability to suppress its own particularity, and thus every other particularity as well, is a new false consciousness, the attainment of which would result in just as much cruelty and inhumanity as that caused by false objectivism. The real and practical unmasking of the false consciousness of objectivism must also show that the subject never completely becomes an object, that the reification of human relations and human consciousness is only a tendency, which, though dominant in the bourgeois era, never successfully eliminated counter-tendencies.

In the essay 'Phenomenology and Bourgeois Society'[42] I have attempted to outline the possibility of a phenomenological reorientation, since the complete isolation of the bourgeois individual, as dictated by objectivism, is only apparent. This individual never ceased to be a social being. The reorientation, then, must not and cannot be a total one. A total reorientation, replacing objectivism with holism and effecting the repression of individuality, would not solve the crisis of mankind. The crisis can be overcome only *by developing the social character of the individual*.

For it is false that 'For the individual, reification and hence determinism are irremovable.'[43] *History and Class Consciousness* is based on the assumption that objectivism is true. Because of this assumption, Lukács can exercise his critique only from the standpoint of a total reorientation. Husserl's ambiguities, however, leave room for a different solution. The standpoint of the totality here is that of the philosopher, whose reorientation is only temporary.

> It can have habitually enduring validity for one's whole remaining life only in the form of an unconditional resolve of the will to take up, at periodic but internally unified points of time, the same attitude and, through this continuity that intentionally bridges the gaps, to sustain its new sort of interests as valid and as ongoing projects and to realize them through corresponding cultural structures.[44]

Philosophy represents the standpoint of the totality, or, as Habermas would say, the emancipation interests of mankind. If it subordinates its own standpoint to that of scientificity as in the case of positivistic determinism, then it does indeed abandon its true mission. This holds true not only when it represents the standpoint of the isolated individual, the private man, the bourgeois, but also when it represents another particularity, i.e., the proletariat. The élitism of *History and Class Consciousness* reveals the false consciousness of Bolshevism, its belief that a self-conscious élite can and should represent a class and, through it, all mankind.

Liberation from every particularity can end only in the terror of the general. The standpoint of a specific particularity amounts to the same thing. If there is a solution, it lies only in the mutual recognition of the most different particularities. The holistic standpoint neither can, nor ought to be achieved. It belongs not to *one* class or to one specific oppressed particularity but to all of mankind. Inasmuch as the unity of mankind is a value only to the extent that the different particularities seek mutual recognition instead of annihilation, the standpoint of the totality, philosophy, should not be realized. If the unity of mankind is a value at all, it is so only in the regulative and not in the constitutive sense. What follows from this for science?

If the holistic standpoint is a point of departure only for critique and not an attainable or desirable reality, we need reject only the universalization of science and not science itself. Habermas writes correctly, but not logically, that

> it constitutes the honour of the sciences to apply their method relentlessly without reflecting on the knower's interest. The sciences are all the more certain of their discipline because they methodologically do not know what they do, i.e., methodological progress within an unproblematized framework. False consciousness has a supportive function.[45]

Habermas is not logical here, for the consciousness of science is *false only in the sense* that it – inevitably – seeks to universalize its world view. Yet we cannot subordinate the technical interest attached to it (and the practical one of hermeneutic science, which is always linked with concrete mankind) to the emancipatory one. Such subordination would mean the totalitarian world order we have just rejected. Thus the consciousness of 'objective science' is not, in and of itself, false. 'Objective science' represents part of our reality: the impossibility of overcoming all objectivity. Science, moreover, does not have the function of creating meaning. In no circumstances can the meaning of life stem from knowledge. Any meaning that stems from knowledge is, for us, transcendent.

Translated by David J. Parent

NOTES

1 Edmund Husserl, *The Crisis of European Science and Transcendental Phenomenology*, trs. David Carr (Evanston, Ill.: Northwestern University Press, 1970), pp. 5 – 6.
2 ibid., pp. 6 – 7.
3 Georg Lukács, *History and Class Consciousness*, trs. Rodney Livingstone (London: Merlin Press, 1971), p. 23.
4 ibid., p. 6.
5 Husserl, *The Crisis of European Science*, p. 71.
6 ibid., p. 299.
7 Lukács, *History and Class Consciousness*, p. 112.
8 ibid., p. 88.
9 ibid., pp. 103 – 4.
10 Edmund Husserl, 'Philosophie als strenge Wissenschaft', *Logos* (Tübingen), 1 (1910 – 11), p. 323.
11 Husserl, *The Crisis of European Science*, p. 299.
12 ibid., p. 283.
13 Georg Lukács, 'The Old Culture and the New Culture', in *Towards a New Marxism*, eds. Bart Grahl and Paul Piccone (St Louis, 1973), p. 21.
14 Husserl, *The Crisis of European Science*, p. 285.
15 Lukács, *History and Class Consciousness*, p. 145.
16 ibid., p. 160.
17 Husserl, *The Crisis of European Science*, p. 52.
18 ibid., p. 53.
19 ibid., pp. 56 – 7.
20 ibid., p. 61.
21 ibid.
22 Lukács, *History and Class Consciousness*, p. 87.
23 Husserl, *The Crisis of European Science*, p. 74.
24 ibid., p. 81.
25 ibid., p. 288.
26 ibid., p. 279.
27 ibid., p. 281.
28 ibid.

29 ibid.
30 ibid., pp. 283, 294.
31 ibid., p. 282.
32 ibid., p. 285.
33 ibid., pp. 286 – 7.
34 Lukács, *History and Class Consciousness*, p. 199.
35 ibid., p. 19.
36 ibid., p. 203.
37 Husserl, *The Crisis of European Science*, p. 12.
38 ibid., p. 13.
39 Lukács, *History and Class Consciousness*, p. 193.
40 ibid.
41 ibid.
42 See *Phänomenologie und Marxismus*, vol. 3: *Sozialphilosophie*, eds. B. Waldenfels, J. M. Brockman and A. Pazanin (Frankfurt: Suhrkamp Verlag, 1978), pp. 115 – 43.
43 Lukács, *History and Class Consciousness*, p. 193.
44 Husserl, *The Crisis of European Science*, pp. 281 – 2.
45 Jürgen Habermas, *Technik und Wissenschaft als 'Ideologie'* (Frankfurt: Suhrkamp Verlag, 1968), p. 165.

6

Notes on Lukács' *Ontology*

FERENC FEHÉR, AGNES HELLER, GYÖRGY MÁRKUS AND MIHÁLY VAJDA

INTRODUCTION (BUDAPEST, JANUARY 1975)

I

When we decided to publish the commentaries written for our friend and teacher Georg Lukács after reading the last version of his book *On the Ontology of Social Reality*, and we reread our 'Notes on Lukács Ontology', it became immediately clear that for various reasons we would have to write a collective introduction to the text. First – not necessarily in order of importance – to provide a few sketchy comments concerning the work's genesis, which is frequently discussed but scarcely known in its entirety.[1]

At the end of 1961 or the beginning of 1962 (i.e., soon after the German manuscript of Volume I of the enormous book *Die Eigenart der Aesthetischen*, was finished), Georg Lukács began a project that he had cherished in his young years – his ethics. (We think it right to speak of the realization of youthful plans in his old age. Although former conceptions were changed when he became a Marxist, every reader of the Heidelberg Manuscripts will recognize their continuity with later works. Likewise, everyone familiar with Lukács can see that in this case he was continuing his lectures at the Free School of Human Sciences: the creation of a contemporary radical ethics, although taking into account his 'reorientation'.) True to his old approach, he mainly consulted primary sources on the subject and took extensive notes. But even during this phase (the latter part of 1962), he toyed with the idea of adding a foreword or a lengthy first chapter to his *Ethics* (in conversations he often gave it the tentative title 'The Place of Ethics in the System of Human Actions'). In it he would formulate the ontological 'basic characteristics' of social existence – all the more so since he was unable to base his ethical conception on 'traditional' Marxist accounts. He often unambiguously discussed the need and the reason for this with us and others.

This work, begun so energetically in the spring of 1963, was interrupted by a catastrophe whose effects and inner torment were even greater than Lukács' 1911 existential crisis, precipitated by Leo Popper's and Irma Seidler's deaths: the death of his wife, Gertrud Borstieber. He had dedicated his *Aesthetics* and the already begun *Ethics* to this woman 'as a modest attempt to express gratitude for more than forty years of life and thought, work and struggle together.' As he confided in intimate conversations, this woman's influence on his life could be compared only with the October Revolution. That was an accurate depiction: it was Gertrud Borstieber's unique personality, a combination of the traits of a *grande dame* of the Enlightenment and a plebeian heroine in a Gottfried Keller novella, that taught him to appreciate the 'ordinary life' he had formerly despised. With her death he saw himself literally confronted with Hamlet's question. His decision was made after almost half a year of inner turmoil. Lukács returned to his desk, from then on under the stern discipline of an unwavering asceticism. As in his younger years, every trace of 'life' was banned from the world, and he tolerated nothing but work as a personal duty in and around himself. The result was that his old dynamic way of thinking surfaced again, and Lukács soon realized that what was needed was not an ontological introduction or a first chapter but an *Ontology*; without this no successful foundation for the ethics would be possible. The final decision was reached in 1964. Lukács began writing without delay.

The following 'Notes' were not written under the ridiculous pretence that they might be equally valuable, but only for the sake of information. As soon as Lukács was finished with a chapter, he usually handed the text over to one of his students. After the entire work was typed (during 1968), he gave the completed manuscript to the authors of this essay and asked for extensive critical comments. He wanted to use these for correcting the proofs or for eventual revisions. Such conversations, five in all, took place in the winter of 1968 – 9; in each case one chapter or a group of chapters was discussed. The debates always extended late into the night and, in view of the theoretical inflexibility on both sides, were often very sharp, though our side was always muted owing to our friendship, love and respect for Lukács. The following 'Notes' were written for Lukács' personal use: they summarize the *main* points of discussion in order to simplify debate. They originated as follows: after we had read individual chapters, we met with Lukács before the proposed discussions and handed our written remarks to Vajda, who edited the papers and blended the common views into a unified formulation. He then gave this written report to Lukács. Unifying the criticism caused no great problem: the fundamental evaluation of the work was the same on all essential questions – especially at the stage of the second reading.

In the discussions with Lukács, essential theoretical differences between us and him arose on some questions; both parties, of course, expected this. As a result of Lukács' 'work-centred' nature, theory was the main line of communication between him and other human beings anyway, but during the last eight years of his work it became practically the only link. Thus in our contacts with him regular theoretical discussions, already substantial, played an ever greater role. Every disputed question had already been discussed while the work was being written. In the debates during the winter of 1968 – 9 Lukács agreed with several of our objections; others he wanted to answer in the final text, which was essentially a revision of the 'first text'. Since our objections seemed to require revision and confirmed his uneasiness that the work had grown beyond its originally intended size, he decided to abridge the book. At first he thought of substituting for the first three chapters on the history of 'ontological thought' a short introduction clearly summarizing the basic ideas. But this attempt also grew longer than originally planned. Therefore, before he had even corrected the proofs, he decided to finish this work, which had grown into an independent book, and to title it *Prolegomena to the Ontology of Social Reality*. He wanted to postpone his decision about the eventual revision and publication of the five theoretical chapters of his *Ontology*.[2]

The writing proceeded very slowly. Furthermore, the last phase was overshadowed by the *awareness* that he was afflicted by an incurable illness, which he bore with exemplary stoicism. The last part (and even we cannot determine whether it is the actual end of the project) was finished in the early autumn of 1970. He was no longer able to read the text, which was deciphered and typed by several people in his last months, since in the last seven or eight months he was unable to work. According to the merciless verdict of 1963, he wanted to await death at his desk, but only a grotesque caricature of a life spent in strict, hard work was granted to him: he was transported to the hospital from his empty desk, now a skeleton of a life devoted to unceasing activity. An expression that he often used when rejecting help, and typical of his unpathetic nature – he used it when someone wanted to relieve him of some of the technical tasks connected with his work – was: 'I have to clean my own dirty laundry.' But he was no longer able to do this.

II

What moral and objective motive can there be for publishing a manuscript written at Lukács' behest for his own use, which furthermore can make no claim to the roundedness of a systematic essay or critical review?

First, the *Ontology* – Lukács' last ambitious work, written while his health was still intact – is now being published in Hungarian, in German and soon also in Italian. Undoubtedly, it is a decisive document for an appraisal of his last period, for an understanding of the problems he dealt with and therefore – in view of the constitution of his personality, equally representative in success or in failure – also for an insight into the entire Marxist philosophical problematic during the last decade. On the other hand, there is the brute fact that he did not regard the manuscript he left us as the final version. Today it would be scientifically irresponsible to 'reconstruct' the revision he planned on the authority of conversations and fragments of discussion. But so much can safely be stated: he generally accepted the existence of a contradiction between the 'two ontologies' mentioned in the following 'Notes', and he found it necessary to eliminate it, although he did not agree, or only partly agreed, with some of our suggestions for its elimination. In view of the fact that the work was unfinished and that he wanted to revise the last version (at least in the direction of eliminating the contradiction we had pointed out), we can state that the 'Notes' are part of the genesis of the work and may provide a better understanding of it.

Secondly, after Lukács' death – partly but not primarily in connection with the publication of his *Ontology* – we were often asked to clarify our own relation to his last creative period, especially since disagreements about the *Ontology* had also appeared in print (in *Der Spiegel*, 14 June 1971). Since our relation to Lukács as students, which we both always admitted and stressed, has become problematic today, we have decided to publish these critical 'Notes' as a document. Thus we are publishing the text unchanged. Only slight abridgements have been made (insignificant recommendations on wording or short deletions).

But precisely because we are publishing an unchanged text, it seemed absolutely necessary to add an explanatory introduction to these 'Notes' for two reasons. First, the text does not provide a *complete* picture of our views on ontology. It would have been superfluous for us to point out to Lukács the fundamental points of our agreement with him: those ideas that we accepted were taken for granted among us. In addition, these 'Notes' elaborate those points that we felt had to be made to warrant revision. Consequently, they concentrate on principal problems without touching on the whole gamut of general methodological questions. We were not writing critical reviews: Lukács had asked us for recommendations for the revision of an already finished text. Although he was very open to counter-arguments and debates, if we had not kept to the framework but had chosen to present once again in writing our own doubts (which were already well-known to him), our friend and teacher would have rightly seen this as impudence.

Moreover, even with the above reservations, the unprejudiced reader will immediately notice that the 'Notes' are extraordinarily *critical* of the work. But this is only the *final result* of a very long process, and it took shape only during our rereading of the completed work. When we knew only the general intentions and individual chapters, our evaluation of the project was much milder. This contradictory relation can be explained as our scientific and moral duty because even before our debates with Lukács we often referred to the work in progress in unmistakably positive terms in the Hungarian philosophical and cultural press.

III

In discussing our relation to the *Ontology* retrospectively, more than a decade after the beginning of the work, we should mention the intense liberating effect that this intellectual enterprise and the setting of its objectives had on all of us. Readers unfamiliar with our intellectual situation at that time will hardly understand this. Although we remain unshaken in our demand to transcend the bourgeois state of the world and convinced that this transcendence can and should be achieved with Marx as a starting-point, since the middle 1950s (i.e., the time when we began to regard ourselves as philosophically independent, thinking human beings), we experienced more and deeper doubts, problems and questions concerning the 'traditional' Marxist philosophical framework. Following Kolakowski, we labelled the 'traditional' framework the 'extensional tendency'.[3]

Since our philosophical childhood, we had sought a 'philosophy of practice'. Here it is unnecessary to describe in detail the close connection between this striving and the fact that we were students of the author of *History and Class Consciousness*, whose radical rejection of his masterpiece we never shared. (Of course, that was also connected with our reception of Gramsci.) Also attributable to Lukács' influence is the fact that in the course of this process of clarification, we held firmly to Marxist philosophy's claim to universality in principle – at least contrary to a few related efforts that appeared internationally. Initially, it was unclear to what extent Marxist philosophy, postulated as 'universal', was distinguishable from the science of the 'most general laws'. This is why, to the extent that we were still at the beginnings of our methodological reflection, in the spirit of the philosophy of *praxis*, we chose in 'self-defence' the solution of dealing with the 'extensional standpoint' in the framework of *sectoral disciplines*. The first important documents of this search were Heller's essay on ethics, written in 1957 – 8 as lectures and published eleven years later under the title *How Free Is Man?*, and Márkus' 1958 study on *The Epistemological Views of the Young Marx* – to mention just two specialized disciplines. This, naturally, brought about an unresolved philosophical compromise, which grew ever more intolerable as we developed. This compromise was not primarily imposed from outside but was dictated by our common feeling that the huge task of 'reviewing the whole' far exceeded our own strength. Given these reservations, doubts, partial attempts to move ahead and uncertainties, it is understandable that Lukács' decision to write *The Ontology of Social Reality* should have had such a liberating effect on us. This experience determined our 'view' for several years as we read the various parts as they were completed, although some scepticism appeared with the very first chapters.

Lukács' decision at that time did not have merely a liberating effect on us: it was also a guarantee of success. We can be accused of overestimating Lukács' general results in the reform of 'traditional Marxism', of not sufficiently clarifying the state of the question (especially methodologically) and of having in the 1960s approached our teacher with the partiality of students. This last statement is certainly accurate as a psychological fact of our development. Yet even those who see the crystallization points of renewal in Althusser, in the Frankfurt School or in Sartre must recognize Lukács' always *representative position* in the last phase of development of Marxist philosophy, which lasted for almost fifty years. Thus our partiality was perhaps more than subjective preferences, and our expectation could probably lay claim to the rank of *hope* as conceived by Bloch.

This 'hope' was reinforced by the most recent philosophical developments. Lukács' great work, *The Specificity of the Aesthetic*, which had been published in the meantime, showed us the outline of such a general philosophical approach. Here we do not wish to deal with the aesthetic content of the work, especially his often challenged position on modern art, which some of us initially shared and dogmatically defended, while others never accepted it, but which all of us have abandoned in the last five years. The philosophical *novum* for us was the *theory of objectification* underlying the entire work. This theory provided a real answer to at least some of the unanswered questions formulated in Marx's philosophy. Since it was philosophically elaborated and seminal, it embodied Lukács' *true* self-critique of *History and Class Consciousness*: the metacritique of the apodictic judgement of the masterpiece of his youth, since the generic character [*Gattungsmässigkeit*] in *The Specificity* was no longer a conceptual mythology. The book was also a grandiose attempt to develop the great generic spheres of objectifications (at least mental ones) from everyday practice and everyday thinking within the framework of a unified conception. At the same time the work laid the foundations for a future *Methodenstreit* by linking the concept of certain great generic spheres of objectification and the values created by them as socio-representative answers to historically delimited concrete situations with their general generic validity. However one-sided and disputable, this provided an answer to the old dilemma of the superstructural character of *historical value products* and their universally valid form: in short, to Marx's Homeric paradox.

This explains our expectations of the *Ontology* and at the same time clarifies what we agreed with: we expected a work that would carry out a synthesis between historicism and analysis on the universal generic level, between practice-centredness and philosophical universality. Like every determination, this was also a negation of numerous trends within Marxism coexisting or appearing at that time. It was, above all, a rejection of the above-mentioned 'extensional conception': the projected synthesis absolutely ruled out the essentially positivistic conception of the 'universal laws' of the 'extensional conception' which homogenized nature and society and therefore eliminated any real human activity. At the same time, it also ruled out those famous reform attempts that sought to go beyond the irresoluble philosophical dilemmas caused by the traditional conception either by means of axiological reforms based on the eternal, hypostasized 'human nature' or by the view that sees society as a complex consisting of the structure of structures. This synthesis also opposed those trends that – whether from the viewpoint of sociological relativism or of epistemological decisionism – identify the philosophy of practice with mere ideology and culture critique. Thus we formulated our expectations of the *Ontology* rather sketchily but also more concretely than as a mere longing for a 'great work'.

Here another personal element is theoretically important for understanding the later differences of opinion. Looking at the title of the work in progress, we accented 'social reality' rather than the naturalistic implications of the 'extensional conception', which we regarded as completely obsolete and methodologically untenable. At that time *Ontology* meant to us nothing more than these demands for a synthesis: the transcending of purely historicizing tendencies without becoming entangled in the net of 'universal laws'. Lukács himself, however, did not clarify his methodological position. After he rejected *History and Class Consciousness,* he ignored the fact that the book had created a 'philosophical situation' (the 'situation' of a Marxist historicism elaborated at a high level of generalization, which paradoxically excluded generalizing systems as 'reified'). This philosophical situation had to be dealt with in a methodological way, which he himself wanted to overcome. While he wanted to build a 'theoretical system', he still distrusted great philosophical *systems* – a distrust which he had once raised to a theoretical level in the critique of rationalism in *History and Class Consciousness* (and had further articulated in his review of Bukharin's work). Although in his 'Extorted Reconciliation' Adorno one-sidedly exaggerates the hostility towards ontology of *Against Misunderstood Realism* (which is extremely ambiguous and, to a certain extent, suggests merely a rejection of the ontology of an eternal *condition humaine*), those familiar with Lukács know that toward the end of the 1950s he used the expression 'ontology' as invective rather than as a constructive model. Even later, this term for him did not mean much more than an emphatic rejection of the dominant *epistemological approximation*, and was primarily motivated by a polemical attitude toward neo-positivism. We were perfectly in agreement in regard to this last intention. But as for the details of the critique we had serious reservations from the very beginning.

It was with these expectations that we read and interpreted the first chapters of the *Ontology* as they were finished and given to us. The work provided an *incentive* for us to seek to work out the central problems of Marxist philosophy –

but without, of course, claiming the systematic universality of Lukács' book. In the 1960s, then, we undertook a series of studies to clarify and develop the same problems that were undertaken in the *Ontology*.[4] Purely from the viewpoint of the notes written on the *Ontology*, the effect of these studies on us was that while Lukács wrote the book, we developed a common perspective concerning both the problems it tackled as well as the methodological problems it implicitly raised (of course, this did not eliminate mutual violent discussions among ourselves over the details – which still persist today). This common perspective also clarified for us the numerous differences that there were between Lukács' solutions and ours.

To forestall misunderstandings two things should be pointed out. First, as usual, the writings on this subject were read by Lukács while they were still in manuscript. He discussed their major thrust with us, and he always agreed with them – as he stated verbally and in writing. Since our introduction is no psychological study of Lukács, we do not want to analyse those elements of agreement which in some sense were related to our free interpretation of the *Ontology* as it was emerging. Since our discussions with Lukács were intellectual confrontations, completely free and unrestrained, and since we had absolute confidence in his attitude, which was always unrestrained by diplomacy, theoretically unyielding and absolutely candid, we tried to provide a *theoretical* and not a psychological answer to the question: how could he emphatically agree with such work, whose conclusions he rejected? The theoretical solution was simple: he saw in them the continuation and elaboration of *his own last philosophical intentions*.

This agreement on philosophical intentions concealed a perhaps deeper, more essential unity: the evaluation and interpretation of our common ideological situation and task, which Lukács designated 'The renaissance of Marxism'. Since a no-man's-land of scholasticism extended between the great traditions of Marxism and the present, a return to Marx, and the conviction that though no answer can be directly read out of Marx for present problems, they can be theoretically and practically solved only through a rediscovery of his theory's original meaning free of the distortions of 'traditional' solutions, a common perspective on a whole series of issues dealt with in the *Ontology* developed on this common basic ground. They were the natural precondition of the practical-social orientation of Marxist philosophy, the recognition of the central role of the category of 'labour', the treatment of ideology as an actual force (not merely as a 'superstructural reflex') and the careful treatment of the central categories of alienation, which for decades had been unjustifiably relegated to the background despite the fact that they give a basis to real historical interpretation and so on.

Secondly, in order to reconcile our always emphatic and sincere feeling of solidarity and the paradox of our disappointment with the solutions proposed in the finished manuscript, we must stress the continuing genetic nature of the experience that culminated in the autumn of 1968 with the rereading of the manuscript. Naturally, our initial enthusiasm had in the meantime changed into scepticism concerning even decisive key points. We could no longer claim a distinct experience of liberation in conversations and intellectual meetings. The most important of these conversations took place between Agnes Heller and Jürgen Habermas in May 1966, on the occasion of a lecture in Frankfurt. Habermas showed considerable interest in Lukács' work: at that time the *Ontology* was already a topic of philosophical 'gossip' in West Germany but was completely unknown in terms of both content and text. When Heller summarized the content of the finished chapters and further plans, Habermas rejected the plan itself. To him, an effort of this sort seemed to contradict in principle the Marxist view of history in seeking to reintroduce the great systems of rationalism which belonged to the 'historical past'. Although carried out in a spirit of friendship and mutual respect, the discussion was heated: even then we did not *exclusively* accept the Frankfurt attempt at a positive solution – i.e., that every category can be investigated only in its concrete historical manifestation (one of the best examples of this is precisely Habermas' *Die Strukturwandel der Oeffentlichkeit*, and its approach is not too different from ours, as can be seen from Heller's book, *Renaissance Man*). But when we went over the discussion among ourselves, it had a different effect; it aroused *methodological doubts* concerning the *Ontology* in two senses. First, it suddenly cast light on a fact that we had only vaguely felt, i.e., that the project's basic methodological principles had not been fully thought through; secondly, it raised once again the century-old dilemma of *Marxism as philosophy*: how historicity (history as the only science, to cite Marx) can be reconciled with systematic universality.

At this point we can outline only the *most essential* problems of discussion that united us in the autumn of 1968 in relation to the completed text of the *Ontology*. Since it involves major philosophical problems, the following list can be replaced only by extensive studies or multi-volume monographs.

1 *The denial of the possibility of the dialectic of nature* and doubt that the creation of a comprehensive picture of nature is the task of philosophy. Although *History and Class Consciousness* never constituted 'orthodoxy' for us, we accepted this idea without reserve. Thus we were especially disappointed by a few negative apodictic judgements in the *Ontology* concerning certain stages of development of natural science. We felt that they were drawn by analogy from Lukács' annoyance with 'modernistic' phenomena as a result of his concept of *decadence* rather than being based on competent judgements. All this did not, of course, mean the denial of the objectivity of self-existent nature; it meant only that nature as a philosophical theme obtains in the active material and spiritual relation of nature and society, i.e., as a decisive social problem.

2 *The rejection of the reflection theory* in epistemology (even within the framework of a realistically oriented epistemological effort). As can be seen from Fehér's and Heller's numerous works written during the 1960s on Lukács' *Aesthetics* and on concrete aesthetic questions, for a long time we tried to expand and transform the concept. Thus, for example, in aesthetics we tried to replace it with the concept of mimesis (Lukács' work actually offers indications along these lines) until we discovered that the category was useless. In Márkus' and Vajda's writings on Wittgenstein, Husserl, perception, etc., as well as in parts of *Everyday Life* dealing with epistemological aspects, it became evident that we were unable to accept the *Ontology's* outspoken hostility to epistemology in the form of the alternative of *either* ontology *or* epistemology.

3 The emphasis on the idea of historical progress is an indispensable principle of socialism and of the practice aiming toward socialism – a principle that gives order and 'meaning' to the past in terms of *today's historical situation*. If the selection and arrangement is right, this principle must have a 'basis' in past history; therefore it is not arbitrarily selected, but it cannot lay claim to any inevitable historical sequence. Accordingly, we rejected the naturalistic 'conception of growth' even in economics.

4 In this connection we interpreted *historical determinism* only in the sense that for human beings born into ready-made conditions, there is a range of movement limited only by these conditions – a narrow or broad circle of possibilities of development and alternatives, whose realization depends only on the totality of consciously or unconsciously integrating human activities. We rejected 'socio-historical laws' 'independent' of human activities and their utility within a non-naturalistic conception.

5 *The central role of the concept of value within our perspective*. At this point we can formulate our relation toward the *Ontology* less polemically because, as readers of these 'Notes' can see, we found no truly consistent conception of value in Lukács. Basically, he was undecided whether to regard value as *only an economic category* or also as a 'moral' one. In his youth – as can be seen from the *Heidelberg Manuscripts* which came to light after his death – this category was crucial. After he became a Marxist, however, he came to regard the whole question as 'ideological mystification'. But on this point the *Ontology* vacillated between the two poles, neither of which (nor both together) we shared with him, as was most clearly formulated by Heller after certain debates and in agreement with all of us: value is a very general category belonging to the origin and essence of society. The discussion that ensued concerning this category concretized the divergent interpretation of *ideal objectifications* both in Lukács' *Ontology* and in our common view.

Since objections about content always involve *methodological* divergences of opinion, it is not surprising that our conversations were summed up in a 'definition' of philosophy that did not coincide at all with the 'practice' of the *Ontology*. The formulation is contained in Márkus' 1968 article on 'Debates and Tendencies in Marxist Philosophy' which, paradoxically enough, characterized our common perspective as 'socio-ontological'. This article was so much the result of our conversations and debates that all of us could literally call its conclusions our own:

> The task of philosophy consists in shaping the alternatives of the *present* into conscious questions (and answers) by investigating today's underlying conflicts within the *total development* of mankind, by discovering the relation of alternatives to historically created values and thereby explaining their significance, their 'meaning', from the viewpoint of all of human development. In this sense, philosophy is really nothing more than a constantly renewed 'summary of the general results . . . that can be abstracted from the observation of man's historical development' (Marx) – a summary that always originates in the present and is the real ontology of social existence understood as history from the viewpoint of the development of 'human beings'.

We are, of course, aware that this formulation is not yet an answer but at best the outline of an answer not to the question: 'What is "the right" structure?' but to 'How do we visualize a possible Marxist philosophical "structure" on the given level of the world situation of human thought, in the context of lessons drawn from many bitter fiascos, but at the same time from ever renewed reform efforts?' We cannot deal extensively with this here but can only indicate where it contradicts the real, though not internally resolved, aspirations of the *Ontology* and how our conception of the nature and structure of philosophy (i.e., *its methodological principle*) tried to answer the previous problems of content.

If the question were asked whether in the debates with Lukács on the *Ontology* all objections were formulated in this coherent form, our answer would be negative. As already mentioned, Lukács knew where our views deviated from his on all topics. A previously mentioned circumstance prevented us from putting forth a summary thesis-like formulation of our views. Lukács had asked for our collaboration to help him correct *his own work*. Personal gratitude and respect for him, along with customary collegial spirit, required that we regard the given manuscript (and not our own divergent opinion) as the point of departure. So a remarkable situation arose, especially after the series of conversations on the *Ontology*. Our point of view on ideal objectifications received a strange confirmation which was also unpleasant for us: once again, it turned out that even if what has already been expressed disposes over no 'material body', it is present and influences thinking as well as action. In the given case, it influenced philosophical action. For another year and a half, until Lukács' illness worsened, the discussions attracted wider and wider circles. By then it had become clear that there were *coherent divergences* and, consequently, the discussions became more and more heated. The man who later would stare death in the face with Spartan equanimity often referred in his last years to Goethe's Aristotelean experience and said repeatedly: 'The developed entelechy really has a right to immortality.' In this 'really' we understood the touching flirtation with the idea of physical immortality hidden behind the cloak of impersonal professionalism. We understood the personal message of trust, so unusual for him: we were happy because this message showed us that his will lived on. But we could not console ourselves with the idea that developed entelechies were *in fact* immortal. In view of the increasingly sharp theoretical debates and the ever more personal atmosphere towards the end of his life, overcast by the painful shadow of extreme old age, another question is justified: why didn't we bring our differences of opinion before the public? Aside from circumstances we do not wish to elaborate on now and which could be considered secondary factors in our decision, we agreed not to formulate *during his lifetime*, as a public polemic against him, the things we had repeatedly said to him in private.[5] He was informed of our decision and agreed fully with it. Did this create some kind of unprincipled unity? To what extent this unity was principled or unprincipled is not for us to judge. About our own motives, with which Lukács was in full accord, we can only say that it was and remains our conviction that there can and ought to be intellectual differences – even essential ones – between philosophers who are in fundamental agreement. Within the same 'school' or the same theoretical circle the existence of marked oppositions under the sign of theoretical divergences and quests for solutions is perfectly normal. What is required is only that they be made clear: one must neither dissolve them nor give up the fundamental ideological unity and solidarity because of them.

'I am a friend of Plato, but truth is a better friend still' – for millennia this proverb has stood as the signpost at every philosophical crossroads. And since the 'Notes' incontestably signal a parting of philosophical ways – within a more comprehensive final and unbroken unity – it would be natural for us to quote this as the conclusion to this Introduction. We will not do so, for reasons which were transformed into moral imperatives by personal experiences and memories affecting our whole lives. In socialism we chose a goal that guides our activity and in which there is no absolute split between truth as an objectification hovering above human circumstances and human relations as ephemeral entities bearing little or no value content and regardable, from the viewpoint of philosophy, as negligible quantities. The great thinker was our friend, and he best proved this in discussions about the work intended as his masterpiece. Those who showed him the inner contradictions of the work he had written as the crown and legacy of his philosophy were the same persons whom he had introduced to the mother-tongue of philosophy and who had learned to think within his intellectual aura. Therefore his attitude in responding became an unforgettable message and obligation for us. His cool discipline did not reveal a trace of the great burden of his destiny, in many respects tragic, that loomed ahead. He had to begin his work of summing up at an age when Hobbes could do nothing more than play tennis. Here his marginal comments, which expressed his agreement or showed his intention to consider ideas, are our witnesses, since for the first time in his life he was contemplating, on the basis of remarks by students, whether or not to correct or revise the work he had thought to be finished. His Socratic joviality, which he had adopted in old age from his favourite sage, and his inexhaustible energy of argumentation, which seemed to belie his years even in his physical gestures, together with such understanding of the opposing viewpoint, with such respect for polemical philosophical intentions, gave those evenings an unforgettable atmosphere.

Georg Lukács firmly believed in the truth of his standpoint, and yet when we claimed the truth for our side and outlined our views, which were opposed to his in decisive respects, he accepted them as justified *though* contestable. The basic intellectual attitude we shared, summed up in the term 'revolutionary tolerance', uncompromisingly rejects every perspective that does not seek a liberated human race or regards this 'regulative idea' as an obsolete illusion of this century and feels no duty towards it. Our basic intellectual attitude supports a theoretical collaboration based on critical understanding with all efforts that, as witnessed by their words and deeds, aim at the realization of these goals. This 'revolutionary tolerance' had long lived in us as an intention, but now it was crystallized into a concrete principle in the course of these conversations. This was the *philosophical message* of the long debate that transformed our unfading memory of our teacher and friend into a didactic model of thought.

NOTES ON THE FIRST PART OF THE *ONTOLOGY*

I

In our judgement, the first part contains two ontologies, contradictory in many essential points. The first regards the process that begins with the humanization of man through labour as 'necessary in reality' (incidentally, we do *not* understand how the 'real necessity' of any process is distinguished from logical necessity), as a process in the economic sphere which, understood as the 'essential sphere', is *always completely realized* through human mediations and, on the phenomenal level, with numerous variations, even through accidents.

The second conception: with the humanization of man through labour, there arose the *possibility* of the development of the three fundamental factors.[6] In 'prehistory' these tendencies develop independently of human will, but by no means necessarily. Since the continuity of human history is assured by the objectifications of needs, abilities, activities, etc., the field of operation of human action is determined by the objectifications that have already been made. This field of operation therefore determines alternative possibilities, whose solution, undertaken in this or that manner, decides the course of development for longer historical periods. We can speak of necessity only with regard to the inner movement of some formations, not in relation to historical transitions.

The most important factors pointing to the first conception of the *Ontology*

We drew first from the chapter on Marx, for although most statements of the previous chapters point in this direction, the coexistence of the two ontological conceptions is nowhere as clearly perceptible as there.

1 You state for the first time on pp. 295 – 6 (but repeat it frequently later on – in fact, the whole of the second part of the Marx chapter is expressly built on this), that the economic sphere is the *essence* of the process of reproduction (it is at the same time also the terrain of necessity), but everything else belongs to the *phenomenal* sphere (and accordingly constitutes the terrain of contingency). Consequently, capitalism and socialism differ only in the phenomenal sphere (which, incidentally, most drastically contradicts the paper on democratization). [8]

2 The sharp distinction between social existence and social consciousness: this is a problem extending through the entire work, which is given many completely different solutions in all the chapters (often the various solutions are intermixed even in a single chapter). In the first chapter the relationship of reality (*Wirklichkeit*), being (*Sein*) and reflection remains unclarified. On page 4: 'If this [the central position of the dialectical reflection of objective reality] is neglected, then there necessarily results a constant intermingling of objective reality and its ontologically always directly subjective reflection.' In the chapter on Marx, page 306: 'Marx everywhere sharply separates the two components: social reality, which exists independently of whether it is more or less correctly known, and the method of its most adequate understanding possible.' We would like to point out that in the chapter on labour, consciousness becomes a specific form of *non-being* (p. 481) and *non-reality* (p. 476). From the above-mentioned distinction between being and consciousness (or reality and consciousness!) it follows that in several places Marx's statement 'They don't know it, but they do it' is understood not only as a typical phenomenon of prehistory but as a *universal socio-ontological fact*. In our opinion, all this is incongruous with statements pointing in the direction of the second conception of ontology, claiming that human consciousness does not have an epiphenomenal

character but has a decisive socio-ontological relevance, as it turns out later in the chapter on ideology.

3 The course of history is constituted in the laws that determine its entirety and whose negation leads to irrationalism (p. 401). Most noticeably in the passage on page 376: 'the sequence and separation of economic formations, the kinds of class struggle possible in them, are in their great underlying tendencies strictly determined by the general laws of the economy.' The consequence is the complete qualitative identification of natural laws and social laws in statements to the effect that nature and society differ only in their complexity, in the quantitative divergence of their effective factors. The application of physical analogies in the treatment of social phenomena (e.g., statistical laws) points in the same direction.

4 The first three chapters point in their entirety in this direction (with the exception of the analyses of Wittgenstein and Heidegger and the passage on religious needs), by raising it to a basic question whether philosophy *occupies itself* with epistemology or with ontology, and not whether its point of departure is the isolated (necessarily exclusively knowing) individual, or social totality. That a philosophical standpoint based on ontology can be just as negative and amenable to manipulation as one based on epistemology is not even considered (with the only exception of an ontology that starts from the conception of transcendence). The denial of all possible forms of ideal objectifications seems especially important from this viewpoint (cf. the chapter on Hartmann), since Comrade Lukács evaluates even the mere *existence* of Hartmann's natural ontology as a positive thing, while at the same time proving that this natural ontology *can* provide *no* basis for a materialistic socio-ontology.

The factors pointing to the second conception of ontology appear first when Comrade Lukács criticizes traditional Marxism: (1) cf. the ontological relevance of consciousness (p. 411); (2) on the 'Homer problem':[9] social continuity cannot be reduced to economic development (pp. 436ff); (3) traditional Marxism replaced the alternatives by a mechanical conception of necessity; (4) the false dualism of being and consciousness in traditional Marxism (p. 425).

II

The first three chapters raise problems that are not specifically socio-ontological but generally ontological and, occasionally, naturally ontological. But with respect to natural ontology these attempts at a solution contain several contradictions. (1) A few passages give the appearance that philosophy, in reference to the natural sciences, has the task of criticizing them. But in that case it is unclear whence this critique could proceed. It often seems as if the basis of this critique were the standpoint of common sense. (2) Elsewhere the argument gives the impression that philosophy itself is called on to solve certain problems of transition between various spheres of nature. (3) Sometimes a conception seems to glimmer through that the task of natural ontology is the synthesis of the facts and laws discovered by the various natural sciences, the construction of a total image of nature. (4) In many cases, however, a conception appears to the effect that philosophy must not meddle at all in problems of the knowledge of nature.

Consequently, it remains unclear whether a natural philosophy is needed or whether philosophy can be satisfied with adopting the world image presented by natural science (presupposing, at any rate, the existence of nature). But if we assume the standpoint that a separate natural ontology is indispensable, then we must decide how it is to be conceived. In this respect, there are again two different standpoints. (1) Natural ontology formulates the most general laws of nature (i.e., such as apply to nature's great spheres of being), namely, that laws undergo only a change of form in the transition from one sphere to the other. (2) Natural ontology is clearly historical, i.e., it describes the particular categorical structures of the respective spheres of being.

In regard to natural ontology, two factors appear with which we can in no way agree: (a) the positing of a universal evolution of nature (this inescapably implies teleology!); (b) a concept of being (*Sein*) so general that is presupposes only a quantitative difference in regard to the reality of nature and social reality, to contrast the concept of consciousness with this being. (Being and reflection: the sharp distinction of reality and reflection without considering that reflection is an element of the social sphere of being itself.)

III

A few important partial remarks. The critique of Einstein (from p. 46 and, later, pp. 103ff), which deals with no questions affecting the basic conception of the book, should be omitted. This would be all the more advisable since Einstein's statements on the relation of physics and geometry are not suited for the critique of neo-positivism. For neo-positivists assume a diametrically opposite position on the question. According to them, mathematics (including geometry) consists of analytical sentences in contrast to the synthetic-empirical character of physics. Classical neo-positivism is characterized precisely by its sharp contrasting of geometry and physics and not at all by the claim that geometry is part of physics. Among positive remarks made in the course of the critique there are also some that are not exact: e.g., 'First, geometrical statements are not at all logically proven. . . . Secondly, such sentences need no substantiation in physical reality.'

On page 133, there is another unwarranted statement in the critique of Einstein. We have in mind here the space – time continuum. Einstein repeatedly emphasized that the four-dimensional space – time continuum constitutes a 'homogeneous', undifferentiated co-ordinate system only in mathematical formalism (which would correspond with the comments on mathematics as a homogeneous system), but in physics the four co-ordinates are not equivalent in their interpretation; the co-ordinates of time and space are not interchangeable there, for the simple reason that time is irreversible.

In the chapter on Hegel, it is not clear what you mean by Hegel's two conceptions of ontology. That the philosophy of nature was described on p. 205 as the high point of Hegel's system completely retracts the basic idea of the book *The Young Hegel*.

THE CHAPTER ON LABOUR

I

In our view, the greatest defect of this chapter is that the problem of objectification remains unsolved – indeed, is not even posed – which is the same reproach that Comrade Lukács levelled against his own *History and Class Consciousness*. This has severe structural consequences for the whole conception. Labour appears exclusively as the positing and the realization of the goal. Not a word is said to the effect that labour is an act that creates social objectivity, and so the side of labour that, according to Marx's view, brings about the historicity of social being is neglected. As a result, the problem of the genesis of individual goal-positing hardly appears at all. It follows that the individual workers' goal is either a reflection of biological needs – transformed into consciousness – this assumption excludes the development of needs, and implies that human needs cannot at all emerge – or, if this goal is the autonomous product of consciousness, then it is consciousness that creates and carries sociability.

Our proposal is that Comrade Lukács insert a new section analysing the problems of the objectification of the labour process, the sociability of the goals posited in the labour process and the historical genesis of needs.

II

Neglecting the problem of objectification[10] causes difficult problems in the treatment of the alternative character of the labour process. Since the social goals objectified in the tools or means of labour and their genesis are excluded from the scope of analysis, the goal of the labour process always appears as something pre-given, and the alternatives of the working individual are restricted to a choice of means and methods for achieving the pre-established goal. On p. 488 Comrade Lukács even states that only the means have an alternative character. This narrows down the whole field of alternatives: alternatives exist only for the individual. No social alternatives can exist within this conception. Of course, if we interpret alternatives always as an act of consciousness

(p. 484), always as a recognized alternative possibility (p. 488), then we must necessarily differentiate the social alternatives from the objective social possibilities. But the reduction of the problem of alternatives to the mere aspect of means leaves no room, on the social level, either for conscious alternatives or for objective possibilities. This narrowing down of the alternative problem would be eliminated by the insertion of the recommended new section: it would become evident that the sphere of possible goals is determined by the objectifications which previous generations produced in history, but within this sphere working individuals in the labour process can themselves choose not only the means for realizing the goals, but also the goals which they want to achieve.

III

That the various fundamental categories of social ontology came about in labour does not mean that labour can serve as the model for all heterogeneous forms of activity: the categorical structures of various forms of activity are obviously fundamentally different, as is clearly shown later in the analysis of reproduction.

IV

The considerations on the relation of theory and practice (pp. 513 – 16) should be omitted, since they are not at all clear. Anyway, the whole problem is analysed where Comrade Lukács deals with ideology. Here – if we consider the viewpoint of the *Aesthetics* – the question is completely out of place. In the everyday forms of activity, theory and practice form an inseparable unity.

V

Likewise we recommend that the analysis of the category of value be moved to the chapter on reproduction. Here it fully suffices if you reiterate the following (p. 516ff.): moments of the normative, of the *ought* (*Sollen*) appear already in labour. To us this proposal seems justified because there are many contradictions in the analysis of value, both within this chapter and among the different chapters. A few examples: you claim on p. 526 that value is nothing but the principle of evaluation of the manufactured product; at the same time it turns out, on p. 546, that value does not necessarily contain a conscious factor. Or you claim several times that value (all sorts of value, value in general) is reducible to utility and success (incidentally, in our opinion, utility is only an everyday concept: philosophy can find no use for it), but later, with the appearance of moral value, you claim that this cannot be derived from utility. In the chapter on reproduction you even go so far as to regard economic development as neutral (p. 636). The problem of value conflicts remains unresolved. We find it highly problematic moreover, that you divide values into only two groups, economic or moral.

We will return to the problem of value in reference to the chapter on reproduction, but at this point we wish to recommend Heller's work on value and history,[11] which tries, on the basis of Márkus' 'Anthropology',[12] to outline a conception of value.

VI

We have very serious doubts about the proposed solution to the problem of freedom. First, we consider the critique of Engels (pp. 571ff.) to be petty. It does not seize the main point of the view of freedom depicted by Engels. It should be emphasized that here only the freedom actualized in labour was taken into consideration, i.e., man's freedom in regard to nature (social freedom has another meaning even ontologically), and not the problem of freedom in general. Still, we find the solution, even within the framework of these limited objectives, completely one-sided: man's freedom towards his own instincts is also a factor in this respect. (In the later chapters it becomes clear that one cannot speak at all about freedom in general: one can only speak of freedoms.)

VII

We wish to call your attention to the most important parts in which the 'ontology of necessity' is introduced even in the chapter on labour: (a) Consciousness as non-existent (p. 481). (b) The positings of consciousness are, as such, non-existent acts (p. 482). (c) The natural necessity of social events (p. 582). (d) Essence – appearance (p. 542). (e) *Dynamis*, as non-being, non-reality (pp. 485ff.: the plan of a factory) – that something really is, is not determined by its objectivity and its form, but by the function it plays in society. (f) We cannot agree at all with the reduction of consciousness to the reflection of reality: if consciousness were really just this reflection, how would we understand that the realization of that which is formed in consciousness produces something new? (g) The juxtaposition of manipulation and science (p. 574). Practice based on the sciences can also be manipulated!

VIII

A few other problems: (a) We consider it an unfortunate formulation (p. 63) that the object of the ontological positing is either rightly understood or one can speak of no positing. False consciousness! (b) The conception of the *Aesthetics* that science grows directly out of the labour experience is sharply contradicted on pp. 468 – 70. The immediate experiences of labour can also be built into myths.

THE CHAPTER ON REPRODUCTION

I

Theoretical Problems and Objections

1 *Freedom and alternatives.* On p. 623 you write: 'as regards the general ontology of society, the problem of freedom means only that the individual's
situation is increasingly determined by accidents once general economic laws
come to the foreground.' But on p. 624 you claim that it is only the *appearance*
of freedom. Consequently, no ontological relevance can be ascribed to freedom.
We cannot accept this at all. The increasing role of chance in individual decisions would, of course, actually create only the appearance of freedom. But the
problem of *social freedom* cannot be treated in relation to the categories
'necessity – chance'.

As a result of the use of labour as a direct model, the alternative character of
all individual decisions and the problem of individual *autonomy* are not differentiated. The idea of autonomy (whereby one could later return to the real problems of freedom) does not appear at all in this chapter. In fact, the passage on
p. 740 gives the appearance that Comrade Lukács denies the autonomy of individual men. From the fact that questions are always already objectively posed
(here, too, it is not irrelevant what mediations are used to answer them), it does
not follow that man reacts to these questions unmoved by his own inner im-
pulses!

2 We have already indicated in connection with the chapter on labour that the
lack of a separate discussion of social objectifications raises difficult theoretical
problems. One is that *the role of consciousness remains unclarified.* While up to this
point one of our most important objections was that Comrade Lukács contrasts
objective evolution with its merely subjective reflection (consciousness), we can
find here exactly the opposite extreme: *consciousness appears as the bearer of the continuity of social being.* Statements on pp. 647 – 50 allow two interpretations: (a)
Social being-in-itself is also an objective and necessary process, independent of
consciousness, and is merely modified by human consciousness: 'Thus, the process' objective laws are by no means abolished, but at times they are modified,
even decisively.' The statement on p. 647 also points to the same idea, whereby
the meaning of the claim 'without consciousness no sociability' is as follows:
sociability rises to the level of being-for-itself only by attaining consciousness.
(b) In social evolution in general (i.e., from the moment when man ceases to be
a dumb genus, which can, in our opinion, mean only this: he ceases to be a brute
animal) consciousness unambiguously takes on the directing, leading role. Page
647: The continuity of the social progress is guided and steered by the forms
and contents of consciousness; consciousness is the organ of continuity. Page

648: The specific trait of social being, in contrast with all other forms of being, is consciousness as the medium of continuity. Page 743 also speaks of the leading role of consciousness.

In our opinion, this vacillation between two extremes stems from the neglecting of the objectifications (on pp. 652 and 665 the role of the bearer of continuity is assumed by language!).

3 The categorical confusion in the treatment of genericness (*Gattungsmässigkeit*) is another consequence resulting from the neglect of objectifications (pp. 635 – 8, and pp. 645 – 61). The categories of *dumb (stumme) genericness*, *genericness in itself (an sich)* and *genericness for itself (für sich)* are not clearly differentiated. Actually, the category of dumb genericness is identified (although not unambiguously) with genericness in itself on the one hand, that of no-longer dumb genericness with genericness for itself on the other. The result is statements such as: the transcendence above the state of dumb genus has its source in the world market (p. 636): no-longer-dumb genericness still appears in dumb form (p. 645). etc. At the same time, we find formulations such as the following: man's genericness-for-himself really originates with labour (p. 646).

Besides the fact that the general line of thought is completely confused by this, our basic objection is that the essential idea expressed here, that genericness-for-itself can only be a category applicable to all mankind, contradicts the basic conception of the *Aesthetics*. If science and art are for themselves generic objectifications, then it would follow from the above remarks that they could not have come about before the existence of the world market.

The identification of dumb genericness with genericness-in-itself also leads to the identification of ontological reproduction with biological reproduction and the identification of the last two with the economic sphere (p. 706), which we cannot accept.

4 Our basic objections are that Comrade Lukács – leaving the specific terrain of social ontology undetermined – excludes several fundamental questions of reproduction from ontology. On page 620 you state that politics is not a part of social ontology (although you analyse it extensively in the chapter on ideology); in numerous passages (and increasingly more in the following chapters) you refer many questions – basic ones from the viewpoint of social evolution – to ethics, etc. In our view, social ontology should comprehend society as a whole, and if detailed studies of a few parts belong to special disciplines, this cannot mean that any parts of the whole transcend ontology.

This chapter too clearly shows that the problem of value remains completely unresolved. On page 630 value grows with existential necessity from labour; while on page 636 value is ontologically secondary; the economy (and production in general) is neutral. On page 638 value appears as being-in-itself; and on page 756 all values are transferred to ethics: they lie outside ontology. A few statements clearly exclude the problem of value from ontology: on page 726 the separation of ontology and value is set at the foundation of Marx's materialist view of social being. Here you claim that all normative statements are arbitrary.

5 We do not agree with you in understanding the social totality as a complex – composed of complexes – within which only one of the complexes (the economic one) is dynamic and so powerful that it determines the movements of all other complexes (pp. 700 – 1).

II

Theoretical Objections on a Few Partial Problems

1 The treatment of the division of labour is inadequate. It contains several statements that contradict Marx's ideas: e.g. you identify the origin of the division of labour with the origin of handicrafts; on page 613 you say that the technical division of labour (what is that?) originated in primitive times. On page 614, then, Marx's idea is explicated to the effect that the division of labour came about with the separation of mental and physical labour.

On the division of labour we make two recommendations. (a) Use Marx's distinction between natural and social divisions of labour, or rather natural and naturally given (*naturwüchsig*) divisions of labour, as your point of departure. (b) Do not interrupt the analysis of the problem of the division of labour by interjecting the treatment of needs, food, sexuality and education. These parts should be removed and dealt with before the study of the division of labour.

2 Our problems with respect to the analysis of language are as follows. (a) We disagree that language supposedly evolves further: we do not understand what this is supposed to mean at all. For what you state on page 593 – that language is becoming capable of naming ever more objects – does not bear scrutiny. It follows from that nature of language that every object ought to be nameable. (b) The relation of thought and language remains unclarified. Consequently, on page 665 language turns out to be reflection. What does it reflect? (c) On page 653, animal language and conventional human signs cannot be identified! Humans have agreed on conventional signs *by means of language*.

3 Antiquity cannot be called a slave society; especially its essence should not be seen in slave-holding (pp. 621, 711, and throughout the whole chapter). On the last point, where you deal with the development of social formations on the basis of Marx, you also characterize it in a completely different manner.

4 We have problems with the analysis of law. Our main objection is that your judgement of its role is completely negative. You never mention that the origin of positive law constituted great progress. You also do not take into considera-

tion the fact that persistence in legal forms, even in the contemporary historical period, plays a far more positive role than a negative one. One cannot look down at law from the heights of communism. A few unacceptable details are also linked with this basic view (p. 688). The concept of justice is said to arise as a reaction to the formal character of law (you disregard the fact that there is not only a moral but also a legal justice, and that the two are not identical). Law appears purely as a means of class oppression. You do not consider law as the off-spring of Greek democracy. You brand every effort at the rational regulation of law as reactionary positivism, without considering how significant the French Revolution's return to Roman law has been, etc.

Other remarks on the question of law: (a) An analysis of the relation of law and property is missing. (b) It is not true that law and ethics were identical in antiquity (p. 676)! (c) What does it mean to say that law is a reflection (pp. 683 – 4)? And what about the other statement, that it reflects the economy (p. 686)? (d) It is not true that morality arose as a reaction to the formal character of law (p. 688).

III

A few of the objections already listed are also connected with the problem of necessity. Other such passages include, on p. 591, the stagnation of the productive forces as a mere appearance. The development of the productive forces always takes place necessarily, and undeterredly. (But from p. 599 on, the line of thought is reversed, and you condemn the point you have just made as positivism.) Secondly, although the sequence of social formations is not pre-ordained, it is necessary.

THE CHAPTER ON IDEOLOGY

I

1 We recommend that Comrade Lukács omit the first two points of the chapter – except for passages discussed below, which should be treated elsewhere. The abridgement of the book – which we have already agreed with – would, in any case, be desirable, and the two main points mentioned add hardly anything new to what was depicted in the preceding chapters. The first point (the ideal [*das Ideelle*] in the economy) is almost entirely repeated from the chapter on labour but is at the same time less clearly organized. The second point (on the ontology of the ideal moment) likewise reiterates earlier points without providing the analysis of the ideal moments. The content of the categories dealt with should be more precisely circumscribed. In the text, objec-tification (*Vergegenständlichung*) refers to the process of objectifying human abilities in general, and also (in objective and non-objective form) objectified

human abilities themselves, etc. A distinction must absolutely be made between these, otherwise the reader cannot find his way in the text. The category of externalization (*Entäusserung*) also has two meanings: it means the development of the subject's abilities in history through his objective activities, but also the *way and manner* the subject is expressed in his objective activity. Moreover, the reader ought also to be reminded that here Comrade Lukács does not use the term 'externalization' in Hegel's and Marx's sense of the word – as a synonym for alienation (*Entfremdung*) – as he did in *The Young Hegel* (there alienation is called *Entäusserung* even in the chapter title).

2 On pp. 873 – 5, you deal with the problem of the historicity of needs. The point ought to be transposed to the chapter on labour; we expressly suggested in that context that this problem should be dealt with there.

II

Here we summarize our remarks on the use of the pair of categories essence – appearance. Our main points have already been made in connection with the previous chapter. The altogether too ambiguous use of this pair of categories extends through the entire work. Now we list the most frequently occurring interpretations, with the help of examples. (a) Essence is surplus value, whose appearance is profit. (b) Essence is capitalism, whose appearances are its concrete forms that differ depending on time and place (French, English, etc). (c) Essence consists of three underlying tendencies of human history – among their appearances is everything that is determined by these factors or constructed upon them. (d) Essence is the fact of nature that the Earth turns on its axis, while its appearance is the Sun rising and setting. (e) The development of essential human forces has the emptying of the individual as an appearance.

Since Comrade Lukács uses the pair of categories in such different contexts, its content is completely blurred. In our view, it deals with very different things. A more precise contentual differentiation would be all the more necessary since the grouping of unrelated problems should not be done for merely semantic reasons. One of the most striking examples of this occurs when Comrade Lukács deals with Goethe's question of duration and change immediately after the analysis of the relation between surplus value and profit. But the latter bears no relation to the former: what does it mean to say that surplus value is duration in the change of profit? What is more important is that this ambiguous use of the category pair results in the confusion of principles.

1 The use of these categories, as in example (a) above (Marx also used the two categories in this sense as coherent and systematically applied technical terms), uncovers a social ontological problem of fundamental importance: namely, that as long as the teleological positings move in the phenomenal sphere, the given

formation cannot be transcended. (For Marx, bourgeois political economy is the reflection of the phenomenal world.) Once this interpretation of the *essence – appearance* category pair is terminologically confused with other problems (e.g., the relation between content and form), then Marx's entire conception loses its sharpness.

2 The problem of essence and existence plays a fundamental role in Marx (the *Ontology* also points to this in precisely the same terminology in the analysis of Engels' critique of Feuerbach). But, again to preserve Marx's distinct contributions, this problem should be sharply distinguished from the problem referred to in point 1 above.

III

The whole chapter is now dominated by the second ontology, but here too some formulations tend to contradict this conception: on page 980, the development of essence is independent of teleological positings. The statement that the total historical process reveals a non-teleological character does not mean that anything could happen in society which is not the result of teleological positings. Page 1000: human decisions only speed up or slow down the developmental process of necessity – essence. *Wesen* is determined independently of these. By whom or by what? Again on page 1000: objective social determination and human activity are mutually factors of development. Page 1013: economic development is essentially necessary. (This clearly contradicts the thesis that it is a question of tendencies.) Page 1023: the development of essence is independent of human activity. Page 1025: the area of necessity and essence, the area of freedom and appearance. Page 1027: the area of necessity is, even in communism, independent of conscious positings (cf. the essay on democratization).

IV

Other Problems

1 The concept of ideology depicted on pp. 951 – 2 is too general: if ideology means only that every appearance is determined by the circumstances of its origin, then ideology is identical with sociability or with reality itself.

2 On page 955 the statement is made that ideology exists only in societies with opposing interest groups. This does not fit the facts: e.g., magic is also ideology. On the other hand, Comrade Lukács also holds the view that there will be ideologies even in communism.

3 Page 967: the functional interpretation of ideology should not lead to

regarding the relation of ideology and truth as completely irrelevant. The problem should absolutely be dealt with.

4 Page 989: we simply do not understand the statement that law is epistemologically false.

5 Why does politics belong to the phenomenal sphere (p. 994)? In addition, we have several other problems about the ideas on politics. Politics is not clearly differentiated from political ideology. Problems of power and of the state are missing from the treatment of politics. The problem of the content of political objectives is not even raised. So politics is equated with tactics, for the positing of a right politics becomes identical with a successful political positing.

6 We cannot accept that reification (*Verdinglichung*) is nothing but the congealing of processes. The problem is not an epistemological one. What was said in *History and Class Consciousness* is still valid today in this regard (p. 1052).

THE CHAPTER ON ALIENATION

I

We disagree with the *basic conception* of this chapter: according to it, alienation (or more precisely, alienations) is a category that applies only to individuals, i.e., it is a theoretical category of personality but not an historical one. (What you stated in the last chapter of *The Young Hegel* and in the monograph on Marx contradicts this.) In this chapter of the *Ontology* alienation is a phenomenon in all societies only to the extent that in them the majority of individuals live a generally alienated life. The statements on alienation in *The German Ideology* contradicting such an individual-oriented interpretation are not even mentioned in this chapter. From *The German Ideology* it is clear that in Marx alienation is not a collective term for various negative phenomena, but the main factor of prior history: 'This congealing of social activity, this consolidation of our own product into an objective power over ourselves, that grows beyond our control, frustrates our expectations, voids our calculations, is one of the main factors in previous historical development. . . .'[13]

The following is also clearly formulated for the first time in *The German Ideology*: that the social division of labour and alienation constitute (even in the mature Marx) inseparable factors of prior history. The chapter, however, does not analyse the problem of the division of labour at all. We would like to remind you that in your monograph on Marx you did not discuss alienation with reference to the individual, despite the fact that there you studied Marx's development only up to the *Economic and Philosophic Manuscripts*, where Marx regards alienation, if not by reference to the individual, at least from the standpoint of the individual.

Of course, one of the problems stressed in the chapter – the discrepancy be-tween the development of human abilities and the development of human per-sonality (a phenomenon produced by alienation) – is the way alienation is mediated. In Marx, however, it is a question not of a discrepancy between the ability and personality of the same man but of a discrepancy between the development of objectified *abilities* of the human *genus*, and the impoverishment of the individual's personality (and ability).

As a result of the basic conception in Comrade Lukács, the struggle against alienation and the struggle against subjective projections of alienation are iden-tified, which turns out to be equal to – and likewise we cannot agree with this – the struggle of the individual against his own alienation. We also regard – within the world of alienation – the struggle against the crippling of per-sonalities and other effects of alienation as important factors. But this is not the struggle against my own alienation. Comrade Lukács goes so far – especially on the first point – as to state: the individual is capable of abolishing his own alienations even independently of his concrete social situation. But this can only mean the transcendence of alienation in consciousness.

II

In regard to two categories, we sense underlying conceptual unclarities.
1 *Genericness.* Neither the category of genericness-in-itself nor that of genericness-for-itself is clearly explained. The use of the two categories gives the appearance of being applicable to the human genus (indeed, even to the historical process) and at the same time also to single human individuals. As to the social process, genericness-in-itself seems to mean irresistible economic development (p. 1132), in contrast to genericness-for-itself, which means the consciousness built upon the genericness-in-itself, the known objectifications, while in reference to the individual genericness-in-itself would mean particular-ly in contrast to the non-particular individual dedicated to a cause, to genericness-for-itself. In one place (p. 1130) you speak of the genericness-in-itself and genericness-for-itself of the artist as a human individual.

2 *Reification.* Again, it is not clear what this means. It seems – exactly as in the ideology chapter – to be a stepping out of the process, the rigidification of pro-cess, but at the same time it is also identical with false consciousness, with com-modity fetishism, etc.

III

We do not agree with you regarding the transcendence of alienation as a 'by-product' of socialist revolution. Your work on Marx, your essay on democ-ratization, etc., are built on the correct (in our opinion) conception that the tran-scendence of alienation is a fundamental moment of communism, as communism is a society without alienation – i.e., unalienated, genuine history. However, in many places of your political analysis the insight breaks through the fact that the revolutionary movements of our day are directed expressly against alienation.

Translated by David J. Parent

NOTES

1   These remarks are very sketchy. All data are reconstructed from memory; later philological studies will have to undertake an exact reconstruction of the genesis of Lukács' work on the basis of his copious correspondence.

2   These five theoretical chapters resulted from the omission of the chapters on the ontological views of neo-positivism and religion and on Hegel and Hartmann. Despite the title, the chapter on Marx is systematic rather than historical and is closely connected with the chapters on work, reproduction, ideology and alienation.

3   This systematization is 'extensional' because it determines the object and task of Marxist philosophy by defining Marxist philosophy – by contrast with the *particularity* of the phenomena studied by the specialized sciences – as the contemplation of the *most general structures and laws* of nature, society and thought.

4   These were: György Márkus, 'Marxism and "Anthropology"' (1965); Agnes Heller, 'Value and History' (1965), 'Everyday Life' (1968), *Towards a Marxist Theory of Value* (1969), published as a special issue of *Kinesis*, III, 1 (Spring 1971); Mihály Vajda, 'Objective View of Nature and Social Practice' (1966), 'On the Boundary of Myth and Reason' (1967); and Ferenc Fehér, 'Is the Novel Problematic? A Contribution to the Theory of the Novel', *Telos*, 15 (Spring 1973), pp. 47–74. Other philosophers and sociologists in Hungary at that time also held views close to our own. But here we speak only for ourselves.

5   Something should be said about 'secondary factors'. In *Deutsche Zeitschrift für Philosophie*, 11 (1969), R. Beyer published, under the title 'Marxist Ontology – an Idealistic Fashion Creation', a critique of the conversational, introductory summary of the *Ontology* that appeared in the book *Conversations with Georg Lukács* and in the lecture 'The Ontological Foundations of Human Thought and Action', written in 1970 for the Philosophical World Congress in Vienna, which briefly summarized the entire work. Although Beyer's critique, written in a decidedly libellous tone, did outline some aspects of the problematic of ontology as method and could have spurred on a philosophical discussion, Ferenc Fehér's reply on behalf of all of us in *Magyar Filozófiai Szemle*, 1 (1970), rejected the possibility of philosophical discussion with such a partner, who transformed a theoretical question into a thoroughly unfounded and malicious ideological and political denunciation.

6   The first factor is the tendency for the amount of work necessary for the physical reproduction of man constantly to decrease. The second factor is that the naturally given (*naturwüchsig*) is originally dominant in work. In later development work

becomes more and more socialized with the division of labour that springs from work and everything based on it. Social categories form, so to speak, an increasingly cohesive stratum that rises above the psychologically given existence of man and modifies him. The third factor is the progressively more developed integration of societies that belong together. (This and all other footnotes were written in 1975 to help the reader.)

7   Page references are given for the original typescript.

8   This is a reference to a manuscript on questions of socialist democratization written by Lukács in the second half of 1968. To this day only a short section of it has appeared in print under the title 'Lenin and the Question of the Transition Period', in *Lenin* (Budapest: Magvetö, 1970).

9   'But the difficulty lies not in understanding that the Greek arts and epic are bound up with certain forms of social development. The difficulty is that they still afford us artistic pleasure and in a certain respect they count as a valid norm and as an unattainable model.' Karl Marx, *Grundrisse*, trs. Martin Nicolaus (Harmondsworth – Baltimore: Penguin, 1973), p. 111.

10   Editors' note: the authors use *tárgyiasulás* (objectification) here in relation to work and *objektivàciò* (objectivation) in relation to the whole complex of the externalizations of various dimensions of human subjectivity.

11   Agnes Heller, 'Value and History', in *Alltag und Geschichte* (Berlin – Neuwied: Luchterhand, 1970), and *Towards a Marxist Theory of Value*.

12   György Márkus, 'Marxism and "Anthropology"'.

13   Karl Marx, *Werke*, vol. 18 (Berlin: Dietz – Verlag, 1958) p. 33.

7

Lukács' *Ontology:* a Metacritical Letter

GÁSPÁR M. TAMÁS

Nous sommes tous des idealistes allemands!
From Bloch's obituary for *Rouge*

Dear Agnes, Ferenc, György and Mihály!

When your criticism of Lukács' *Ontology* was published,[1] I signalled my
dissatisfaction in a letter. It was Ferenc Fehér who encouraged me to set out my
objections in more detail. As it happened, I was glad to seize this opportunity,
particularly as I was thus obliged to think through the problems to their end –
by contrast with those who regard Lukács, according to André Gluckmann's
memorable *aperçu*, as one of the *maîtres-penseurs* who are not worth reading.
You, however, lean towards the opposite extreme. By contrast even with
Lukács' own attitude, and as a result of your own intellectual biography, you
look upon him as a living partner in debate. The most serious failure of your
collective writing is that you do not treat the last phase of Lukács' work as an
objectivation, as a form, as merely the document of the history of an attitude.
This may be a moral stance, and it would blunt the edge of my polemics if I
considered as an object, on ideological grounds, what was (and is) subject – I
would be doing precisely the same as the philosophy that I abhor and try to ex-
pose. In this matter, however, the same ruthlessness is called for as that applied
by Lukács in his Dilthey obituary. Criticism has respect for the subject only if it
detects the generality in it that appears in the guise of sovereign self-
consciousness. You are confronted with a man who thinks on the level of sharp
self-consciousness, or so he contends. For my part, however, the alarming sign
is the extent of tradition and a certain type of ideological usage of language
which 'thinks itself' in one of the greatest thinkers of the century (and perhaps
the history of philosophy).

154

The dimensions of the failure are gigantic. The only representative modern philosopher of form and culture, Georg Lukács, like his protagonist, the young Hegel, embarked on the enterprise of rationalizing the unrationalizable. As a consequence, he had to attempt that which is beyond the limits of endurance of both form and logic, *the transformation of his choice into law*. I already hear the objection: is this not precisely what all philosophies do? But on this side of the Rhine all modern philosophies are philosophies of practice, whose formative principle is the categorical imperative, the principle of generalization. If my maxim can serve as a principle of 'general legislation', then we are already on our way towards the promised land, but this is true only if my maxim is indeed generalizable. To presuppose the 'legislation' of the maxim as something that has already been completed, to describe it as objectivity and to infer the rules of 'right' choice from it, this is precisely the structure that remains hidden in the Stalinist *diamat* and is revealed by Lukács' *Ontology*. Bloch's 'categorical optative' avoids this pitfall, but at the cost of eliminating all possibilities of a discursive description. In order to rescue the possibility of the description of objectivity, Lukács transforms his choice into law (practical schema) by *recognizing* the former as a law (ontological schema). The substratum of this recognition, of transforming practice into theory, choice into knowledge, is Being.

For Lukács, Being is simply a metaphor of everything in which his choice *can be recognized* as a law, as real, as realized, in which free choice appears as truth deducible from objectivity corroborated through (self)-affirmation. Of course, certain other types of objectivity are conceivable too, from which choices and options different from his are deducible. All actions and social facts disapproved of by the philosopher offer proof of this. These objectivities and types of Being are of second-rate quality. Being proper is that which supports the conclusions that can be drawn from the domain of 'species values' (*gattungsmässige Werte*) – in other words, from Lukács' own value choice, his voluntary option. The contrasted sphere of Being (more precisely, the statements made about it) will be less objective or will simply cease to be objective altogether. According to Lukács, what is Being and what is object(ivity) cannot be defined by epistemology that has been enlarged into a mythical adversary, since in it Being and the existing entity are separated from the assertions that assert Being-about-something and describe the existing. The arbiter is perforce ontology, whose only subject-matter proper is objectivity on the progressive level of 'species-Being' (*Gattungsmässigkeit*). It is easy to discover what the former means: the revolutionary institution or organization resulting from the objectivation of revolutionary faith. 'Objectivity is not a determinant . . . attached to Being which it shapes (?) in a certain way, either in its capacity of existing or through the cognitive consciousness. It has to be strictly discerned: every Being, in so far as it is Being, is also objective' Lukács writes.[2] We can have recourse only to what is objective. Selective will is justified by what selective will (individual or collective) objectifies. However, selective will selects from among forms, pre-existing objectivations. (Incidentally, the fact that the objects of our choices, as objects, already bear the imprint of a free choice, in that we select from a domain created by others, is the main source of hesitation, anxiety and failure – but I will return to this.) These objectivations, the terms of our choices, have, through their compelling 'existential' force, brought history to the stage at which it is now to be found. However, history marches towards 'species-Being-for-itself' (*für-sich-seiende Gattungsmässigkeit*), towards the promised land: both waste products and the real successes of objectivity will be equally justified in it. Human history is promoted only by what has been, and is, and will be the object of options in its *objective* capacity. *Object* is only what is part of the history of 'species-Being'. The following will serve as an example: 'The development of social Being has been realized by its own dynamics; in other words, it can only be conceived of as a movement aimed at the real totality of human species.'[3] Being as such is the upshot of its own teleology as such; Being evolves gradually towards itself.

And sometimes it does not even matter if Being is non-Being.

Acts of transgression of the bounds of totality of Being are going to be built into one of the 'world views' of praxis whose truth may remain highly problematic in an objective sense, whose false reflections, however, may be presented in the consciousness, in this practical agent of social reproduction, as Being, sometimes even as a supreme type of an actually conceived of and restrained Being. Thus it becomes possible that certain objects which are non-existent, but whose concepts may fulfil an important function in social life, guide and determine certain social activities in a practical sense.[4]

What is part of the history of 'species-Being' is 'object', so it will become Being even if it does not exist in the ordinary sense of the word.

What is recourse (*recursus*)? What is the quest for Being? In what sense does the statement 'This should be so' differ from the statement 'This is so'? The categorical imperative of theory, the formative principle of generalization, makes obligatory only such propositions as 'In all instances when A is the case, B will also be the case.' But the mere assertion that 'A is the case' is the affirmation of my cognitive deed, of my own self as an active cognitive subject. For in a proper sense 'A is the case' is neither a synthetic nor an analytic proposition. Voicing such a tautology serves only the transposition of the metaphor of the lingual (descriptive) cognitive act into a sphere sanctified by ideology. It serves its perpetuation in the 'existential' substratum of truth. Thus the chosen ideology, the chosen values, attain to an indirect affirmation by positing this very affirmation as something external.

The exact list of the divergences between you and Lukács (pp. 133 – 4), a lucid summary of the critical aspects of your views formed in the 1960s, is already *lingua franca* for my generation. Together with the results of Kolakowski, Kosik and the *Praxis* circle, they are part and parcel of that secret syntax that shapes the language of all of us. I am aware of the irritation provoked by the 'philosophy of praxis' of the 1960s, by political fiascos and blind alleys, but I do not share it. I feel and see a kind of continuity between your (our) efforts then and now. Moreover, despite the undeniable caesura, the unchanged goal has remained the elaboration of a 'philosophy of praxis', from the Erlangen School and Apel to Mihály Vajda's new romanticism, to mention only the extreme poles. This 'philosophy of praxis' is not in search of Being in order to justify the absolute character of its choices, pretending that they are unique, so to speak, by virtue of a 'naturally given'' objectivity. Rather, it attempts to fathom whether its maxim can serve as a principle of 'general legislation'. At least it ought to do so, if the spirit and the (self)-criticism of 1968 are still part of its intentions. The Feuerbachian critique of abstract *recursus*, the Marxian-Lukácsian critique of reification, the anarchist critique of institutions, the Frankfurt School's critique of consumption – all of these, the entire Leftist tradition, are opposed to the quest of Being, the recursive ontology, the tradition of St Anselm.

Anselm intended to give to his work – written precisely 900 years ago – the first document of the quest of Being, the title *Fides quaerens intellectum*, ('Belief in Quest of Intellect'). But the *Proslogium* could have also been entitled *Intellectus quaerens existentiam* ('Intellect in Quest of Being'). These two claims have been merged for 900 years at least; perhaps they always were. When, 600 years after Anselm, Descartes returned to the ontological proof of God's existence, he did *not* thereby return, as I have tried to prove elsewhere, to Augustine or Anselm. With Descartes, recursive philosophical structure, this fundamental configuration of all doctrines combined with existential faith, characteristic of medieval thinking in its genuine, unipolar version, was bipolar. Individual thinking (in a way, individualization as a principle) provided the foundation for Being, and God found proof in the abstractness of Being. Faith itself is part of recursive thinking here; the creed is not an original fact but a proposition inferred. The circular character of this idea has become intensified in modern (Lukácsian) ontology, which was intended to deduce the communist creed. In an ominous parallel to a simplified version of Heidegger, in Lukács' collectivity, the independent Being of human society is self-justifying in nature. 'Since . . . man is . . . a responding being, his role in this historical process is to give such replies to questions raised by society as are capable, in their consequences, of promoting, obstructing or modifying the active tendencies.'[5]

Philosophical polemics against alienation crystallize the frozen opposite of its own endeavours. Here the individual is merely *ens per accidens* with no other *raison d'être* than to be the *dunamei on* of objectively existing universal (society) and its substantial character, its potentially existing entity, its vehicle, the category that renders Being possible. Once again, objectivation has devoured the individual, this time under the aegis of philosophy of history. Nothing but hypostatized institution attains to a specific existence. Lukács writes:

> 'Species-Being' is the fundamental character of all existing entities in a fundamentally objective way. The elimination of its 'elemental dumbness' may, therefore, alone turn into an existential basis and a touchstone of all human efforts striving for rendering Being conscious in its universality and reality.[6]

The basic element of faith, human universality, can be separated, just as with Guillaume de Champeaux, as the essence of individuality. 'The abstractness residing in the single individual', treated so critically by Marx, returned from history to theory. Latent essence becomes here 'existential fundament' by being vocalized, by being represented and fought for, as it were; this is its feed-back and affirmation. This manner of thinking is also circular for the reason that Lukács returns to the methods of pre-Cartesian *recursus*. Only what has been projected by medieval philosophy as objectivity on God and eternal truth is reincorporated by Lukács as an idol, as an untranscendable immanence into the 'this-worldliness' through the (probably unconscious) internalization of certain modern experiences. But through this projection 'this-worldliness' ceases to exist precisely in its specific substance to a far greater extent than in the most radical mysticism that denies 'this-worldly' reality. For the converse of mysticism, the other side of 'self-created vacuum', is the God-provoking dictum: 'If I were not, you would not be either.' With Lukács the constellation is irreversible. Everything was decided at the beginning of time; in the heart of all acts we can locate the almost mystically interpreted knowledge that is independent of the knowing agent. The rationalization of 'this-worldly' faith (correctly, idolatry) revokes and invalidates the mere fact of post-Kantian philosophical development. It is rendered as follows: 'Objectively speaking, each act of work already contains the realized transition from what we are merely acquainted with to what is known to us even if the latter does not possess a conscious mirror-image in the consciousness. . . . "They are not aware of it but they do it." '[7] Let us, for the time being, disregard the *non sequitur*, which is only proof of Lukács' efforts to find his way back to the theses of his *Aesthetics*. We should rather concentrate on the fact that, according to this statement, there is a 'known-in-itself', a *cognitum per se*, independent of any consciousness! But who would be its subject? Lukács' formulation is unmistakable: 'it seems as if general human 'species-Being' is a mere abstraction by contrast with these acts, even though it is this force that determines the direction of the main trend of the ultimate analysis.'[8] Despite all provisos and quibbling, this is the most extreme kind of conceptual realism, which is only aggravated by the denial of transcendence: the latter eliminates the last systematic criterion. What remains is faith in the value-concept of 'species-Being' as a result of total induction, but some shadow is cast even on this by the circumstance that the existential basis, the essence of inducible facts, is the very value-concept tacitly anticipated.

For his part, Anselm makes emphatic use of the transcendental caesura, while seemingly denying man's specific being:

> For what is one thing on the whole, and another in the parts, and in which there is any mutable element, is not altogether what it is. And what begins from non-existence, and can be conceived not to exist, and unless it subsists through something else, returns to non-existence; and what has a past existence, which is no longer, or a future existence, which is not yet – this does not properly and absolutely exist. But thou [God] art what thou art, because, whatever thou art at any time, or in any way, thou art as a whole and forever.[9]

Obviously, here we are confronted with a specific interpretation of Being. Only that whose complete self-identity can be stated proves to be Being. This is the Being of absolute substance. Anselm, like Heidegger, considers time to be the characteristic feature *par excellence* of mortal beings, but for Anselm, by contrast with Heidegger, this is not at all the index of existence. Anselm questions God in the following way:

> Or, in this way also dost thou transcend all things, even the eternal, because thy eternity and theirs is present as a whole with thee; while they have not yet that part of their eternity which is to come, just as they no longer have that part which is past? For so dost thou ever transcend them, since thou art ever present with thyself, and since that to which they have not yet come is ever present with thee.[10]

It is thus that Being, opposed to time, can be established. The object of faith, *credendum*, attains to its adequate existence, which is the Being of absolute substance. But what kind of existence accords with the subject of which we are predicating time – more specifically, history? History is the absolute *accidens* of species-Being, as Franz Brentano defines it.[11] Absolute accidents (*accidens*) are the constituents that assert something about substance in an absolute way (that is to say, not merely in its relation to something else) and 'innerly' (that is to say, not only giving it a name externally). Brentano further distinguishes within the class of accidents those that do not coexist and perish with the subject, as the former do, but remain inherent in the subject as long as a *causa efficiens* retains them.[12] He terms them, in the wake of Aristotle, *paskhein* (from *pati*, to endure). Brentano further contends that to the extent that a subject contains such a *paskhein* insufficiently (not totally) and the 'affecting' substance too is its carrier and support, it will become an accident of this substance as well, only in a different way. What has been called endurance in relation to the receiving substance will be action in relation to the 'affecting' substance (*poiein*). In Brentano's view, it was apposite of Aristotle not to include *paskhein* and *poiein* in his roster of categories in the group of relations, for here subject is an absolute substratum, a carrier (*absolutes Tragen durch das Subjekt*), even if for the accidents to be sustained (*Getragenwerden*) other means, too, are necessary.

All these are precious and important items of information, for they reveal the structure of modern ontology based on 'this-worldly' faith and the myth of history. Despite its being a product of decay in every respect, in the last phase of Lukács' philosophy enough of the earlier 'sentimental', reflected way of its author's thinking has been preserved for these two subgroups of 'absolute accidents' to be distinguished instinctively from one another. If historicity is *paskhein* in 'species-Being', then 'human endeavours aimed at rendering Being conscious in its universality and reality', intervening in objectivity-in-itself (to wit, the élite of the revolutionary working-class movement), Marxist philosophy à la Lukács, institutions promoting 'species-Being', are together *poiein*. The latter brings about the substantial sustaining (*Getragenwerden*) of historicity within this class, of *paskhein* as 'absolute accident'. Transcending the parallel but more subjectivist formula of 'imputed (class)-consciousness', Lukács reverses the topological order and the hierarchy of species essence attributed to history. *This* hierarchy would abolish the very concept of 'species-Being', would dissolve it into relatives (*relativa*) – and, as is well-known, *relativa sunt entia rationis* (relative concepts are [only] ideal entities). As a result of the original hierarchy, Being, this universal symbol of confirmation of the truth of its assertion, of its confrontation with man, would slip through his fingers anew. Once again it is Anselm who formulates this unambiguously: 'nothing is true except by participating in truth and therefore the truth of what is true is in that which is true; but the thing stated is not in the true statement and therefore it must be called not the truth of it, but the cause of its truth.'[13] But it is not only Being that confirms the truth of this proposition; the reverse is also the case. Given the identical extension of subject and predicate, true propositions can be made about all specific Being 'that which is what it is'.[14] According to Anselm, there is supreme Truth, which, of course, coincides with Being *sui generis*, and participation in Being becomes identical with participation in supreme Truth. From this homogeneity and the impossibility of choice follows. In this methodologically praiseworthy world there is no room for evil, for hiatus, rendering it possible for the good to *make its move*.

Anselm writes:

> Truth is, therefore, in the essence of all things which are, because they are that which they are, in the supreme Truth. . . . If therefore all things are

what they are there, they are without doubt what they should be. . . .
But whatever is that which it should be, is rightly. . . . Therefore
everything that is, is rightly.[15]

If we believed that this is so only in a theoretical-methodological sense, we
would commit an error. For Anselm explains:

> Nothing is more properly called the truth of thought than its rightness.
> For the power has been given us to think that something is or is not, to
> the end that we think that that which is, is, and that that which is not, is
> not. Wherefore whoever thinks that that which is, is, thinks as he
> should, and consequently the thought is right. If, therefore, the thought
> is true and right for no other reason than that we think that that which is,
> is, or that that which is not, is not, then there is no other truth of
> thought than rightness.[16]

As a result, Anselm must have been clearly aware of the *practical* meaning of his
own thesis. What is *esse*, however? Franco Volpi, in his analysis of the Brentano – Heidegger relationship, reminds us[17] that the existing is, according to
Aristotle, *homonumon* (*aequivocum*) and he adds: 'Being is *aequivocum* with
regard to the single entities, the necessary precondition of polysemy, since it is
not [a single] entity.' In ontologies that rationalize faith, homonymy of Being
becomes substantially simplified.

Ens per accidens exists in the same way as the substantially existing, but it exists to a lesser degree. Instead of *aporias*, we attain to hierarchy. The ontological
proof of God's existence also rests on this consideration. For mysterious
reasons, Being is in a way more valuable than non-Being (it is enough to think
of the fact that Being is affirmation in the ultimate analysis, the symbolic affirmation of the truth of our own propositions). The hierarchy is ready, so we
may turn to the demonstration:

> For, it is possible to conceive of a being which cannot be conceived not to
> exist; and this is greater than one which can be conceived not to exist.
> Hence, if that, than which nothing greater can be conceived, can be con-
> ceived not to exist, it is not that, than which nothing greater can be con-
> ceived. But this is an irreconcilable contradiction.[18]

Apparently, the counter-arguments of Kant (and of others, among them Marx)
are relevant. Moreover, Marx takes into consideration not only the logic but
the topology of the argument as well. The argument is characteristically hierarchical: it confirms Heidegger's suspicion; it presupposes something that exists,
the self-existence of the self-affirmation of hierarchy.

But Anselm's Being *par excellence* exists prior to and beyond everything: 'Is it
because they [the things] cannot exist at all without thee; while thou art in no

wise less, if they should return to nothingness? For so, in a certain sense, thou dost transcend them.'[19]

Can the same proposition be stated of Lukács' conception of Being? Obviously not. If the entirety of single individuals perished, the concept of 'species-Being' would not have even a functional relevance. It is not, then, a genuine substance. Thus human beings and their separated Being (what they fight out for themselves, what 'fights out itself' for them) are related to one another. As we know from Brentano, for Leibniz the *relativa* are ideal, intellectual entities, *entia rationis*; they subsist in God for eternity (*Gedankendinge Gottes*). Brentano's solution of the problem is the following. He assumes that if the *relativum* exists, that which we imagine *modo recto* has to exist; that which we imagine *modo obliquo* does not. And the concept of *relativa* is this: they are determinants that dictate whether those related things that we imagine are being imagined *in recto* or *in obliquo*.[20] Should all this be applied strictly to Lukács' vision of man in his last period, the conclusion must be that human beings have to exist according either to *visio recta* or to *visio obliqua*. Were we, then, to consider the role of *paskhein – poiein* in this sphere and the fact that that which is itself related (the object of faith, 'species-Being') is the determining factor in the sense of 'Being' outlined above, we should be able to distinguish between substantial and particularist, unnecessary and necessary, human beings. Georg Lukács once wrote that he understood Stalinism in a deeper sense than did Stalin himself. This is proven here in a tragicomic way (not, of course in relation to 'socialism in one country' versus 'permanent revolution', to which the *aperçu* alluded). I have no doubts about Lukács' humanistic intentions. His analysis of Being, defined through his faith in an exclusively theoretical, ontological way (even though he trespassed beyond the bounds of the recoursive structure and, in his case, its totally sophistical, circular version), could only be approached through a radical philosophy of praxis, an aporetic analysis; otherwise our preferences would become untranscendable universals, since paradoxically they would be 'this-worldly' and hence refutations of humanist intentions.

Somewhere in the *Ontology* Lukács reproaches modern theology for being no longer in search of an ontological proof of God's existence – in other words, for having renounced *recursus ad existentiam*. In a way he attributes this failure to 'bourgeois decadence', spreading through even the Church. Undoubtedly, Lukács represents in his *Ontology* more ancient principles and methods than modern theology; in addition, all this is aggravated by perfect immanence, the absence of any criteria. For if we take seriously the remarks in the *Ontology* about alternative, pluralistic development,[21] then some room ought to be granted to good and evil, to choice, to voluntary decision (*Willkür*). But where 'all that which is, is rightly' and that which is not 'rightly' does not even exist in a proper sense (cf. 'the main trend of existence'), there everything gleams, unmoved, in a Byzantine totality. But what if all this is only the object of faith, only history in its existence *sui generis*? The doubt arises in Anselm as well: 'But if through thine eternity thou hast been, and art, and wilt be; and to have been is not to be destined to be; and to be is not to have been, or to be destined to be; how does thine eternity exist as a whole forever?' And the answer also clarifies why 'species-essence' (*Gattungswesen*) has to include (for heuristic reasons) the collectivity of human beings: 'all things exist in thee. For nothing contains thee, but thou containest all.'[22] The only difference between the two standpoints is that God (even the God of ontology) can be addressed, but 'dumb species-Being' (*stumme Gattungsmässigkeit*) gives voice to statements by itself or it is vocalized by institutional philosophical *poiein*. However, in voicing statements it destroys its own universality.

I have termed the Lukácsian categories of Being 'hypostatized institution'. Of course, a strong element of criticism is inherent in this interpretation, since, together with Agnes Heller, I regard a 'world without institutions', a 'world of proud human beings', as our ultimate hope, even if, once again in harmony with her, I have reservations about the Utopias of immediacy. My question, however, is the following: *does institution 'exist'?* Obviously, it does not. It consists of *n* number of human beings who follow procedures and commit actions related to themselves, other persons, objects and relations as a result of a voluntary decision, according to established rules. The individuals participating in these actions remain individuals – in other words, existing entities proper; the institution itself is a series of actions. Attributing a proper, ontologically definable existence to this series of actions, practical in nature, within the sovereignty of pure (theoretical) reason, considering it to be an objectivation, just like a finished classic work of art or a legal codex, even with certain typological qualifications, is tantamount to the transposition of the emphatic affirmation of Being originally attached to the truth of statement (see the Cartesian conceptual structure, a bipolar recoursive one) to the terrain of practical reason.[23] But all this is amplified by the abstract image of Being, of theoretical reason void of options. *Mutatis mutandis:* Being, 'species-Being', as the substratum of singular entities and independent universals, do not exist. They are hypostases of the regularities of existing beings, acted and endured, practical in nature. Just as not all human individual actions can be included in the 'Being' of the institution, but only the ones that can be institutionally regulated, similarly the Lukácsian 'ontological sphere', which is equally not *capax omnium, capax universi*, will become separated. Not all that which exists can be included in it, unless it *appears* in the light of its values.

Similarly, the sexual act is not institutional in character unless it is performed in a brothel, in exchange for payment according to a fixed tariff, or within the framework of marriage sanctioned by state and Church. Just as individual love either does not appear at all from an institutional viewpoint or is qualified as a deviation or an anomaly, even when tolerated, similarly individuality does not appear from the viewpoint of a Being that is conceived of neither practically nor epistemologically, only nominally defined and *evaluated* from an ontological theoretical viewpoint. Just as one can readily detect the self-regulating mechanism of the early capitalist, liberal market economy without state intervention in the 'cunning of reason', that heuristic, metaphysical principle of Hegel's philosophy of history, so value-centred but non-reflected and non-practice-oriented ontology is the theoretical counterpart of East-European domination of institutional and organizational order – this time, however, through the infringement of the categorical imperative of theory.

The Lukácsian ontology is not generalizable; its principle is not a principle of all existing beings, which is one of the obligations of theory. Particularity does not participate in Being, though not for moral but for Manichaean onto-theological reasons. (Particularity is identical here with the sphere of existence of all human beings who do not meet the criteria of communist faith, with all that which is, according to the old eschatology stemming from 1919, *not yet* complete, universal, free, social, creative, etc.) Everything which is not good (here) seems not to be evil for Lukács but non-existent. As a result, no *eros* of compassion, solidarity, commiseration should be assigned to such things. Obviously, no justification of their annihilation is necessary for the simple reason that they do not exist.

Needless to say, this ontology is not identical with the spirit of 1937. Its conclusion is a kind of institutional – statist – reformistic enlightenment. Anyone who wants to partake of the value sphere, attractive in itself, to participate in Being (in other words, in justification), is invited to do it. In this case, philosophy will also participate in the conceptual clarification of his or her problems. Thus philosophy renounces universality. This is where the dogma of development concludes, of necessity. As soon as a theory does not describe *that which is* but that *which should be*, and does not define this as Utopia, or *eskhaton*, or practical moral choice, then the 'developmental tendency' opted for or posited by the philosophy in question turns into a principle of *Being*. Since by definition that which is *opted for* is not identical with that which *exists*, then if the former is the sole criterion of the 'Being quality' of the latter, instead of the freedom of alternatives, we shall be witnesses to the struggle between brightness and obscurity, Being and non-Being. In addition, all this is imbued with a contemptuous view of the legions of daemons: according to it, the daemons will, in a manner of speaking, 'grow peacefully into socialism'.

We have been familiar with this view of things since St Anselm: Being *sui generis* turns into the only Being. The free act of creation (of whose irony Schelling wrote so magnificently), if it is circumscribed and unique, both displays and prohibits freedom. The freedom of the creative spirit creates Being out of non-Being. Being came into being. It is here; it is, but it bears the traces of its having been created, the marks of the fact that it is the upshot of a free deed; thus its emergence was not destined by fate. The ontologically based image of freedom creating Being condemns to humiliating anxiety the individual who thus has to feel that his fate is no fate at all. Antigone has to consider that perhaps Creon is right; Achilles that perhaps Patroclos' death is Patroclos' private affair. This holds true particularly if the creative spirit is 'this-worldly'. Without hierarchy, the creature cannot understand why he or she is obliged to accept precisely *these values*. If the free act of the creative spirit is not opposed to the mere potentiality of *all* givenness stemming precisely from its very Being, then there are two consequences. On the one hand the act of allotting Being to the Being of creatures through the universality of the value sphere makes the Molotov – Ribbentrop pact, Hitler's role as the negative repository of the 'morally good' within our philosophy of history and the general revolutionary defeatism demanded by a minority of the Fourth International equally acceptable. On the other hand, for want of a radical contrast, the potentiality, the 'received' and mediated character, the self-transcendence of the given goes to waste; potentiality is identical with Being; there is no emergence, unless the institutional and organizational *poiein*, representing the value sphere of species-Being, interferes. Being comes into being whenever a particular aspect of the life of creatures coincides with a predestined stage of the philosophy of history of progress. Should anything (dare to) attempt to exist outside this framework, it will fail. Since, however, the creative spirit ('species-Being-for-itself') is not visible, instances of its surfacing will only be marked *a posteriori* by revolutionary theory; faith in it remains, literally, blind faith, faith in the eventual possibility of our deeds becoming justified, in the chance that embers will glow on one of the altars of heteronomy.

In his *Memoirs* the celebrated Hungarian poet Gyula Illyés recounts an illustrative conversation with Ervin Sinkó, a contemporary and comrade of Georg Lukács in the 1919 Revolution. Illyés asked Sinkó when he would form a final opinion of his own Christian commiseration (he had released counter-revolutionaries during the Revolution who later became mass murderers). The answer was profound: 'When I have lived for eternity.' In fact, *disharmonia praestabilita* makes judgement possible only when 'we have lived for eternity'. Then light will have been shed upon whether what we considered to be valuable was indeed valuable.

Anselm's view is clear and simple:

> Since all beings, which are other than this Spirit himself, have come from non-existence to existence, not through themselves, but through another; and, since they return from existence to non-existence, so far as their own power is concerned, unless they are sustained through another being, is it consistent with their nature to exist simply, or perfectly, or absolutely, and not rather to be almost non-existent? . . . and since, whatever he is

himself, he is not through another than himself, that is, than what he is himself, ought not his existence alone to be conceived of as simple, perfect, and absolute? . . . And . . . whatever is known . . . but scarcely to exist, or to be almost non-existent – this assuredly may be rightly said to be in some sort non-existent. According to this course of reasoning, then, the creative Spirit alone exists, and all creatures are non-existent; yet, they are not wholly non-existent, because through that Spirit which alone exists absolutely, they have been made something from nothing.[24]

To reiterate: this is a conception underlying the whole of Lukács' work. The non-subjective creative spirit, which allocates Being to Being, is just as free a creator as Anselm's God. Since, however, it is contrasted as objectivity to objectivity, it does not create the creatures (*de nihilo aliquid factae, scil. creaturae*) but affects them in a coercive way through the agents (work, etc.) of progress. Anselm's God pushes creatures from non-Being to Being, that of Lukács ('species-Being') devours, annihilates them. The strategy of annihilation is twofold. In work, Lukács' 'God' is established under the aegis of objectivity; technological purposiveness swallows subjectivity (what is diagnosed by Marx as loss of essence precisely in work becomes here a triumphal march). In communication, however, it is up to the individuals to grasp the message of the 'Gospel', as a compulsion bearing down on their subjectivity. Here compulsion *addresses* them. What is important *in work* is repetition (as opposed to particularity), seriality, the fundamental constituent of *modern technological oppression*;[25] *in language*, the emphasis on Plan, the persuasion to purposiveness. Lukács writes:

> In the process of work, the dominant role of 'species-Being' becomes manifest in such a way that its repetitive features come to the fore, and the individual is taken into consideration only so far as is consistent with the elimination of error, to the extent that this is possible. At the subjective pole a trend is discernible: the objectively optimal (in other words, that which is on the level of 'species-Being') is preferred to the actualization of purely particular individual methods.[26]

Moreover:

> It is no objection to this statement of fact that the optimal usually comes first, as an individual achievement. In the long run it prevails [!], for as far as its substance is concerned, it was originally on the level of 'species-Being', *capable* of generalization, not a mere particularity.[27]

And what proves that the 'optimal' was formerly on the level of 'species-Being'? The fact that it has prevailed. This is the only visible criterion. Of course, many things prevail in the 'integration of integrations', in the world

of today, and this ontology does not intend to justify all of them.
How does all this look with respect to communication?

> Originally, language is an instrument to enforce acts of teleological
> positing whose telos is to induce [!] other people to perform certain other
> teleological acts. The final goal always remains action on the level of
> 'species-Being', performed through work. But this can only be achieved
> through the consciousness of others. This 'being on the level of species-
> Being', this transcendence of one's own particularity, can be aroused only
> through the most variegated means, in the most various ways. To the
> tendencies that are evident in work itself personal injunction, addressed to
> those performing work, is added.[28]

Obviously, this exceeds enlightenment in that this 'arousing' of 'species-Being'
has an existing substratum: the agent of progress, the hypostatized *revolutionary*
institution.

It becomes very clear under semantic scrutiny to what extent Lukács tries to
shed the burden of subject. Language is the instrument of teleological acts,
which induce, even coerce, people to perform new teleological acts.
Teleological acts implement new teleological acts, and in the spirit of this
definition, this instrument is derivative of the generality of coercion. Something
that is void of subject ('positing goals') transforms subjects into its objects. Subject is the object of object, the object of projected activity. What is this
something that is capable of teleological acts and is *not* subject? It is the collectivity acting according to formalized rules, the bureaucratic institution alone,[29]
that is capable of this. This collectivity mobilizes people, 'arouses them to
species-Being' (once again: *not* to subjectivity); it solicits action on the level of
'species-Being'. But how? Lukács' answer is most telling: this can only be
achieved through the consciousness of *others*. Of course, these other human beings can also be the constituents of the institution. The penal code is to be applied both to the prosecuting attorney and to the judge (by contrast with the
capitalist, who is not exploited, whose workforce is not appropriated by a certain kind of generality). Part of the institution is the person who is institutionalized and *only in so far as* he or she is institutionalized. 'Personal injunction
to human beings' can also be applied to the repository of 'species-Being' – for
instance, to the member of the revolutionary élite – but, of course, not
everyone can issue injunctions to 'arouse species-Being' on the appropriate
level. This is a privilege that is not accorded to *'other persons'*. Clearly, the concept of subject should be broadened here. What can the subject look like whose
language serves only to stress further the emphasis on the objective constituents
of work? (What constituents? The natural ones? The alienated ones?) No
doubt, this seems to be very close to the exact description of the slave. *In-
strumentum vocale*, as the ancient put it.

The philosopher has to violate his own common sense and logical lucidity in order to operate with a 'God' that has to be conceived of in part in a pantheistic way (for the 'human species' is allegedly related to all specimens in some way) but to which, at the same time, certain intentions, values, have to be attributed (in their entirety, constituents of 'species-Being') which, therefore, cannot be totally 'absorbed' by the generality of totality. The following considerations ought to be reconciled with each other:

1 The human being is a specimen of his or her species; as a result, there is an inherent 'species-Being' in him or her.

2 'Species-Being' is not yet a completed fact. (a) It has to be 'fought out'. (b) It will develop – in other words, there is no 'species-Being' in the individuals (not yet, not enough).

3 Because of the variety of individuals, groups, classes, societies and the like, the descriptive concept of humankind is almost devoid of content; however, as far as space, time, qualitative differences are concerned, its value-concept limits the number of those who can participate in it. On the other hand, all human beings are related to 'species-Being'.

4 'Species-Being' also means consciousness.

5 Nevertheless, since not everyone is on the level of 'species-Being', not everyone is universal human being, 'species-Being' is hidden in the inner core of the particularity of each human being *unconsciously*. 'Species-Being' is not (not entirely) conscious therefore.

6 There is a dialectical struggle in human being between (a) generalization and (b) individualization (for instance, in the medium of language). The more individual (the more specified) the human being and the word, the more general it is at the same time, the more he/she/it is on the level of 'species-Being'.

In order to resolve the above-mentioned dilemmas, there is a distinction in the *Ontology* between 'species-Being-in-itself' and 'for-itself'. But who and what transforms the former into the latter? Who and what is the agent of progress?

> The progress of humankind from 'species-Being-in-itself' to 'species-Being-for-itself' is a process that takes place in human beings, ultimately in each human being, in that the merely particular human being becomes inwardly detached from the one in whom 'species-Being-in-itself' struggles for life, even if this struggle assumes primitive or awkward forms. The ultimate character of the leap finds its expression in the fact that even the particular human being is related to 'species-Being'; its mere 'species-

Being-in-itself' becomes manifest through teleological acts; the specimen is not merely biologically related to his or her species. All this concludes, of necessity, in acts of objectivation, in which the human being consciously [!] creates something of social relevance, even if he or she is not aware of [!] doing so, as has repeatedly been demonstrated by Marx.[30]

The philosopher's vain efforts are obvious; the dilemma cannot be resolved. Why? The 'non-species-Being' is also 'species-Being': it is this contradiction alone that has remained in this philosophy a vestige of the original value-option of Marxism, of the hope of emancipation. The non-conscious consciousness, through which the representative of the 'species-Being' is on the level of 'non-species Being' – the man of 'non-species Being' being, nevertheless, on the level of species-Being and producing 'something of social relevance' – is altogether an anachronistic residuum of the 'cunning of reason', of Hegelianism. But this Hegelianism, unlike the considerations in *History and Class Consciousness*, Hegelian not only in character but also in quality and significance, is no longer authentic.

What results from Hegel's scepticism is the sanctification of anything that exists. This is why it became a source of inspiration for conflicting political movements, legal doctrines and the like. Moreover, in terms of Hegel's tenets the 'cunning of reason' could be reconciled even with *laissez-faire* liberalism. We have gradually come to know that legitimist mercantilism was not so far removed from Hegel's intentions, which were reconcilable with the Prussian ethos of state to which so many hackneyed reproaches have been addressed. The standpoint 'Do whatever you want; it will turn into World Spirit anyway' makes all kinds of *a posteriori* apologetical attitudes possible. But a modern (more precisely, bureaucratic modernizing) system of institutions that liquidates *laissez-faire* demands legitimation in advance. *Not everything* striving for Being suits its interests. What is being mediated by non-conscious consciousness is not a matter of indifference to it, for the modern institutional system is *formalized*. It is not the results but the plans that need justification, for the system can legitimate the elimination of spontaneity only by reference to 'objectivity', 'necessity' or 'science', according to whose laws it acts. Apologetics *a posteriori* are no longer needed.

It was in the late 1950s that Kolakowski irrefutably unmasked the real contents of the vulgar version of *diamat* (even if the result of this operation has been ignored by many – for instance, by Althusser). In the case under scrutiny we are, however, confronted with a genuine philosophy, which is demonstrated by, among other things, the added fact that Kolakowski's criticism of the *political* doctrines of the time, of the 'deep structure', can be applied to Lukács' text. For Lukács, in contrast to official Marxist – Leninist exercises, did express the 'deep structure'. The fundamental element of one's belonging to the human species is then one's participation in acts of objectivation generating societality (i.e., abstraction) without being aware of this. The heroic-cynical philosophy that treats masses pushed into the revolutionary turmoil in a moralistic, Machiavellian manner has become obsolete (*History and Class Consciousness*). Its place has been taken by a detached, sceptical philosophy of the non-subject (*das Subjektlose*), which imposes objectivity itself on this consciousness (*Ontology*).

Lukács, like so many others in the socialist working-class movement, could not acquiesce, in that his choice of human wealth, longed-for emancipation, was merely a 'pious wish'. He could not accept the inescapable, namely, that his hope could draw its general relevance only from the validity of the maxim of his practical option. Certain nineteenth-century socialists believed that the guarantee of their faith *was not morality* but science: political economy. Certain twentieth-century socialists have believed that the guarantee of their faith *is not morality* but science: a doctrine that is known as Marxist philosophy. Socialism is no longer merely a 'pious wish'; it is a fact. It is mobilized not only by the uncertain longing for freedom but also by the firm command of necessity, and yet it becomes freedom.

This is why Lukács could not conceive of the universal of *human species* in a nominalist way. This is why it was beyond the reach of his late philosophy to realize that the *human species*, both as a descriptive and as a value-concept, was unsuitable for the purposes of assertion, even the assertion of Being. Ought may be transformed into Being in action, but this procedure cannot be described. Lukács' intention was to transform Ought into Being through the metaphors of his *Ontology*, but he merely transformed Being into Ought. The existing became an emphatic, daemonic moral commandment – more precisely, one kind of the existing, the institutional organizational, rule of the bureaucratized élite. (Of course, it should be added to all this that *within* this framework Lukács was an advocate of democratization and reform, of cultural freedom, but – let us face facts – these are political concepts of very limited value.) No doubt, socialism has to find its way back from 'science' to Utopia in order to wrest emancipation from its false idols. An affirmation of humanity based on the philosophy of history is an impossible undertaking. Simone Weil wrote: 'We do not like humanity; we like this human being. This is not a legitimate love; the only legitimate love is that of humanity. But to love deity and this particular god: this is one and the same love.'

Transforming values into Being means that we select no longer from values but from human beings. This is how necessary and unnecessary, developed and underdeveloped, civilized and uncivilized, mentally sane and mentally ill, normal and perverted, active and passive, talented and untalented, resourceful and unresourceful, winning and losing, potent and impotent, attractive and unattractive people come about. Their elimination, one way or the other, becomes a mere epistemological problem. Where is the world view that regards human beings as equal? Where is the philosopher who knows, as Simone Weil did, that it is hunger that counts in human beings, not their capacity to provide a certain type of food for our cannibalistic love? At this point, the left, the radical philosophy, is highly imperfect, although it is precisely at this point that it has to be perfect. Of course, it is ridiculous to explain all this to you. When Lukács transformed his choice into law, much more consistently than naive metaphysics (that of Nicolai Hartmann) or the similar but much more hieratic *diamat* did in constructing pyramids out of the material of strata of Being, he confused two theses that should not be confused. One is that we have to believe in our chosen value absolutely; the other is that we have to believe that our chosen value is absolute. Obviously, we chose our leading values for the reason that we believe them to be good and true. If, however, it belongs to our chosen values that all subjects are of equal value, all are 'God sons', if we do not infer the inferiority of women, slaves and barbarians from the fact of their being in a subordinate position, if we like hunger, and not food, in the human heart, then we cannot believe that values may be derived from human existence itself. If we believe this, we ought to reject, through the *recursus*, together with human values, the value of humanity as well. On the one hand, Lukács' ontology identifies Being with the Good and the True because for him it is only the Good and the True that 'truly' exist. On the other hand, it separates one from the other, in order that the True and the Good should be elevated to higher and higher rungs of the ladder of philosophy of history, finally to merge, on the level of *parusia*, with Being in eschatology. All this is connected with the dual nature of institution.[31] Institution seems to be materialization ('Being'), whereas it is in fact only a series of action ('choices', 'voluntary decisions'). This myth is the clue to *coercion*.

Should the monadically ('logically') arranged system of rules (law as 'objectivation', as 'Being'), be Being, how would it bring Being into being? It renders choices homogeneous and uniform, but this is still an algorithm, a blueprint for regularities to come. If Being were identical with regularity, with institutionally rendered algorithms (which are seemingly the telos of the institution), then there would be no need for the institution, for it would coincide with human Being. It is of vital interest to the institution that it should claim to be the representative of some value, the repository of *one* of the tendencies ('general interest', 'progress', 'economic balance', 'revolution', 'national pride', 'the exemplary water supply of the city', etc.) and at the same time to enforce this tendency as the *only* postulate of Being *sui generis*. If that which it represents is *Being itself*, why should coercion be needed for its regulation? If that which it represents is not *human Being in itself*, however, and if it should indeed need coercion for its regulation, what can make it legitimate? It can be legitimized only through the assumption that it is somehow the emanation of human existence *sui generis*. In the main, this ambiguity is needed in order theoretically to sustain the state.

In Marx's analysis the same thing applies to the institution, as the general, symbolic regulator of modern society, with respect to money. Originally, money was the representative of values; later values became representative of money: 'Money implies separation between the value of things and their substance. Money is originally the representative of all values; in practice this situation is inverted, and all real products and *labours* become the representatives of money.'[32] And if we substitute, in a further quotation from Marx's text about the indirectly social character of production, 'institution' for 'money', 'activity in a general sense' for 'production', the Marxian critique of alienation works amazingly well:

> The very necessity first transforming individual products or activities into *exchange value*, into *money*, so that they obtain and demonstrate their social *power* in this *objective* (*sachlichen*) form, proves two things: (1) that individuals now produce only for society and in society; (2) that production is not *directly* social, is not the 'offspring of association', which distributes labour internally. Individuals are subsumed under social production; social production exists outside them as their fate; but social production is not subsumed under individuals, manageable by them as their common wealth.[33]

Neither is human life simply the 'offspring of association'. But *in what sense* does fate, existing outside human beings, exist? What becomes external? Whether its consciousness is messianic or paternalistic, revolutionary institution intends to conceive of itself, and to be understood, as the objectivation of human essence. To this end, it has to operate with a twofold concept of Being. One of them is the sum of 'existential' acts (whatever they may be), from which, through the detour of Leninist 'total induction', the correct decisions are *deduced*. The other contains a qualitative element in which 'right' decision is the index of Being – and if the yardstick of 'rightness' of decisions is the quality of the Utopian totality, then the circle is complete.

Lukács writes: 'Social life is a complex consisting of complexes whose reproduction is, in a multifaceted and multi-lateral way, interdependent with the process of reproduction of relatively independent partial complexes, but it is always totality that prevails within this interdependence.'[34] I have already criticized the absurd doctrine of the interrelationship between the whole and its parts,[35] so I am not going to return to this. Let us instead imagine a situation in which one thing is prevalent rather than another. Of course, it is conceivable that in a complex structure a partial element will prevail, and that we will declare it to be the 'real thing' (such as sensuality, or addiction to music in one period of one's life, about which others make the comment: 'This is it! *Finally*, he has found himself!'). But this is a metaphor for our value-choice. In our evaluation something is *now* 'the real thing' because we prefer the prevailing partial element ('He has "found" himself because *in our estimation* amorous blushing or musical devotion "suit him"'). In other words, the statement 'This is the real thing' can simply be substituted for another: 'This is "a good" (or "a right") thing' (according to clearly defined criteria), or the claim 'That is his real self!' for another, more honest one: 'The propensity I prefer has prevailed in him!'

Without doubt, institution, that specific ideological idol that conceals the coercion stemming from practical and arbitrary choices of groups of individuals, has to be formulated in the spirit of the *Ontology*. But why should philosophy do this?

In a sense, this seems to be a fatal constellation. The universals from which Claude Lévi-Strauss' structural ethnology departs, from which he constructs the individual, are similar to the Lukácsian concept of 'social Being'. Each individual is but a cutting, a collage constructed from a few universals; the individual character of individuals is assigned by statistical regularities, or planned and designed by the quadratures of operational research. But Lévi-Strauss wants only an insight into the ultimate, divine trick of potential versions; he is certainly not intent on planning games ahead. Lukács' universals must not intersect each other; they are *principles* and *protagonists* of the game. Categories such as a royal flush, the ace of hearts, a new player in the game are interchangeable in his case. The reason for this is not confused thinking, not even excessive enjoyment of *metabasis eis to allo genos* (the ontological leap). The reason is simply this: the cards must always be played close to the chest; they should never be turned up. The universals must be prevented from intersecting each other; the emergence of a genuinely individual character must be preempted. For the individual tolerated by this philosophy is the one 'which' has to become *universal*, according to the prescriptions of the Plan. In other words, 'it' has to be emancipated from the misery of 'its' individuality so that 'it' can cease to be individual. Moreover, as we have seen, this is *not* Utopia, a pious wish, but a command of Being, as it were, since man is (*sauf erreur*) universal by the circumstance of his being, his existing. But all this has to happen in time; 'species-Being' has a history, from 'Being-in-itself' to 'Being-for-itself'. As a result, the human being's own essence looms large in front of him or her. As a result, the human being's essence is his or her telos. As a result, what is not the telos of the human being must be the human being's essence. The essence of the human being whose essence is not this (or who has a *different* essence) is non-essence (*Unwesen*). But if the criterion of the human being's human character is human essence, what sort of being is the one whose essence is non-essence? This specimen is not a human being, or 'it' is a 'human-being-in-itself', which is the same thing. What can this being do?

'It' can be educated. 'It' can be *incorporated*.

If this happens to 'it', 'it' will appear. 'Its' Being will acquire the grammar of the language of institutional philosophy, a process similar to the one in which the body, if it becomes vocal through sexuality, 'starts to exist' with the aid of Lacan's psycho-analytic philosophy. Non-communicative, erotically reposing body, non-communicative, socially passive Ego, are dumb and invisible. They find their verification only in the *act*. Through the act, however, potentiality, indispensable to the freedom of choice, expires. If philosophy bears in mind only the *act*, not the potency (moreover, if it preserves for itself the privilege to define which is which), it will have, of necessity, to draw the ultimate conclusions of conceptual realism and to declare freedom meaningless. Freedom does not result from the abstract and sentimental declaration of human dignity; the reverse is the case. This is what is suggested (though not in so many words) by Ernst Bloch's analysis of natural law. Any human undertaking (such as hope, for instance) can be completed only if it is projected. To this end, however, conceptual space is needed, which is expropriated by the institution, representing the intentions of the bureaucratic élite. True, the myth of natural law has tried to occupy this conceptual space, on behalf of freedom. But this symbolic action cannot be renewed. Besides, it has the weakness of knowing only *dunamei on*, not genuine *dynamis*. *Potentia qua potentia*, this 'dumb' quality that resists interpretation according to the abstract 'grammar' of ontology, is at least part of the conceptual space of freedom and projection. We are inclined to regard as heterogeneous, impure and random all that cannot be measured by the specified character of our universals, which seem to be, in the light of our values, alien or inferior. Bloch did not hesitate to shed light on the space of *potentia*, of project: desire, *déjà vu*, the guess, crime fiction, the philosophy of *Selbstporträt ohne Spiegel* make vocal even the entity that has no voice, but not with Freud's intent and manner: in order to institutionalize, socialize and cure all this, simply so that we might understand *precisely* what is not universal. The assignment has already been formulated by Feuerbach, but it has remained merely an assignment.

In my view, either the left will become nominalist or it will betray its chosen values. Either – or.

But I may be wrong.

Fraternally,

Gáspár M. Tamás

Translated by F. Fehér

NOTES

1   See pp. 125 – 53 above.
2   Georg Lukács, *On the Ontology of Social Being*, 3 vols. (Budapest: Magvetö, 1976), *Prolegomena*, III, p. 311. I always quote the Hungarian edition.
3   ibid., vol. 3, p. 275.
4   ibid., p. 256.
5   ibid., *Prolegomena*, p. 60.
6   ibid., vol. 3, p. 43.
7   ibid., p. 54.
8   ibid.
9   St Anselm, *Basic Writings*, trs. S. N. Deane, (La Salle, Ill.: Open Court Publishing Co., 1962), *Proslogium*, ch. XX, p. 27.
10 ibid., p. 26.
11 Franz Brentano, *Kategorienlehre*, ed. Kastil, 2 Abt., I, 3, para. 7.
12 ibid., para. 8.
13 St Anselm, 'Dialogue on Truth', in *Selections from Medieval Philosophers*, ed. and trs. Richard Mackeon (New York: Charles Scribner's Sons, 1957), ch. II, p. 153.
14 See Brentano's distinction between the proper and the improper meaning of Being, *ens, ens per accidens* and so on: Brentano, *Kategorienlehre*, 1 Abt., I, 5, para. 1.
15 St Anselm, *Dialogue on Truth*, ch. VII, pp. 163 – 4.
16 St Anselm, *Dialogue on Truth*, ch. III, pp. 156 – 7.
17 Franco Volpi, *Zeitschrift für Philosophie* (Frankfurt), 32, 2 (1978), p. 27.
18 St Anselm, *Proslogium*, ch. III, p.8.
19 ibid., ch. XX, p. 26.
20 Brentano, *Kategorienlehre*, 2 Abt., III, 1, paras. 3, 7.
21 Although I do not know whether we should do this or what we should understand by the concept. Any notion of development should at least differ from simple change in that it should denote that something will change from 'less' to 'more', from 'worse' to 'better', in *some* sense. If this change is alternative in nature (in other words, if it can be this or that, if it can also be 'regress'), what does progress mean? Eventually, it can denote nothing but insistence on an earlier terminology.
22 St Anselm, *Proslogium*, ch. XIX, p. 25.
23 See my 'The Limits of Methodical Doubt', the Preface to the Hungarian edition of René Descartes, *Discours de la méthode* (Bucharest – Cluj: Kriterion, 1977).
24 St Anselm, *Basic Writings, Monologium*, ch. XXVIII, pp. 88 – 9.
25 See Simone Weil's essays on Taylorism.
26 Lukács, *Ontology*, vol. 2, 'Reproduction', p. 197.
27 ibid.
28 ibid.
29 Here I do not use the adjective 'bureaucratic' in the Weberian descriptive, typological sense but in the way that Castoriadis uses it: with an evaluative, historical connotation.
30 Lukács, *Ontology*, vol. 2, 'The Ideal and the Ideology', p. 409.

31   S. Cornelius Castoriadis, *L'Institution imaginaire de la société* (Paris: Seuil, 1975), *passim* but esp. pp. 194 – 200.

32   Karl Marx, *Grundrisse (Foundations of the Critique of Political Economy* (Rough Draft), trs. Martin Nicolaus (Harmondsworth – Baltimore: Penguin, 1973), p. 149; Notebook I, chapter on money.

33   ibid., p. 158.

34   Lukács, *Ontology*, 'Reproduction', p. 258.

35   See *The Spell of Barbarism* (Bucharest – Cluj: Kriterion, 1977).

8

Lukács' Later Philosophy

AGNES HELLER

In discussing the philosophy of the older Lukács one ought not to confine one's analysis to the post-Second World War period alone. For the continuity of his later philosophy with his theoretical efforts of the 1930s is so crucially important that even his final two works, *The Specificity of the Aesthetic* and *The Ontology of Social Reality*, in which he attempted to break, partially or even totally, with his earlier position, remain incomprehensible if we do not approach them from the standpoint of the philosophical premises embodied in the writings of the pre-war and war period.

The decisive break within Lukács' theoretical *oeuvre* was his repudiation of *History and Class Consciousness*, which continues to be regarded as the paradigmatic expression of his theoretical activity. Very much by contrast with other, later acts of self-criticism, Lukács' repudiation of *History and Class Consciousness* was sincerely meant. His recantation had two motives. One of these is widely known and acknowledged; the other has attracted no attention whatsoever. The first motive is to be found in the existential choice that bound him to the then existing Communist Parties and, in consequence, to the Soviet Union and to the Third International. I call this an 'existential' choice because it stood above and beyond all possible criticism, because it could be called into question neither by fact nor by argument. Had Lukács insisted upon the conceptions embodied in *History and Class Consciousness* he would have relativized that choice, which, precisely because it was existential, had for reasons of principle to be absolute. Anxiety and frustration on the one hand, the critical spirit on the other, could motivate him only *within* the framework of this existential choice. But it was this very frustration and anxiety, and also this critical spirit, that gave him his second motive for recantation. Lukács often remarked to us, his disciples, how crucial the reading of the *Paris Manuscripts* was for his self-criticism: the discovery of the concept of human species and of the central role, in Marx, of 'species essence' (*Gattungswesen*) was a great intellectual shock for

177

him. 'Class' cannot take the place of 'species' – that was how he now came to conceive Marx's position – but it was just such a substitution that had characterized *History and Class Consciousness*. Obviously, the reception of a book depends primarily on our needs at the time of its publication and our attitude to the created work. The shock that Lukács felt at this confrontation with the Marxian concept of human species was a response to his own anxiety and frustration, to the unrest of his own critical spirit. We are thus, of necessity, confronted with a paradox: Lukács' repudiation of *History and Class Consciousness* was motivated *both* by the existential choice of an absolute *and* by the anxiety elicited by that very same absolute. Nor should this be in the least surprising. Kierkegaard knew that despair and faith *together* characterize our relation to the absolute, and that paradox itself is nothing other than this connection. It is only in terms of such a paradox that one can understand Lukács' life and philosophy from the 1930s onwards. Lukács believes in his God, yet at the same time he recognizes all the dirt and horror of 'God's created world' and contrasts this extant world with an ideal world that would be commensurate with his God. This is why all those who see in him the representative of Stalinism (such as Isaac Deutscher, among many others) are right, while those who see him as Stalin's greatest philosophical adversary are also right. For until his very last years, when his belief in the absolute became shaky, he was both.

Once he had recanted, there were two courses open to him: either to restructure his own philosophy in order to create a new philosophical edifice or to resign philosophy altogether. Had he chosen the first course, he would have been compelled, according to his existential choice, not only to accept but also to practise the universal metaphysics of *diamat*. It was not only his sense of philosophical good taste that made the latter move repulsive to him but also the paradox that I have just described. He was left, then, with a choice: he could either give up all great philosophy or he could engage in a masquerade. And he chose to engage in a masquerade, for behind the mask of literary criticism, behind the mask of the history of philosophy, was hidden a confession of his commitment to the human species and to the individuality through which the human species is represented.

The only truly great work of that period in his life is *The Young Hegel*, a philosophical biography that is at the same time an autobiography, since Lukács interprets Hegel's intellectual development from the viewpoint of his own. Hegel's *magnum opus*, *The Phenomenology of Spirit*, was the crowning act of his youthful efforts, just as *History and Class Consciousness* was the crowning act of Lukács'. Great ideas come to maturity before their reconciliation with reality. This is where Lukács' story of Hegel ends, for it was here that his own terminated. He did not want to, nor could he, proceed towards reconciliation. For faith in the absolute is no reconciliation: that is precisely the paradox.

The Popular Front policy of the Third International made it too easy for him to stand as the living representative of this paradox, however. His anxieties, his frustration, his critical spirit – all could be acted out and confirmed within 'what was allowed' and with a pathos that seemed to be both politically and morally justified. He experienced the irrational and demoniacal, but he identified it with Nazi Germany – that is to say, he saw it as embodied in the Other; with regard to the Other, the question 'How has this come to happen?' could be formulated. Thomas Mann called these times 'morally good'. In the collective struggle against Nazism everything non-Nazi was whitewashed; all other conflicts were suspended, all question marks eliminated. To be or not to be? That was the question for European culture. Lukács felt he was justified in conceiving 'his' absolute as Ormusd marching against Ariman.

The most problematic result of these efforts was *The Destruction of Reason*, a two-volume pamphlet that was at the same time a demonology. Lukács pursued the problem of responsibility: what facilitated the reception of Nazi ideology? What paralysed the German intelligentsia's capacity to resist? And he found the responsible agent in that tendency of traditional German philosophy that he described as irrationalism.

Lukács was not alone in his attempt to attribute all the horrors of the twentieth century to various philosophies. The belief that there are no innocent ideas was very widespread. Popper in his *Open Society*, or Horkheimer and Adorno in their *Dialectic of Enlightenment*, trod the same road of *a posteriori* construction. In Popper's view, it was not only Hegel and Marx but also Plato himself who could be considered responsible for all forms of totalitarianism. Horkheimer and Adorno (in contrast to Lukács) saw the root of the evil in a certain interpretation of rationalism. All of these works were characterized by a kind of demonology, for they split philosophies into good and bad ones. It is sufficient to glance at Popper's title: 'open society' embodies the Good and the opposite tendency is designated as the 'enemy' in order to show these demonological inclinations.

A historico-philosophical theology and teleology – one that does not hold water if it is examined critically – is being construed here from a legitimate human attitude. What is legitimate in the human attitude? The authors of these demonologies were philosophers themselves, and it is the obligation of all philosophers to query all the possible consequences of their own ideas in order to avoid what is dangerous in them and to take the risks involved therein as a personal commitment. Responsibility is a moral, not a historico-philosophical category, however: ideas themselves cannot be responsible, but only the persons representing them. Nor can the philosopher be held responsible for all possible interpretations of an idea, for he cannot foresee or have prior knowledge of its reception. The limit of his foresight is precisely the limit of his responsibility. Whoever wants to regard responsibility as the infinitude of the possible receptions of his ideas has only one way out: silence. This would mean, however, the end of all philosophizing – indeed the end of all speculative thinking, of all interpretation – and this would involve no small risk. If a thinker is responsible only for the foreseeable consequences of his ideas, it follows, then, that it is not the ideas themselves (precisely because they are not persons) but the recipients who bear the responsibility. The belief that there are no innocent ideas ignores the responsiblity that lies in the expounding of ideas, in the mediating of a certain interpretation for others.

Such a historico-philosophical extension of the notion of responsibility leads to a certain lack of moderation in one's judgement of the idea that one is criticizing: critical objectivity is liquidated and bias comes to the fore. That is how Hegel becomes a feudal reactionary (according to Popper) and Max Weber an arch-conservative burdened by prejudices (according to Lukács). Certain features, sometimes even certain statements, will be abstracted from the whole of a philosophical construction and artificially emphasized in order that the thinker may be placed within a diabolical circle and thereby annihilated.

It follows from this demonology that although evil can be identified with the untrue, the identification of the good with the true becomes impossible. For if the good embodied the true, there would be no room left for the triumphant intervention of the devil. The power of the demon resides precisely in his ability to uncover the weak points of the Good and to hide behind the appearance of truth.

That is why Lukács (of whom alone I am going to speak from this point on) is compelled to duplicate philosophy's division into two. Side by side with the dichotomy of rationalism and irrationalism, identified with good and evil, a second dichotomy appears – the dichotomy of metaphysics and dialectic. In Lukács' opinion, the weakness of rationalism was to be found in its metaphysical methodology: had it proceeded in a dialectical manner, irrationalism would not have had any field for argument. To put it simply: had all rationalists been Marxists or Hegelians, irrationalism would not have developed, or at least it would not have become widespread, and consequently Nazism would not have possessed any kind of ideology and could not possibly have become victorious.

This train of thought expressed a Socratic optimism on the one hand, an illusion on the other.

Socratic optimism became manifest in Lukács' unassailable confidence in reason and in the rationality of all persons. In his view, there is not a single problem assigned by the world that cannot be resolved by rational argumentation, and the rational solutions to these problems will be recognized as solutions by all those confronted with the same problems. Rationally conceived thoughts lead to rational modes of behaviour. Lukács was very fond of the Marxian assertion that ignorance is a demon leading us towards the worst sorts of tragedy, though he modified the question by maintaining that false knowledge is an even more dangerous demon than ignorance. Indeed, this is a standpoint very characteristic of the Enlightenment, and as a philosophical norm it is not only respectable but is also one of the fundamental norms of all philosophizing.

The illusion inherent in these thoughts stemmed directly from the central paradox in Lukács. To insist on rational, critical thinking on the one hand, to believe in the absolute on the other, led to ambiguity. The legitimate belief that all problems of the world can be posed and resolved in a rational manner, and that these acts of posing and resolving problems will be comprehensible to all persons, is tacitly replaced by another: all problems *have already been solved* once and for all, but because of their class limitations, philosophers have not understood and accepted the solutions. Absolute truth has been brought into the world with Marxism. After Karl Marx, nothing in the world can be considered, either in principle or in fact, to constitute an intractable problem. There is nothing new under the sun. Absolute knowledge has already been born and remains hidden only for those who hesitate, only for those who will not, and cannot, accept it. The struggle *against* myth and *for* rationality is being conducted, then, from the standpoint of myth: for Lukács, there is no theoretical way out of that vicious circle.

However, the circularity inherent in Lukács' thinking is not equally evident in all his analyses. Obviously, it is least apparent at those points where the dialectic is not yet represented by the absolute: in the critique of pre-Marxian irrationalism, the irrationalism of Schelling, Schopenhauer, Kierkegaard. At such points Lukács' powerful analytic capacity reveals itself. However, the further we move forward in time, and especially when we come to the philosophy of the twentieth century, the more distorted the analyses we meet as a result of the paradox. The one-sidedness of global interpretation of a given 'idea world' is highly legitimate in philosophy: from this point of view, Lukács' interpretation of Nietzsche, for example, can be regarded as legitimate. But one-sidedness is not legitimate when global understanding is not even intended, for then what emerges is not an 'understanding misunderstanding' but rather a pure distortion of the 'idea world' that one is criticizing. It was Lukács' faith in the absolute that led him, in his critique of the philosophies of the twentieth century, to such a distortion. It was a redundant procedure which, as has been mentioned, was characteristic not only of Lukács but also of the Manichaean way of thinking of the whole epoch. It should be said, to Lukács' credit, that very much by contrast with his contemporaries, he managed not to distort the classic authors.

The year 1953 and the events of the years that followed freed Lukács from the necessity to canalize his anxieties, his frustration and his critical spirit. The absolute itself had expressed these anxieties, this frustration and criticism in the person of Khrushchev and in the gesture of the Twentieth Party Congress of the Soviet Union. The road to great philosophy was open once again. There was no longer any need for Lukács to question the absolute; yet, at the same time, his thinking could now move in a less fettered manner. He broadened his fixed and narrow frame of reference, opening up the possibility of a *positive* philosophy. The work on the great *Aesthetics* commenced.

Lukács planned that the *Aesthetics* would consist of three parts. The first part (actually published under the title of *The Specificity of the Aesthetic*) would be the application of 'dialectical materialism', the second the application of 'historical materialism' to the realm of aesthetics, and the third part a synthesis of the first two, a theory of artistic genres. The fact that in practice Lukács relinquished the whole enterprise after having written the first part, that he intended to write an ethic but actually wrote an ontology, was far from accidental and cannot be ascribed to his advanced age. The first part of the *Aesthetics* made the second part impossible; we shall see later on why this was so.

Lukács' return to great philosophy meant a (relative) return to the way of thinking of his youth – not to *History and Class Consciousness*, however, but rather to the *Heidelberg Aesthetics*. One could assume, perhaps, that the return to his first, not his second, positive philosophy was dictated by his choice of subject-matter. However, a question ought to be raised: why was *this* subject-matter chosen? If we recall that the literary essays of the 1930s had expressed a renewed interest in the categories of human species and of personality – indeed, that it was precisely from this renewed interest that they arose – then we shall understand that the choice of aesthetic signified a continuation of these earlier efforts that developed, in fact, out of the process of self-criticism in which Lukács engaged with regard to *History and Class Consciousness* and which also motivated that same self-criticism. This is why the Marxist Lukács decided to return to the main work of his pre-Marxist period, to a work that has never been published, to a work that had long been almost forgotten by him.

But if Lukács resumed the fundamental categories of his youth, the methodology of his late *Aesthetics* and that of his youthful efforts were essentially different. The work of his youth is characterized by a reversal of the Kantian way of posing the question. Lukács' question runs as follows: 'Works of art exist, but how are they possible?' The first part of this formulation stands, but the second part, together with the question mark attached to it, is dismissed or simply ignored. There exist works of art, and these works of art have a function within human life and within human activity: it is this *function* that is queried, not the possibility. That is to say, questions regarding methodological presuppositions are brushed aside: one cannot inquire about the existence of the works of art, for it is something ultimate, something given, behind which one cannot penetrate.

In place of the reflexive, sentimental attitude of Lukács' early philosophy, we are confronted here by a naive philosophy. It must be admitted that from the beginning Lukács had been fascinated by a certain type of 'philosophical naivety'. It is a well-known fact that what he appreciated greatly in Ernst Bloch was the latter's 'philosophizing in an ancient manner'. There are, however, two levels of naivety: the 'still naive' and the 'already naive'. The first type of naivety ontologizes in the conviction that it can grasp and describe the only true knowledge. The second type has already passed through the purgatory of criticism, either in a personal sense or through the medium of philosophical debates. Here naivety is a bold operation, a wager, a conscious attempt to find one's way back to an attitude that is regarded as the only fruitful one. At first glance, Lukács' *Aesthetics* seems to be a 'still naive' philosophical construction. The rejection of the epistemological approach and the acceptance of the theory of art as mirroring reality are undoubtedly signs of that 'still naive' character. Only when one analyses attentively the intellectual structure of the book, and takes into consideration the new shades of meaning that Lukács attaches to the old categories, can one readily conceive how *modern* – in the positive sense of that word – the whole enterprise is, how far it is characterized by the second type of naivety.

Why did Lukács dismiss the question of how works of art are possible after having proclaimed their existence? Because in an operation very similar to that of modern existent‍‌‌‌. ‌‌‌‌rts from the priority of existence to essence. The question of how works of art are possible is aimed at conceiving and grasping essence. Precisely because the question of essence has been raised, the aesthetics of the youthful Lukács turns out to be a theory of communication. Approaching art from the angle of its existence *prior* to its essence eliminates the problem: whatever exists *prior* to its essence exists in an ultimate sense. According to the later Lukács, the essence of art is a result, the result of a development. And it is because he adopts this kind of approach that his late aesthetics became not a theory of communication but a philosophy of history.

In what way does the essence of art evolve from its existence, according to Lukács? The abstract forms of the so-called aesthetic reflection (such as rhythm, symmetry, proportion, ornamentics) on the one hand and magical mimesis on the other embody only the potentiality of essence, not essence itself. Existence proves to be essence only in the synthesis of these two forms of existence, which takes place at the same moment as the emergence of the 'world-like character' of the work of art. The world of art becomes independent, and in this same process it becomes essential.

Together with the emergence of its 'world-like' character, every work of art becomes an individuality; and at the same time, and precisely for that reason, art – as an entirety of individual works of art – becomes the memory of mankind. It is not hard to see that here the question of individual and species is raised, and that the essence of art is conceived of as the unity of individuality and species. Lukács outlines in his *Aesthetics* a philosophy of history within which the unity of individual and species appears as the truth of history.

Indeed, for Lukács the unity of individual and species was the truth of history, and he was well aware that this type of philosophy of history can be drawn up only in the form of an aesthetics, for when one approaches not art but the totality of societal life, one inevitably stumbles into impasses. As we have seen, the first blind alley was *History and Class Consciousness*, in which the categories both of species and of individual were missing, and the concept of class was substituted for them. One of the functions inherent in the construction of *History and Class Consciousness* was, however, wholly identical with that of the later aesthetics: namely, the objective of solving the problem of correct, not false, consciousness. Lukács wanted to find a way out of the vicious circle of universal fetishism: how can one attain to a true and correct consciousness in an alienated, reified society? His answer at the time of *History and Class Consciousness* was that the consciousness imputed to the being of a certain class represented true consciousness itself. In its details, this solution still played a role in the later Lukács – as one can see by reference to what I have said about *The Destruction of Reason*. But this is not the end of his search, for he attempts to find the solutions of the problem of fetishism in the unity of species and individuality, and in the literary essays of the 1930s and the 1940s he formulates this solution again and again on the basis of a theory of personality. The main result of the theory is that the rich and many-sided development of personality is identical with 'species character' (*das Gattungsmässige*). But this solution could have no historico-philosophical relevance for Lukács. The unity of individual and species *in life itself* is an *Ought*, at least when we conceive of it as something generalized, an Ought that is imaginable only as the consequence of defetishized consciousness and has, precisely for that reason, no defetishizing function. Some entity has to be found that already represents in itself the unity of individual and species and provides that, through its adoption, it will give to all the possibility of rising to true, defetishized consciousness. This entity, according to Lukács, is art itself.

Art is the objectivation whose function is defetishization. In their enjoyment and understanding of a work of art, all individuals rise to the level of 'species character' (*Gattungsmässigkeit*); a unity of individuals constantly comes about as defetishization of consciousness is accomplished. In catharsis all individuals acquire the memory of mankind and, together with that memory, they fulfil the postulate: 'You must change your life.'

Here we are confronted, however, by substantial problems that remain unresolved in that philosophical construction, even though within this Lukács does suggest several possible ways of resolving these problems.

The whole thesis regarding the principal defetishizing function of art stems from the conception of art as unity of individual and species. But his assertion itself needs proper foundations.

Whether all works of art can be viewed as individuals, as self-contained personalities, depends on our conception of art as a whole. *Hamlet* or the B minor Mass are undoubtedly self-contained in this sense, but can one view an individual *Lied* or a play as self-contained? They have an undoubted 'world-like' character (they are neither magical nor purely decorative). It will already be clear that the separation of the essence of art from its existence implies not only an historical but also a structural division. It is not 'art as such' that corresponds to the essence of art. Like all concepts of essence, this too is a value-concept.

But this value-concept finds its proper foundation in a theory of objectivation.

The book starts with the separation of art and science from everyday life. Though everyday thinking contains in embryonic form all the elements of artistic and scientific knowledge, these forms of knowledge represent species as such only if they separate themselves from everyday life, only if they rise, as independent worlds of objectivation, above what is *quotidien*. Only a work that has separated itself from everyday life and thinking can be considered to be artistic in essence. That is why the defetishizing function belongs not to art in general but exclusively to the great objectivations of art. The latter are, however, genuine 'work individualities'. The value-concept of art corresponds to those artistic objectivations that have 'worked themselves out' of everyday life.

It is the category of validity that explains how great works of art, as 'work individualities', embody species as well. Here we find the answer to Marx's question about why the normativity of the Homeric poems has not expired, even though our world is radically different from the Homeric universe. The eternal validity of historically evolved formations, a fact in itself, would not be conceivable if we did not assume that in their individuality they represent at the same time the essence of our species: as human beings, we encounter our own selves in their protagonists and destinies. They speak to us because through them we are able to speak to ourselves.

A hermeneutic circle is present in this act of foundation: the validity of works of art is evidence of their being on the level of 'species character', and their being on the level of 'species character', is accounted for by the fact of validity. But since no closed philosophies (or those that seek to be closed) can avoid the hermeneutic circle, I want merely to call attention to the problem without entering into a detailed criticism of it.

The real problem appears only when we confront this concept of art with the Lukácsian theory of decadence. If the great work of art, according to its very function, is defetishizing, how is it possible to conceive of nearly the whole of modern art as an expression of fetishistic consciousness? The idea that modern art does not separate itself from everyday life would lead to an untenable position, and Lukács emphasizes again and again just the opposite: the widening gulf between everyday thinking and the world of modern arts. The individuality of these works of art cannot be questioned either. And what about their 'species character'? This is precisely the point of departure for the Lukács of the literary essays: he questions the 'species character' of modern art. If, however, the validity of works of art is evidence of their being on the level of 'species character', the procedure, according to Lukács' own standards, is illegitimate, for how could he know that these works will lose their validity in the future? The whole tendency of Lukács' own *Aesthetics* ought to have led him to abandon his feeling of *ressentiment* against modern art, for within his own aesthetic there was theoretically no room for such a judgement. The fact that he dismissed the concept of realism from his aesthetics – or, more precisely, that it appears in his aesthetics in a much more sporadic, more accidental way – shows that he himself became sensitive to this tendency of his own work. The conscious solution could not, however, be achieved.

Another, no less important problem remains unresolved in Lukács' conception. If everyday life and thinking is fetishistic and if defetishization takes place only in the sphere of art (that is, in the creation and reception of works of art), how does man manage to create works of art at all and to experience catharsis in his enjoyment of them? It is unconditionally true that works of art possess an evocative power and that through this power they can homogenize our being (as Lukács put it: they transform the 'whole man' into 'man's whole'). It is also beyond any doubt that the works suggest the suspension of our most heterogeneous forms of activity – but why do we understand this suggestion, why are we prepared to accept that suspension at all? In short: whence stems the need for art? If our everyday life and thinking were thoroughly fetishized, if we could elaborate no individual relation to species, or at any rate if we felt within ourselves no desire for such a relation, how could art, through its evocative power, elevate us to the level of 'species character'? Further, how could creation itself come about? The analysis of the aftermath of the receptive experience in Lukács is as rich as his dissection of what leads up to it is arid.

Lukács himself was partially aware of this deficiency, and that is why he attached a chapter on the psychology of art to the work. He wanted to explain our 'openness-for-art' through the postulation of an artistic sense, in order to find a foundation for man's special capacity for conceiving the essential through the preconceptual, that is, through sensual imagination (*Anschauung*). Here we can safely ignore the fact that in his attempt to carry out this task Lukács employs a primitive psychology, for this is quite secondary from our point of view. The important thing is that in his attempt to provide a psychological foundation for the artistic sense he relinquishes his own conception in order to analyse a problem that, from the viewpoint of his own philosophy, is secondary. If one takes as one's point of departure the fact that works of art exist, without inquiring after their possibility, if one places existence ahead of essence, the analysis of the artistic sense has no place at all within the conception. What would have a place in it, however, is precisely the analysis of the social need for art-as-essence (and not for its existence, which is a premise of the theory). That, however, cannot either be conceived or understood through the analysis of the artistic sense.

In this regard, the aesthetic of the later Lukács is very near the work of his youth. In the early work, however, the gap between fetishistic everyday life and the defetishized work of art had been conceived in terms of a tragic world view of eternal misunderstanding. This tragic conception is replaced in the later Lukács by a naive optimism. There is no longer any trace of the tragic in the pluralistic structure of reception; pluralism is simply conditioned by the un-determined objectivity of the work of art itself. All understandings are equally essential, for in them man rises to species. As has already been mentioned, the possibility of this elevation is never directly questioned. But we are provided, indirectly, with an ontological rather than an epistemological solution. In brief, Lukács simply *asserts* the identity of all non-identical human types of reality. Ac-cording to him, in all spheres of the humanly created world the same categories of being (such as inherence, substantiality, causality, accidental and necessary, space and time) are at work. The categorical unity of the world guarantees the possibility, the completeness and the equality of rights of all receptions. We do not need to demonstrate that this solution was conceived in the spirit of the 'first naivety'. The choice of optimism rather than the tragic led Lukács to bypass the problem of fetishism and to return instead from the 'second naivety' to the 'first'. But this theoretical impasse in no way undermines the legitimacy of Lukács' philosophical undertaking.

I have already mentioned that in this work all the concepts of *diamat* are pro-vided with a new content and a new meaning. The category of reflection is re-placed by that of mimesis, with reflection being understood as mimesis. Mimesis is used in the ancient sense of the word: the imitation of 'ethos'. 'Ethos', in Lukács' understanding, is 'species character' that becomes manifest through in-dividual deeds and destinies. A work of art is mimetic if it grasps the species in the individual and represents thereby the sphere of the so-called 'particular' (*das Besondere*). The 'particular' is a category that Lukács borrowed from Goethe, on which, as a propaedeutic to his aesthetics, he even wrote a short study. In the booklet the concept is still quite formal; it is only in the more voluminous elaboration of the *Aesthetics* that its meaning and function become truly understandable. Through his intensified subjectivity, the artist attains to objec-tivity; through his extremely profound and sensitive experience of time he reaches the level of species. This experience of time, which, in the Hegelian sense of *Aufhebung*, is being cancelled and preserved at the same time, con-titutes the eternity of the temporal, the universal validity of what has emerged in the historical *here and now*. The formal principle of this *Aufhebung* is the 'particular': it is in the 'particular' that individual experience, risen to the level of species, becomes form.

The Specificity of the Aesthetic is, as I have mentioned, a philosophy of history. In and through art the question of the truth of history emerges and is solved. Here, however, we have to raise (and resolve) a further question: what is the status of the central category of the philosophy of history here – the category of evolution?

On this central issue the book is ambiguous, and it is in this ambiguity that its greatness resides.

Lukács commits himself to evolution, referring constantly to the evolution in art. But he also holds that art manifests, in the form of the particular, a 'species character-being-for-us' (*für-uns-seiende Gattungsmässigkeit*) from the very moment that its essence arises out of its existence – that is to say, when it becomes 'world-like'. In brief, there is no evolution with regard to art's manifestation of human essence. Individual works of art appear in succession, but they are not ordered hierarchically above and below each other: they are equally legitimate offspring or gods of history. Epochs advantageous or disadvantageous for art follow one another, without altering the equally valid character of great works of art.

There is only one train of thought in Lukács to which it is legitimate to apply, even relatively, the concept of evolution, and this is the chapter on art's 'struggle for liberation'. And yet the title of the final part of the chapter is 'Basis and Perspective of Liberation'. Works of art – as unities of the individual and the species – have always represented the immanence of humankind and are, in fact, objectivations of this immanence. Myths and religions, because they are expressions of transcendence, have always been enemies of art, even at times when art has made use of mythical and religious subjects. Only in a free-world, a world without myths and religions, will art be 'homebound' again, returning to the everyday life of man. Lukács still insists on his absolute, but this absolute is no longer identical with a movement, a class or a party. The absolute is simply the proclamation of Karl Marx – since that proclamation the world of freedom is open to us. But it is open only in principle, not in fact, as it seemed in *The Destruction of Reason*. *The Specificity of the Aesthetic* concludes with a critique of Stalinism as having hampered the actualization of that prophecy. It is only the world of freedom that is also a world of evolution. Art demonstrates that the unity of individual and species is possible. Its essence is a guarantee of the possibility of an evolution on the level of 'species character'. But that evolution itself is an *Ought*. Lukács himself does not use the word 'Ought' but speaks, rather, of *perspective*. The philosophy of history inherent in this aesthetics is conceived in the spirit of hope (in the sense of a *guaranteed* hope). And that is precisely why the work can easily be placed, as a real masterpiece next to *History and Class Consciousness*. If one has the courage and determination to surmount the obstacles of obsolete categories and over-documented analyses, one enters the promised land of philosophy. It is easy to see why Lukács renounced the writing of the second, 'historical', part of his aesthetics: in fact, *he had written it*. The division of the undertaking into a 'dialectical materialist' and an 'historical materialist' part, a division accepted uncritically from *diamat* orthodoxy, proved in theoretical practice to be nonsensical.

The Ontology of Social Reality, a work that was originally envisaged as an introduction to his ethics but later took on gigantic dimensions, lags in every respect behind both the conception and the actual realization of the *Aesthetics*. Written when he was very old, but nevertheless before the beginning of his fatal illness, this was the last book that Lukács completed. The failure of the book cannot be attributed to his age, however. He himself mentioned often the so-called 'period of consequences' in life, and it was his lot to experience one at the end of his life. The paradox in life took its revenge on the work.

When he accepted the paradox, he withdrew consciously from great philosophy. He took over the conceptual arsenal of the official *diamat* without reservation, but his frustration, his anxiety and his critical spirit kept him from formulating, with the aid of these categories, something positive in the form of a philosophical system. In his last period, however, the absolute had changed: it was only Karl Marx, as source and prophecy, that had to be regarded as absolute. The slogan 'the renaissance of Marxism' exactly expressed this resolution. *Diamat* appeared no longer as the continuation of the theoretical legacy but as the opposite, its distortion. The 'genuine' Marx had to be uncovered and the *real* succession to his ideas, in the form of a philosophical construction, had to be found; that was the 'assignment'. The fact that he kept accepting the source as absolute, however, made him still captive to his prejudices of the 1930s, 1940s and 1950s. Non-Marxist philosophy after 1848 could be understood only as 'bourgeois decadence' in all its manifestations, since it was blind to the prophecy. Lukács could not see what was obvious: the fact that great philosophy in the twentieth century is no longer bourgeois, since for him the non-bourgeois was identical with the acceptance of Karl Marx as *the* absolute. That is why he turned his back on all problems formulated as such after Marx and why he combined two attitudes: the dogmatic, with regard to Marx, and that of 'first naivety' as an 'unbracketed contemplation of essence' (*Wesens-schau*) – not an infrequent combination.

In *The Specificity of the Aesthetic* Lukács had a reliable Virgil: art itself. Moreover, with regard to the understanding of art he did not, in fact, turn his back on modern conceptions, for it was his conviction that in so-called detail even bourgeois thinking could raise relevant questions. In great philosophy, however, this was impossible, in his view, and *Ontology*, precisely because of that bias, proved to be a failure.

The word 'failure' is a harsh one. Its use would not be appropriate if the book represented something coherent, but inner coherence is missing from it. This giant of a work, many thousand pages long, is full of logical contradictions, of diametrically opposed conceptions of the same problem, of empty repetitions, of gaps in the process of argumentation. Nevertheless, something up-to-date glimmers through this jungle of impressions, showing that it is not a complete failure; it is still the product of one of the most significant intellects of the twentieth century. The written work of Lukács parallels in this regard the imaginary work of art in Balzac's *Le chef-d'oeuvre inconnu*, in which an admirably shaped leg in the middle of a spoiled but colourful canvas bears witness to original artistic genius and to the underlying genius of the artist and the venturesomeness of his thought.

Indeed, the reconstruction of historical materialism is an up-to-date endeavour and it was not by chance that Habermas' title occurred to me. For one of the leading and constantly recurring ideas in Lukács' work is the conception of evolution as 'pushing back nature's limitation'. According to Lukács, this operation has three aspects or, more precisely, three parallel forms of appearance. The first is the development of the means of production, the second the generalization of the human integrations and the third the socialization of human nature – all aspects that are grasped by Habermas in terms of work and interaction or as the evolution of production and collective morality. Lukács' category has the advantage, however, that all three can be expressed in one. Here I set aside all critical objections to the theory. What I seek to show is only that Lukács, despite his deliberately chosen isolation, did not lose his feeling for what was on the theoretical agenda.

Philosophy is no domain of the tragic. A paradigmatic failure elicits here no catharsis, either in the creator or in the recipient. The recipients learned from Lukács precisely what he learned in his youth from Ernst Bloch: philosophy is not dead. It is too soon to bury it; the task should be approached in a different manner. The man who created the work was dissatisfied with the created work, but dissatisfaction is not a tragic feeling. It was neither despair nor faith that led Lukács onwards: the absolute character of the absolute had tacitly been called into question. 'We live in an age of Utopian socialism,' he often said in his last years. 'Everything should be started anew.' To start anew involves not anxiety and frustration but courage, the courage of the critical spirit.

But Lukács had no time left for a new critical beginning.

Index

absolute, the, 178, 181 – 2, 188 – 9, 190
   see also essence; totality
absolute reason, 119
absolute sinfulness (culpability), era of, 49, 53, 57, 64, 80
absolute spirit, 10, 11, 111
absolute truth, 181
accidents, 137, 159 – 60
act, and potency, 174
action, 89, 113, 138
   individual, 163
   see also praxis
Adorno, Theodor, 72, 88, 94, 95, 131, 179
Ady, Endre, 44, 57, 62, 65
aesthetics:
   and ethics, 86
   Lukács' early and late work on, 2 – 3
   and mimesis, 134
   sphere of, 102 – 6
   see also art; artist, the; Lukács, works (various)
alienation, 80, 83, 89
   art transcending, 12, 15
   as crisis of culture, 4, 8 – 20
   and externalization, 148
   Hegelian, 111, 148
   individual, 150 – 1, 157 – 8, 172

Marxist, 79, 132, 172
   students' comments on, 150 – 2
   suffering from, 93
Althusser, Louis, 130, 169
annihilation, 165 – 6
Anselm, Saint, 157, 159, 160 – 2, 163, 164, 165 – 6
anthropology, classicist, 91 – 4, 96, 98
appearance and essence, 96 – 9, 148 – 9
aristocracy, spiritual, 68, 69
aristocratic:
   ethics, 84
   fetishism, 78 – 9, 96 – 7
   realism theory, 95 – 7, 100
   Stoicism, 93
Aristotle, 85, 86, 159 – 60, 161
art:
   L's early view of, 2 – 3, 10 – 14
   L's later view of, 182 – 90
   Bloch's concept of, 69, 70 – 1
   and defetishization, 3, 94, 184 – 7
   essence of, 183 – 8
   and essentialism, 96 – 9
   life-shaping, 10 – 14
   philosophical role of, 69 – 71, 74
   and philosophy, 5
   and political commitment, 86
   popular, 100
   psychology of, 186 – 7
   and realism, 94 – 100

art (cont.)
  and species character, 182 – 8
  Utopian function, 2 – 3, 15, 70
  works of, 2, 10 – 14, 20, 182 – 8
  see also aesthetics
artist, the, 97 – 8, 187
  and audience, 12 – 13, 105 – 6
  life of, 57 – 9
  as realist, 94 – 8
  tragedy of, 13 – 14, 19 – 20
  women as, 54 – 7
attitude, 111 – 13, 117 – 19
audience:
  of art form, 12 – 13, 100, 105
  of ideas, 179 – 80
authentic being (soul), 6, 7 – 9,
  14 – 15
  Being, 155 – 74
  see also life; soul
avantgardism, 71, 80, 94

Babits, Mihály, 57, 62
Balázs, Béla, 24, 25, 65, 74
Balzac, Honoré de, 87, 99, 190
barbarians, 61, 102, 171
Bartók, Béla, 95
Becher, Johannes, 102
Being, 155 – 74
  authentic, 7 – 9, 14 – 15
  and creation, 164 – 5
  ethical democracy, 80, 96, 100, 101
  ontologization of appearance and
    essence, 96 – 8
  and Ought, 80, 87, 101, 170
  proper, 155
  social, 144 – 5, 156, 174
  and values, 170 – 1
  see also Lukács, works *(On the Ontology
    of Social Reality)*; species-Being
Benjamin, Walter, 71, 72, 97
Berdyayev, N., 95
Beyer, R., 152
Bloch, Ernst, 24, 94, 154, 155
  Geist der Utopie, 63, 66 – 7, 70, 73
  hope, 79, 91, 130, 174, 190
  Marxism, 67

  philosophical relationship with
    Lukács, 63 – 72, 79, 80, 183, 190
Bolshevism, 1 – 2, 122
  see also Marxism
Börne, L., 86
Borstieber, Gertrud (wife of Lukács),
  126
bourgeois society, 77, 78, 83, 120 – 1
  crisis of, 16 – 19, 107
  culture of, 80, 81, 94 – 5, 189
Brecht, Bertolt, 66, 78, 79, 80, 94, 100
Brentano, Franz, 159 – 60, 161, 162,
  175
British classicism, 88
  Enlightenment, 76, 87, 88, 91, 181
Budapest, 31, 32, 33, 35
Bukharin, Nikolai, Lukács' review of,
  131
bureaucratic, the, 78, 164, 169, 175
  élite, 170, 174
  institution, 163 – 4, 167, 170 – 4
  see also state

capitalism, 75, 84
  alienation, 80, 83
  anti-, 78
  and art, 94
  and Brecht, 79
  and classicism, 81
  crisis of, 109
  and democracy, 82
  in 1950s, 101
  and rationalism, 88
causality, 91
  see also fate; necessity
Champeaux, Guillaume de, 158
change, 66
  transforming nature, 80 – 1
  transforming society, 21, 69
  see also evolutionism
choice, 155 – 6, 160, 162, 172 – 3
  existential, 177 – 8
  and law, 155, 171
  of values, 170 – 1
  see also will
Christianity, 96, 165

Church, the, 162
class, 184
  prejudices, 83
  reduction, 78 – 9, 98
  and species, 120 – 1, 178
class-consciousness, 68 – 9, 112, 121,
  184
  see also Lukács, works *(History and
  Class Consciousness)*
classic, the, 75, 80
classical German philosophy, 7, 10
  Weimar period, 75 – 106
classicism:
  European, 88
  Lukács', 79 – 94, 101 – 2, 106;
    anthropology, 91 – 4, 96, 98; ethical
    democracy, 81 – 7; supremacy of
    reason, 87 – 90
Comintern (Third International), 75,
  102, 177, 178
communication:
  art and, 12 – 13, 183
  domination-free, 83, 84 – 5
  of individuals, 34 – 41, 44 – 7
  lack of, 48, 174
  language, 48 – 50, 104, 145, 146,
    166, 167
communism, 101 – 2, 151 – 2
  see also Marxism
Communist Party:
  German, 78
  Hungarian, 1, 81
  Soviet Union, 78, 177; 20th
    Congress, 101, 181
community, 66, 69
  spiritual, 69
competition, 18
consciousness, 143
  class-, 68 – 9, 112, 121, 184
  and culture, 48 – 50
  false, 117, 120, 121, 122 – 3, 184
  in human development, 114
  religious, 66
  self-, 48 – 9
  social, 138 – 9
  and social being, 144 – 5

species-Being as, 168 – 9
constructivism, new, 80
conventions, 49, 50 – 1
  and relationships, 34 – 5, 36, 37 – 8, 44
created work, 29 – 30
creation, 164 – 6
  aesthetic, 105 – 6
criticism, 154, 179 – 83
  Lukács' self-, 177 – 9
Croce, Benedetto, article on, 10
culpability (sinfulness), absolute, era
  of, 49, 53, 57, 58 – 9, 64, 80
culture:
  and barbarism, 102
  bourgeois, 16 – 19, 80, 81, 94 – 5,
    107, 189
  and classicism, 80 – 1, 102
  and consciousness, 48 – 50
  crisis of, 3 – 5, 13 – 16, 19 – 20
  desire for, 50, 53, 61
  European, 101 – 2, 109, 111
  proletarian, 80
  and science, 117

de Lisle, Leconte, 95
death, 93, 136
  of Irma Seidler, 44, 54, 57, 58, 60,
    126
  of Lukács' wife, 126
  and tragedy, 53
decadence, 81, 94 – 5, 133, 185
  bourgeois, 162
decency, moral, 85
defetishization:
  aristocratic, 78 – 9
  and art, 3, 94, 184 – 7
democracy, 68 – 9
  see also ethical democracy
demonology, 179 – 80
Descartes, René, 88, 114, 116, 157
desire for culture, 50, 53, 61
despair, 178, 190
destiny, 66
  see also fate; necessity
determinism, 119 – 20, 122, 134
  see also fate; necessity

Deutscher, Isaac, 77, 178
development, 111, 162, 175
  historical, 113 – 14
  philosophical, 116, 117 – 20
  of society, 112
  see also evolutionism; history
dialectical materialism, 78, 182, 189
dialectical reason, 98
dictatorship, 76, 94
Dilthey, W., 4, 22, 89, 154
disease:
  of personality, 104 – 5
  social, 93 – 4
Döblin, A., 94
Dostoevsky, Fyodor, 25 – 6, 37, 80, 86
  and Bloch, 70
  Utopia of, 15, 24
doubt, 133
drama:
  audience of, 100
  Brechtian, 79
  History of the Development of the Modern Drama (Lukács), 1, 2, 16, 19, 25
dualism, 67, 92
  life/soul, 6 – 7, 9 – 15, 23

Eckhart, Johannes, 38
economics, 67, 138 – 9, 146, 164
  and labour, 116, 137
  and science, 114
economy, political, 170
education:
  in literature, 86 – 7
  in morality, 85
  of personality, 104 – 5
  for public life, 83, 85
Eichendorff, Joseph, 76
Einstein, Albert, 140 – 1
Eisler, G., 94
élite:
  bureaucratic, 170, 174
  cult of the, 78 – 9, 122
  revolutionary, 167
  see also aristocratic

emotions, 92 – 3
Engels, Friedrich, 143, 149
English rationalism, 88
Enlightenment, 76, 87, 88, 91, 181
Enzenberger, M., 94
epistemology:
  and essentialism, 97 – 8
  and ontology, 139
  and rationalism, 90 – 1, 96
  and reflection theory, 134
  see also knowledge
equality, 170
Erlangen School, 157
Ernst, Paul, 53, 59, 80
  Lukács' letters to, 24, 74
essay form, 5
essays, Lukács' period of writing, 25, 27 – 8, 29
essence:
  and appearance, 96 – 9, 148 – 9
  of art, 183 – 8
  of human being, 173
essentialism, 96 – 9, 104 – 5, 106
ethical democracy, 81 – 7, 89 – 90, 96, 100, 101
  pluralism of, 86 – 7, 90, 106
ethics:
  collective, 84 – 5
  of duty, 15
  Kant, 77, 84
  and law, 59 – 60, 147
  of Lukács when young, 13 – 21
  of Lukács in 1960s, 125 – 6
  and religion, 63 – 72
  Tactics and Ethics (Lukács), 2, 64, 67, 84
  tragic, 64, 68
  and values, 145 – 6
  see also morality; Ought
Eurocommunism, 101
Europe, Eastern, 101, 164
Europe, in 1950s, 101
European classicism, 88
European culture, 101 – 2, 109, 111
European history, 114 – 17

everyday life ('ordinary'), 6 – 8,
11 – 12, 14, 19 – 20, 104 – 6, 126,
185
everyday thinking (*Lebenswelt*), 103
evil, 160, 162 – 5, 179 – 80
era of absolute sinfulness, 49, 53,
57, 64, 80
sin, 30, 64
world abandoned by God, 63 – 5, 71
evolutionism, 90 – 1, 103 – 4, 113 – 14,
188, 190
existential analysis, 46 – 7
existentialism, 5, 94, 102, 183
expressionism, 70, 74, 94
extensional conception, 129, 130 – 1,
152
externalization (*Entäusserung*), 148

faith, 2, 42, 44, 63, 157 – 9, 161, 162
and despair, 178
and ethics, 63
and science, 170
fate, 14, 16, 17 – 18, 165, 172
causality, 91
constructed fate, 48
destiny, 66
determinism, 119 – 20, 122, 134
see also necessity
feelings, culture of, 92 – 3
Fehér, Ferenc, 74, 134, 152, 154
Ferenczy, Karl, 39, 62
fetishism, 184 – 7
cultural, 88
Marxist, 78 – 9
and rationalism, 90 – 1
and realism, 94 – 100, 106
Feuerbach, Ludwig, 174
Fichte, Johann, 9, 64, 69, 74, 79, 80
Flaubert, Gustave, 91
form, 10 – 13, 20, 23, 24, 28 – 30, 58,
61, 70 – 1
Bloch and, 70 – 1
'the particular', 188
Soul and Form (Lukács), 5, 25,
27 – 33, 57
Forster, Georg, 76, 95

France, Anatole, 86
Frankfurt School, 88, 130, 157
Frederick the Great, 86
freedom, 64 – 5, 143, 144, 164 – 5,
170, 174
and art, 188
and choice, 155 – 6, 160, 162, 174
and creation, 164 – 6
and God, 64 – 5
and labour, 143
and socialism, 170
French classicism, 88
French revolution:
of 1789, 76, 147
of 1848, 81, 94, 95
Freud, Sigmund, 91, 174

Galileo Galilei, 114 – 15
generalization, 155, 156, 166, 168
generic character, *see* species-Being
genius, 12
George, Stefan, 28
German classical philosophy, 7, 76,
110
Weimar period, 76 – 106
German Communist movement, 78
Germany:
Nazi, 179, 180
Potsdam, 77
gesture, significance of, 34, 36, 37 – 8,
44
Gluckmann, André, 154
God:
and art, 69 – 71
as creator, 164 – 6, 178
and ethics, 63 – 72
existence of, 157 – 9, 161 – 3, 168
replaced, 120
see also religion
Goethe, Johann Wolfgang von, 77,
81, 86, 87, 136, 187
Lukács' analysis of *Wilhelm Meister*,
15, 39, 68 – 9, 82, 85, 86
Lukács' writing on, 76, 85, 148
Gogol, Nikolai, 86
Goldmann, Lucien, 5, 72, 88, 98

good, 171, 180
    and evil, 160 – 1, 162 – 5, 179 – 80
grace, 37
Gramsci, Antonio, 129
Greece, ancient, 113
    art of, 95, 99, 153
    Homer paradox, 104, 130, 139,
        153, 185
    literature of, 165
    society of, 16 – 17, 82, 146, 147
growth, conception of, 134

Habermas, Jürgen, 71, 83, 122, 133,
    190
Hartmann, Nicolai, 139, 152, 171
haughtiness, 50 – 3, 60 – 1
health, 93 – 4
Hebbel, Christian, 63 – 4
Hegel, Georg Wilhelm, 9, 74, 77, 82,
    83, 141, 152, 155, 178, 180
    idea of spirit, 7, 90, 104, 111, 169
    Hegelian philosophy, 23, 24, 84,
        90, 169
    The Young Hegel (Lukács), 75, 89,
        141, 150, 178
Heidegger, Martin, 79, 85, 93, 95,
    157, 159, 175
Heine, Heinrich, 86
Heller, Agnes, 13, 78, 85, 129, 133,
    134, 143, 152, 163
hierarchy, 160 – 1
historical determinism, 102, 118, 134,
    139
    see also determinism
historical materialism, 1, 99, 111, 112,
    113 – 14, 182, 190
historical progress, 134
historical value products, 130
historicism, 111, 130 – 1
historicity, 160
    abolition of, 109
history:
    and crisis of culture, 19 – 21
    holistic view of, 110 – 11, 119 – 21
    of ideas, 111 – 13
    laws of, 139

philosophy of, 69, 72, 90, 102,
    103 – 4, 164, 165, 183 – 4, 188 – 9
    and science, 108 – 9
    and species-Being, 156, 159
    see also Lukács, works (History and
        Class Consciousness); past, one's own
Hitler, Adolf, 72, 91, 165
Hölderlin, Friedrich, 76
holism, 110 – 11, 119 – 21, 122
    see also totality
Homeric paradox, 104, 130, 139, 153,
    185
hope, 72, 91, 130, 174, 188, 190
    optimism, 79, 180, 187
Horkheimer, Max, 88, 179
Huizinga, J., 95
human species, 86, 156, 158 – 60,
    162 – 4, 168 – 74, 177 – 8
    essence of, 173
    mankind, 117 – 23
    universality, 158
    value of, 86, 170 – 1
    see also species
humanism, 76, 89, 162
humility, 51 – 3, 60 – 1
Hungarian Communist Party, 1
Hungarian revolution of 1919, 78, 84,
    101, 165
Hungarian Soviet Republic, 81
Husserl, Edmund, 107, 108 – 20, 122

Ibsen, Henrik, 87
ideal objectifications, 134, 135, 139
idealism, ethical, 69
ideology, 132
    ancient Greek, 16 – 17
    Lukács', comments by students on,
        147 – 50
    and rationalism, 90
    self-deceptive, 79
Ilyés, Gyula, 165
immortality, 136
impressionism, 8
individual:
    and alienation, 150 – 1, 157 – 8, 172
    and art, 183 – 8

and bourgeois society, 83
freedom, 144
in ordinary and authentic life, 6 – 21
problematization of, 17 – 19
relationships with Other, 28 – 30
self-creation of, 104 – 5
self-respecting, 53
and species, 118 – 22, 156 – 8,
162 – 3, 165, 168, 172 – 3, 182,
183 – 8
uniqueness of, meeting, 44 – 6
and universals, 173 – 4
see also personality; self
individuality, 55
moral, 48, 163 – 4
instincts, 92
institution, 163 – 4, 167, 170 – 4
bureaucratic, the, 78, 164, 175
institutions, 82 – 3, 169
irrationalism, 24, 88 – 9, 92, 101, 110,
139, 180 – 1

Jacobins, 76, 85, 100
judgement, 30, 52, 58, 60 – 1, 165
justice, 147

Kafka, Franz, 96 – 7
Kant, Immanuel, 67, 161
art, 23, 105
epistemology, 91
ethics, 77, 84
Lukács' opposition to, 92
philosophy subsequent to, 88, 89,
90, 158
Kassner, Rudolph, 27, 31, 45, 53
Keller, Gottfried, 82, 83, 85, 86 – 7,
93, 126
Khrushchev, Nikita, 181
Kierkegaard, Sören, 69, 178, 181
haughtiness, 84, 85
Lukács' essay on in *Soul and Form*
14, 15, 27, 28 – 9, 34, 43, 57, 59
and Regine Olsen, 27, 28, 30, 34,
43, 61
Kleist, Heinrich, 76, 92

knowledge:
false, 180 – 1
objective, 119
and power, 117, 118, 120
and rationalism, 90, 91
and science, 109 – 11, 115, 122 – 3
self-, 91, 119 – 21
totality, 119 – 23
true (dialectical reason), 98
see also consciousness; epistemology
Kolakowski, Leszek, 129, 157, 169
Korsch, Karl, 80
Kosik, K., 157

labour:
and alienation, 150
division of, 18 – 19, 146, 153
humanization through, 137, 152 – 3
Lukács' students' comments re,
141 – 4
and money, 172
one's own, 116
and totality, 94
see also production; work
Lacan, J., 174
language, 145, 146, 166
evolution of, 104, 146
ideological, 154
private, 49
and teleology, 167
words, 47, 49
see also communication
Lask, E., 23
law(s), 146 – 7
causality, 91
and choice, 155, 171
of history, 139
moral, 59 – 60
natural, 139, 174
and science, 108 – 9
Lebensphilosophie, 8, 9, 10, 23, 24, 79
left, radical, 72, 76, 174
Leibniz, Gottfried von, 162
Lenin, Vladimir Ilyich, 90, 153, 172
Lessing, Gotthold, 85, 86, 103
Lesznai, Anna, 1, 24, 68

Lévi-Strauss, Claude, 173
liberalism, 129
life:
    creation of one's own, 29 – 30
    and culture, 4 – 5, 16, 20 – 1
    external, 71
    and form, 10 – 13, 20, 23, 24, 28 – 30, 58, 61, 70 – 1, 155
    ordinary (everyday), 6 – 8, 11 – 12, 14, 19 – 20, 104 – 6, 126, 185
    and philosophy, 29 – 30, 52
    real (authentic), 6, 7 – 9, 14 – 15, 57
    and the soul, 6 – 15
    and totality, 64
    see also Being
literature, 99, 100
    re education, 86 – 7
    see also Lukács, works (Remarks on the Theory of Literary History; Theory of the Novel, The)
love, 28 – 9, 36, 38, 43, 44, 47, 49, 50 – 8
    of humanity, 170 – 1
    and institution, 163
    and spiritual community, 84
Löwy, Michael, 76
Lukács, Georg:
    early work, 1 – 2, 4 – 21, 23, 25 – 6
    1918 conversion, 1, 3, 21, 69
    relation of early and later work, 2 – 4, 125, 177
    rejection of early work, 74, 80, 131, 177
    in 1930 – 40s, 89, 102, 177 – 9, 182, 184
    in 1950s, 100 – 2, 181 – 2
    in 1960s, 125 – 7, 177
    old age, 137, 189
    last illness, 127, 136
    and Bloch, 63 – 72
    and Husserl, 107 – 23
    marriage, 126
    and Irma Seidler, 27 – 61
    and students, 125, 126 – 37
    and Weimar period, 75 – 106

Lukács, Georg, works of:
    Aesthetic Culture, 2, 5, 22, 25, 60
    Aesthetics, see Heidelberg Manuscripts; Specificity of the Aesthetic
    Against Misunderstood Realism, 131
    Bolshevism as an Ethical Problem, 2
    Destruction of Reason, The, 92, 179, 184, 188
    Ethics, 125 – 6
    Heidelberg Manuscripts on Aesthetics 2 – 3, (Philosophy of Art and Aesthetics) 10, 14, 23, 24, 25 – 6, 125, 134, 182
    History and Class Consciousness, 67, 74, 75, 78, 89, 98, 133, 150; Bloch in, 67; and phenomenology, 107 – 17, 119 – 22; rejected by Lukács, 80, 129, 130, 131, 141, 177 – 8, 182, 184
    History of the Development of the Modern Drama, 1, 2, 16, 19, 25
    Lenin, 153
    Metaphysics of Tragedy, The (in Soul and Form), 5, 14, 64, 65, 68, 71
    On Spiritual Poverty, 5, 25, 30, 37, 68
    On the Ontology of Social Reality, 89, 177, 189 – 90; genesis, 125 – 8; Introduction to by pupils, 125 – 37; critique of Introduction, 152; notes on by pupils, 137 – 52; Tamas' critique of, 154 – 74
    Problems of Realism, The, 100
    Remarks on the Theory of Literary History, 1, 22, 25
    Soul and Form, 5, 25, 27 – 33, 57; see also Kierkegaard, Philippe, Sterne, Storm and Metaphysics of Tragedy
    Specificity of the Aesthetic, The (first part of projected 3-part Aesthetics), 2 – 3, 101, 102 – 3, 104, 105, 106, 125, 126, 130 – 134, 142, 143, 145, 158, 177, 182, 183, 186 – 7, 188 – 9
    Tactics and Ethics, 2, 64, 67, 84
    Theory of the Novel, The, 15, 16, 26, 30, 39, 64, 65, 68 – 9, 70, 71, 72, 82, 85

Young Hegel, The, 75, 89, 141, 150, 178

Makarenko, A. S., 92
Manichaeism, 104, 181
mankind, 117 – 23
see also human species
Mann, Thomas, 30, 57, 60, 85 – 7, 92, 95, 101 – 2, 179
Márkus, György, 129, 134, 135, 143, 152, 153
Marx, Karl, 94 – 5, 102, 161
German Ideology, The, 150
Grundrisse, 153, 172
Paris Manuscripts, The, 79, 177
Marxism, 129, 135, 148 – 9
and Bloch, 67
Lukács' early view of, 1 – 2
Lukács' conversion to, 1, 3, 21
influence on Lukács, 20
Lukács and, 75, 78, 82, 87, 89, 97, 99, 103 – 4, 107 – 8, 110, 125, 130, 131, 132 – 3, 138 – 9, 146, 150 – 1, 152, 177 – 8, 181, 188, 189
and science, 107 – 8, 110 – 12
'Western', 107 – 8
'Mason Kelemen's Wife', 58, 62
materialism:
dialectical, 78, 182, 189
historical, 1, 99, 111, 112, 113 – 14, 182, 190
mathematics, 115, 140 – 1
meaning, and science, 123
see also communication
medieval philosophy, 157, 158
see also Anselm, Saint
Meier, H., 26
metaphysics and history, 20 – 1
methodology, 4 – 5, 20, 135, 180
mimesis, 105, 134, 183, 187
miracles, 41 – 4
modernism, 80
money, 172
'monoethism', 16
Montagne, the (1793 – 4 activities), 82

moral law, 59 – 60
moral personality, 85
moral theory, 84 – 7
morality:
collective, 84 – 5
and faith, 170
and feelings, 92 – 3
Good, the, 160 – 1, 162 – 5, 171, 179 – 80
individual, 48, 163 – 4
subjective, 84
see also ethics; Ought
music, 88, 95, 96
history of, 69
mysticism, 24, 65, 84, 102, 158
myth, 112, 160, 181, 188
anti-capitalist, 78
Irma Seidler as, 52, 55, 58 – 9

Nagybánya, Hungary (artists' colony), 31, 32, 39, 40, 61, 62
naivety, 182 – 3
natural laws, 139, 174
natural ontology, 139 – 40, 141
natural sciences, 114 – 15, 133, 139 – 40
naturalism, 23, 100, 109 – 11, 114
nature, 114 – 16, 133
dialectic of, 133
teleology, 109, 119, 167
transforming, 80 – 1
Nazism, 179, 180
necessity, 66, 137 – 8, 147, 169 – 70
and essence, 149
see also fate
neo-positivism, 89, 131, 140, 152
Nietzsche, Friedrich Wilhelm, 69, 181
Novalis (Friedrich von Hardenberg), 27, 38, 48, 58
novels:
re education, 86 – 7
Lukács, works (*Theory of the Novel*)

object and subject, *see* subject/object

objectification(s) *(Vergegenständlichung)*,
  69, 138, 147 – 8
  cultural, 10 – 11, 13
  ideal, 134, 135, 139
  of labour process, 141 – 2
  social, 144 – 5
  theory of, 130
objectivation, 155 – 6, 158
  cultural, 2, 3, 9 – 13
  law as, 171
  and self, 24
objective knowledge, 119
objective science, 121 – 3
objective spirit, 11
objective world, 108 – 9
objectivism, rationalist, 109 – 11,
  114 – 16, 120 – 3
objectivity, 120, 123, 155, 170
  false, 111
  and subjectivity, 6
  work, 9 – 10, 11, 166
Olsen, Regine, 27, 28, 30, 34, 43, 57
ontologization:
  appearance/essence, 96 – 7
ontology, 155
  natural, 139 – 40, 141
  see also Lukács, works *(On the Ontology
    of Social Reality)*
optimism, 187
  Socratic, 180
  see also hope
Ortega y Gasset, José, 95
Ought, 64, 66, 84, 90
  and Being, 80, 87, 101, 170
  see also ethics; morality

paradox, 178, 189
  see also Homeric paradox
particularity, 86, 163 – 4, 187 – 8
Pascal, Blaise, 88
past, one's own, 91 – 2
  recreating, 27, 28 – 30, 57 – 8,
    60 – 1
  see also history
personality:
  distortion of, 93 – 4, 105

dynamic of, 103 – 5
moral, 85 – 6
and reason, 91 – 2
and species-character, 184
see also individual; individuality; self
phenomenology, and science,
  107 – 23, 138, 148 – 9
  transcendental, 117
Philippe, Charles-Louis, Lukács' essay
  on in *Soul and Form*, 27 – 8, 29, 30,
  43, 50, 59
philosophy:
  definition of, 135
  dichotomy of, 180
  of history, 69, 72, 90, 102, 103 – 4,
    164, 165, 183 – 4, 188 – 9
  living out one's, 29 – 30, 52
  and politics, 169 – 70
  and responsibility, 179 – 80
physics, 115, 140 – 1
Plato, 179
Platonic conduct, 27
pluralism, ethical, 86 – 7, 90, 106
poetry, life, 28
political commitment, 86
political economy, 170
politics, 145, 150
  deep structure, 169 – 70
  and ethics, 21, 69
Popper, Karl, 88, 179, 180
Popper, Leo, death, 126
Popular Front, 76, 178
Potsdam, 77
power, 150
praxis, 89, 107, 112, 129, 156 – 7
predestination, 66
  see also fate
production, 172
  anarchy of, 19
  development of, 114
  forces of, 147
  relations of, 112, 116
  see also labour
proletariat:
  and art, 98

class-consciousness of, 98, 110, 112 – 13, 117, 119, 120 – 1
culture of, 80
French, 94 – 5
international, 75
Lukács abandons myth of, 78
Proletkult writers, 78
Prussia, 169
psychology:
of art, 186 – 7
conventional, 49
Lukács' opposition to, 8, 22, 46, 48, 91 – 2
and morality, 91, 93 – 4
public sphere, free, 83 – 4, 86
Pushkin, Alexander, 86

quality, sense of, 109
see also value

radicalism, 75 – 8, 80, 87, 100
and culture, 94 – 6
left, 72, 76, 174
and science, 107 – 8
radicalisation du mal, 87, 91
rationalism, 87 – 93, 96, 101, 104, 180 – 1
cunning of reason, 169
dialectical reason, 98
and science, 109 – 10, 115 – 17
realism, theory of, 94 – 100, 104 – 6
anti-, 100
aristocratic, 95 – 7, 100
essentialism, 96 – 9, 104 – 5, 106
reality (*Wirklichkeit*), and reflection, 138
reconciliation with, 75 – 6
reason, *see* rationalism
recipient:
of art form, 12 – 13, 100, 105
of ideas, 179 – 80
recreation of relationships, 27, 28 – 30, 57 – 8, 60 – 1
redemption:
and art, 3, 13
in human relationships, 37 – 8, 47

and religion, 64 – 5, 68
and work, 9
reductionism:
class, 78 – 9, 98
theory of art, 99
reflection, 97 – 8, 134, 138, 140, 143, 183
reification, 74, 109, 114, 116 – 17, 121, 150, 151
opposition to, 89, 90
world of, 112
relationships, human, 36 – 9, 44 – 57
conventions and, 34 – 5
recreation of, 27, 28 – 30, 57 – 8, 60 – 1
see also communication
religion, 152
and art, 188
Christianity, 96, 165
and ethics, 63 – 72
and praxis, 112
see also God
reproduction, process of, 138, 144 – 7, 152
responsibility, 179 – 80
revolution, 67 – 8, 75, 78, 79, 80, 101, 167
of 1789, French, 76, 147
of 1830, 94
of 1848, 81, 94, 95
of 1919, Hungarian, 78, 84, 101, 165
revolutionary tolerance, 137
Rickert, H., 23, 26
right and left, 72, 76
Romanticism, 81, 82, 87
Rousseau, Jean-Jacques, 82 – 3
Russian culture, 81, 82, 84
Soviet Union, 78, 177, 181

sanity, 93 – 4
Sartre, Jean-Paul, 79 – 80, 88, 91, 93, 94, 95, 130
Satanism, and art, 3
Schelling, Friedrich von, 164, 181
Schiller, Johann von, 80, 81, 101
Schlegel, Friedrich, 76

Schopenhauer, Arthur, 69, 181
science(s), 107 – 12, 114 – 23
    and manipulation, 143
    natural, 114 – 15, 133, 139 – 40
    objective, 121 – 3
    social, 90, 107, 114
Scott, Walter, 82
Seidler, Irma:
    as artist, 54, 56
    death, 44, 54, 57, 58, 60, 126
    relationship with Lukács; actual
        course of, 30 – 4, 39 – 41; nature of,
        34 – 9, 41 – 50; recreated, 27 – 30,
        50 – 61
    tragedy of, 53 – 8, 60
self, the, 6, 9, 14 – 15
    and ethics, 70 – 1
    loss of, 65
    and soul, 7, 24
    see also individual; personality
self-creation, 105
self-enclosed world, 16 – 17
self-hood, 7, 64, 65
self-knowledge, 91, 119 – 21
self-perfection, and love, 51
self-realization, 9
self-respect, 53, 55, 61
senses, 48 – 9
sexuality, 92, 163, 174
Shakespeare, William, 99
Simmel, G., 4, 8, 20
sin, 30, 64
    sinfulness (culpability), era of
        absolute, 49, 53, 57, 64, 80
    see also evil
Sinkó, Ervin, 165
slave society, 146
social Being, 144 – 5, 156, 173
social consciousness, 138
social formations, development of,
    146, 147
social illnesses, 93 – 4
social life, 172
social sciences, 90, 107, 114
socialism, 1, 79, 81, 106, 134, 136,
    170, 190

    in Lukács' early works, 74
    in 1920s, 75, 76
    in 1950s, 101
    and religion, 65
socialist democratization, 138, 153
socialist parties, 1920s, 75
socialization, 190
society:
    closed or open, 16 – 17
    transformation of, 21, 69
solitude, 52 – 3
soul, the, 6 – 15
    authentic being, 7 – 9, 14 – 15
    determination of, 91
    and form, 10 – 11
    history of, 46
    immediacy in, 49
    and self, 7, 24
    Soul and Form (Lukács), 5, 25,
        27 – 33, 57
    see also life; self
Soviet Union, 78, 177
    Russian culture, 81, 82, 84
    20th Party Congress, 181
space – time continuum, 140 – 1
specialization, 110
species, 104 – 6, 177 – 8
    and art, 183 – 8
    and class, 120 – 1, 178
    and individual, 118 – 22, 156 – 8,
        162 – 3, 165, 168, 172 – 3, 182,
        183 – 8
    see also human species
species-Being (species character, generic-
    ness, Gattungsmässigkeit), 168 – 9
    and art, 106, 183 – 8
    arousing, 167
    and class, 79
    and faith, 158 – 60, 162 – 3, 165
    -for-itself (creative spirit), 156,
        165 – 6, 168, 173
    -in-itself, 168 – 9, 171, 173
    non-, 169
    and objectivity, 155 – 6
    students' comments on, 130, 145, 151
    and work, 165 – 6

species essence (*Gattungswesen*), 163, 177 – 8
species-value, 155
Spiegel, Der, 128
Spinoza, Baruch, 86
spirit (*Geist*) 111
  absolute, 10, 11
  creative, 164 – 5
  Hegelian concept of, 7, 90, 104, 111, 169
  objective, 11
Stalin, Joseph, 75, 77, 85, 91, 100 – 1, 155, 162, 178, 188
state, the, 83, 171
  Greek city-, 16 – 17, 82, 85, 146, 147
  Prussian, 169
  see also bureaucratic, the
Sterne, Laurence, essay on in *Soul and Form* 5
Stoicism, 93
Storm, T., essay on in *Soul and Form* 15, 27, 28
Stravinsky, Igor, 95
Strindberg, August, 39
structuralism, 98 – 9, 169, 173
subject, and teleology, 167
subject/object:
  dichonomy, 26, 89
  identity, 110, 112 – 14, 117, 121
  unity, 4, 102 – 3, 120
subjectivity, 6 – 7, 11 – 12, 120 – 1, 166, 167
subjectivization (introversion), 17
suffering, 93
Supermen, 87
superstructure and base, 99
Switzerland, democracy in, 82, 83

Tamás, Gáspár M., 175
teleology, 109, 119, 167
  see also nature
theoretical attitude, 118 – 19
theory, 112, 127
  imperative of, 164
  and labour, 142

practical effects of, 72
Third International (Comintern), 75, 102, 177, 178
time, 109, 159
  and art, 187 – 8
  and space, 140 – 1
Tolstoy, Leo, 86
totalitarianism, 179
totality, 64, 89, 94, 122
  and class, 120 – 1
  created, 70
  and history, 111
  holism, 110 – 11, 119 – 21, 122
  knowledge of, 119
  and science, 109, 122 – 3
  and Utopian art, 2
  see also absolute
tragedy, 5, 85, 187, 190
  of the artist, 13 – 14, 19 – 20
  and ethics, 64, 68
  of Lukács, 60 – 1
  of Irma Seidler, 54 – 8, 60
  of woman, 53 – 4
  Metaphysics of Tragedy, The (Lukács), 5, 14, 64, 65, 68, 71
transcendence, 70, 72, 108, 158 – 9
transcendental phenomenology, 111 – 13, 117
transcendentalism, 110
transformation:
  of nature, 80 – 1
  of society, 21, 69
Trotsky, Leon, 80
truth, 90, 119, 136, 156
  absolute, 181
  Good and, 171, 180
  objective, 108, 119
  and rightness, 160 – 1

universals, 9, 173 – 4
Utopias, 190
  and art, 2 – 3, 70
  and culture, 15
  diversity in content of, 15
  'Dostoevsky', 15, 24
  and hope, 72

Utopias, (cont.)
  and totality, 70, 172
  Spirit of Utopia, The (Lukács), 71, 72

Vajda, Mihály, 74, 121, 126, 134, 152, 157
value, 134, 142 – 3, 145 – 6
  and art, 185
  and Being, 170 – 1
  and essence, 148
  of humanity, 170 – 1
  and money, 172
  species, 155
vanity, 50 – 1, 52
Vico, Giovanni, 113
virtues, 93
vocation, individual, 8
Volpi, Franco, 161

Weber, Max, 4, 175, 180
Weil, Simone, 170
Weimar period of German culture, 75 – 106
will(s):
  collision of, 18
  free, *see* determinism

the individual's, 8, 22
selective, 155 – 6
and self, 14
  see also choice
Winckelmann, Johann, 81
women, 53 – 7
  emotions of, 93
  in literature, 86 – 7, 93
  poets' relations with, 27 – 30
words, 47, 49
  see also language
work(s), 166
  of art, 2, 20; and form, 10 – 14;
    possibility of, 182 – 8
  created, 29 – 30
  cultural, 12
  division of labour, 18 – 19
  judgement of, 69 – 70
  objectivity, 9 – 10, 166
  see also labour
World War I, 24, 25, 78, 99
writers, 91 – 2
  re education, 86 – 7
  political commitment of, 86
  relations with women, 27 – 30